A GUIDE TO THE

MILITARY POSTS OF THE UNITED STATES

1789 - 1895

A GUIDE TO THE

Military Posts
of the United States

1789 - 1895

FRANCIS PAUL PRUCHA

MADISON

THE STATE HISTORICAL SOCIETY OF WISCONSIN

1964

Copyright © 1964 by

THE STATE HISTORICAL SOCIETY OF WISCONSIN

All rights reserved

Library of Congress Catalog Card Number: 64–63571

Publication of this volume was made possible by a grant
from the Lilly Endowment, Inc., Indianapolis, Indiana.

Europe: W. S. Hall & Co., Inc., Amsterdam, London, New York
Canada: Harvest House, Ltd., Montreal
India: Thacker & Co., Ltd., Bombay

Second Printing, January, 1966
Manufactured in the United States of America by
The North American Press, Milwaukee, Wisconsin

Preface

THE United States in the nineteenth century was a singularly unmilitary nation. Americans abhorred a standing army as a danger to liberty and considered a democratic militia the proper means for the defense of the republic. Nor were these principles shaken by foreign dangers. The United States had a certain isolated security, unthreatened by foes. She boasted of her long, undefended borders and looked to the Atlantic and Pacific oceans as protection from attack.

Nevertheless, the United States was not without military frontiers of a sort, and from 1789 to 1895 its regular army posts were a good deal more numerous than most people imagine. Initially the army built a string of artillery posts along the eastern seaboard and eventually similar fortifications on the Gulf and Pacific coasts. But the frontier of most concern and most activity was the western military frontier. These military posts served as a cordon in the West to maintain American authority against the infiltrating influence of the British and Spanish or against the Indian tribes, which for decades caused the federal government more trouble than we are likely to appreciate in the middle of the twentieth century.

These posts, ranging alphabetically from Abercrombie to Zarah, extended geographically from Fort Sullivan on the easternmost tip of Maine to San Diego on the Pacific, and from Fort Brown at the tip of Texas to Fort Pembina on the Canadian border. The troops, sometimes concentrated, sometimes scattered across the West like the spattering of paint from a stiff brush, performed an all-but-forgotten mission on the frontiers. A few of the posts have continued into our times, as garrisons for army troops or as historic shrines of bygone days. Fort Snelling at St. Paul, Fort Dearborn at Chicago, and Fort Sam Houston at San Antonio are almost commonplace names. Other posts have left their names on towns and cities which have largely forgotten the soldiers who first encamped there. But many of the frontier forts have almost passed into oblivion. The sites of some cannot even be ascertained with certainty; some have been completely forgotten, only to be rediscovered and excavated as park sites in recent decades; others stand in dismal isolation, off the beaten path, poorly marked, and unattended.

Even the records have largely been forgotten, and strange as the oversight may seem, there is no satisfactory general guide to the regular army posts established by the United States from its beginning under the Constitution in 1789 to the closing of the frontier period at the end of the nineteenth century. The reader of western stories and the scholar of western history alike have no place to turn for basic information about the military frontier which was such an important part of the nation's westward expansion. No one has separated the major posts from the temporary encampments, or the heavily garrisoned cantonments from the unmanned forts left in the hands of care-takers. Nor is it easy to pinpoint the locations of the regular army posts. It is still more difficult to determine when the army moved a particular fort from one site to another and to trace the succession of names which applied to a single post.

A simple guide, accurate and complete, has long been needed. I have tried to supply that need, overcoming a hesitation engendered by the difficul-ties of the subject with the hope that a scholarly attempt to provide a con-venient source of information is worthwhile, even though errors and gaps in knowledge may still be found.

This book is divided into five distinct parts, which taken together serve as a guide to the regular army establishments of the United States up to 1895. The first part deals with the military frontier in general, as it changed from period to period. This information is summarized on a series of maps designed to locate military garrisons at selected dates—1817, 1822, 1830, 1839, 1843, 1845, 1850, 1860, 1867, 1870, 1878, 1885, and 1895. The size of each garri-son has been indicated by a graded series of dots, so that each map presents at a glance the concentration of troops at a particular moment in time. Taken together, the maps indicate the evolving pattern of the military frontier. The accompanying text notes and explains the significant changes in distribution of regular army troops. In effect, it is a short history of the deployment of American soldiers from 1789 to 1895.

The second part of this book is an alphabetically arranged catalog of army posts in the continental United States. Here are listed all regular army estab-lishments from 1789 to 1895, the latter date being chosen as a round number to mark the end of the frontier conditions which called into being most of the installations. If a post had been established before 1789 but continued to be active after that date, it is included, as are forts established and active before 1895, even though their important history may have come later. Although interest is focused on the western frontier posts, the important forts of the seacoast have been included, so as to give a full picture of army activity.

All the posts listed were regular army installations, established and manned by federal troops or in some cases by state volunteers in federal service. They have not been selected on the basis of title, but on the basis of nature or function. Thus trading posts (very often bearing the title of "fort") or blockhouses erected by local citizens for their own protection have not been cataloged. The titles of army installations were frequently shifted back and forth, so that a single post might have been known first as a "camp," then as a "fort," then as a "cantonment," and finally as a "barracks." Occasionally, the army gave no special designation at all beyond the name of the settlement at which the soldiers were stationed. I have tried to keep my eye on concentrations of federal troops at designated sites, established there for specified purposes by the War Department.

In order to make a usable list of reasonable consistency and length, I have eliminated certain categories of federal establishments. The following types of posts are *not* cataloged:

1. *Strictly wartime establishments of the War of 1812, the Mexican War, and the Civil War.* These were of a temporary nature and were not part of the general military frontier—either for coastal defense or for western frontier defense. However, those posts are included which, though established in the periods of these wars, continued to form part of the over-all system of defense.

2. *Temporary encampments and minor subposts.* Temporary camps established as part of expeditions against the Indians, and posts established with some intention of permanence but almost immediately abandoned or moved, are not included. The line of demarcation was hard to establish with consistency; other compilers might reach different conclusions on a number of these camps, perhaps including some that I have omitted or omitting some that I have listed.

3. *Batteries and minor coastal defenses.* A great many fortifications on the seaboard are not listed here. Many of them operated very irregularly, and few, if any, had separate garrisons but depended upon some permanently established post.

4. *Arsenals and Quartermaster depots.* The army maintained a considerable number of arsenals and some supply depots. These are not included unless they were transformed into regular garrisons.

5. *Forts of the Seminole Wars.* During the Seminole Wars many posts were established in Florida and a few in southeastern Georgia. Most of them had official names and played some part in the defense of the area or

served as bases for the offensive against the Indians. Unless they had a fairly extended existence, they are named in Appendix A rather than in the regular catalog of forts.

For the posts listed in the catalog certain limited information is given. The purpose of the list is to furnish a reference guide to the military establishments, not to give a comprehensive history of each post. I have therefore included only the following information:

1. *The name of the post*, with the designation that it finally had or that it had during its most important period. Temporary names are listed with a cross reference to the final or traditional name of the post.

2. *The location of the post*, with an indication of the present state in which the site is located. Many of the posts underwent changes in site. Significant changes have been indicated; minor moves, which frequently occurred, are not noted.

3. *The dates of the post's existence.* Whenever the information was available, the entry shows the date when the troops first arrived at the site and the date when they left. Other scholars may question some of these entries since the dates of the arrival of troops, of the orders establishing the post, and of the orders naming the post do not always coincide. Similarly, abandonment might be dated from the time when the final caretakers left the site, or when the army turned over the reservation to the Department of the Interior, or when the government sold the property to some private individual. Posts which were still in use in 1895 do not have a terminal date indicated.

4. *The purpose of the post* if not clear from the date and location and if it has some special significance for an understanding of the military frontier.

5. *The serial number of items in the bibliography* which pertain particularly to the post.

The third part of the book comprises a series of seven sectional maps of the continental United States showing the exact locations of the military installations listed in the catalog of posts. Since the base map has detailed topographical information, the reader can see the locations in relation to the physiographic features of the region.

The fourth part of the book is a series of appendixes, containing supplementary information which contributes to a knowledge of the military frontier: (1) a list of temporary forts of the Seminole Wars; (2) a table of annual army strength from 1789 to 1895; and (3) an account of the changes in the territorial organization of the army.

The fifth part is a selected bibliography on military posts. The nature of the entries is explained in the proper sections of the bibliography. The bibliography is not meant to be exhaustive. It is, rather, a carefully selected list of both general works and histories of particular posts.

This guide is the product of uncounted hours of searching and compiling, and I am indebted to many for their help and encouragement. My greatest gratitude goes to the staff members who service the War Department records in the National Archives. Over a period of more than a dozen years they have most generously aided me in tracking down some very elusive data. The staff in the Cartographic Branch of the Archives was also most helpful. Very special gratitude is due Erwin Raisz, who has kindly allowed the use of his "Landforms of the United States" as the base map on which to locate the military posts. A grant from the Midwest Research Committee of The State Historical Society of Wisconsin and the University of Wisconsin aided in the research and the preparation of the manuscript.

Francis Paul Prucha, S.J.

Milwaukee, Wisconsin
February, 1964

NOTE TO THE SECOND PRINTING

Corrected entries have been made in the catalog of military posts for Fort Brady, Fort Canby [Arizona], Fort Defiance [Arizona], Fort Smith [Arkansas], Fort Washita, and Fort Wayne [Oklahoma].

Contents

Maps

A. Distribution of Regular Army Troops, 1817–1895

B. United States Military Posts, 1789–1895

Illustrations

Introduction

WHEN Henry Knox took over the office of Secretary of War in the cabinet of George Washington in March, 1789, he found little to work with. There remained from the Continental Army only a handful of regular troops, and their organization was confused. The military establishment was almost nonexistent, the coastal defenses were in a state of disrepair, and the frontier was seething with unrest, as white pressure upon the Indian country increased the anxiety of the redmen.

The Continental Congress had made some provision for the defense of the West, but when the Washington Administration began, only six establishments on the western frontier could in any sense be considered military posts. Chief of these in terms of traditional importance was Fort Pitt, at the confluence of the rivers that formed the Ohio, which had been occupied by Virginia troops in 1775 and had maintained some sort of watchfulness on the West throughout the Revolution. Nearby was Fort McIntosh, some thirty miles down the Ohio, built by Virginia troops in 1778. Not until after the Revolution, when treaties with the Northwest Indians began, did other forts appear along the Ohio waterway: Fort Harmar, near the mouth of the Muskingum River at present day Marietta, established in September, 1785; Fort Finney, established at the mouth of the Miami River in November as the site of a treaty with the Indians, then moved downriver the next summer to the falls of the Ohio near present-day Louisville; Fort Steuben, on the Ohio fifty miles below Fort McIntosh, established in August, 1786; and Fort Knox, built at Vincennes a year later. It was a small beginning, an initial push of American authority into the Indian lands, and it was not enough to overawe the Indians nor to restrain the aggressiveness of the frontiersmen, who were already probing into Indian lands before the redmen had signed away their titles.

The treaties signed by the Indians of Ohio at Fort McIntosh in January, 1785, and at Fort Finney in January, 1786, did not prevent the incursions of

1

the whites into lands guaranteed to the Indians. The Indians, disgusted with American failure to live up to the treaties, were soon ready to repudiate all the agreements made since the war. A new treaty signed at Fort Harmar in January, 1789, compensated the Indians for lands ceded in early treaties, but it did not insure peace, and soon the state of Indian affairs in Ohio called for additional efforts to subjugate the tribes and make the Northwest Terrritory available for settlement.

The campaigns of Generals Josiah Harmar, Arthur St. Clair, and Anthony Wayne in the 1790's moved the military frontier at once to the west. The old posts along the upper Ohio—McIntosh, Harmar, and Steuben—then passed into disuse and were abandoned. A new chain of frontier fortifications quickly sprang up in western Ohio to replace them. They marked the advance of American troops which culminated in Wayne's victory over the Indians at Fallen Timbers. Fort Washington, established at the site of Cincinnati in the fall of 1789, formed the anchor in this chain and for a decade served as the most important post in the Northwest Territory. To the north of Fort Washington, marking the line of march, were Forts Hamilton, Jefferson, St. Clair, Greenville, Adams, and Defiance—all minor posts which served their brief purpose as bases of supply and of attack and then disappeared when the Indian danger declined and white settlers arrived in substantial numbers. Fort Wayne, established in 1794 on the upper Maumee, remained the only outpost in the area.

A similar, but less well defined story was enacted in the South, where the problems of Indian control were more complex and more serious than in the Northwest. Treaties with the Cherokees, Choctaws, and Chickasaws had been signed in 1785 and 1786, and the more recalcitrant Creeks signed, too, in 1790. But the aggressive whites in Tennessee and Georgia kept the frontier in a state of turmoil, and the young national government came close to despair in its attempts to maintain peace. In the 1790's, garrisons at Forts Telfair and James on the Altamaha River and Forts Fidius and Wilkinson on the Oconee kept a precarious peace on the Georgia frontier, while in Tennessee troops at Knoxville and neighboring areas sought to prevent conflict in a region of dangerous contact between Indians and whites.

Meanwhile, international concerns widened the scope of American military activity. Fear of French machinations in the Mississippi Valley had prompted the re-establishment in 1794 of Fort Massac, an old French fort on the Ohio near its confluence with the Mississippi, and a similar anxiety resulted in the temporary Cantonment Wilkinsonville in 1801. The negotiation of the Jay Treaty with Great Britain brought into American hands the northern posts which Britain had refused to evacuate after the Revolution, and garrisons began their longtime occupation of Fort Niagara, Fort

2

Mackinac, and the post at Detroit in 1796. The termination of the territorial dispute with Spain in the southwest by the Pinckney Treaty of 1795
brought the transfer to the United States in 1799 of Fort St. Stephens on
the Tombigbee River and the building of Fort Stoddert in the same year,
a little to the south. The United States had already established its authority
in the lower Mississippi Valley, with the building of Fort Pickering on
Chickasaw Bluffs (at present-day Memphis) in July, 1797, Fort McHenry
at Vicksburg in the spring of 1798, and Fort Adams at Loftus Heights, in
the extreme southwestern corner of United States territory, in October.

Although the western frontier demanded the first attention of the War
Department, the coastal defenses also had to be attended to. In 1794 a
House committee recommended a series of fortifications, initial appropria-
tions were made, and works were begun at New York, Baltimore, Norfolk,
and Savannah. But no sizable forts of a permanent nature were built along
the Atlantic or Gulf coasts. Instead, defenses rested upon small batteries
or defense-works, many of which had been constructed originally by the
French, Spanish, or English. With the increasing dangers of war during the
John Adams Administration, however, the War Department inaugurated
a new system of coastal defense. In 1798 Fort Independence was begun in
Boston Harbor, Forts Adams and Wolcott in Newport Harbor, Fort Mifflin
in the Delaware River just below Philadelphia, and Fort Moultrie and Castle
Pinckney in Charleston Harbor. These forts became more or less permanent
establishments, garrisoned by artillery troops.

By the beginning of the War of 1812 other comparable posts had been
established along the Atlantic coast: Fort McHenry at Baltimore, Forts Jay
and Columbus in New York Harbor, Fort Constitution at Portsmouth, Fort
Preble at Portland, and Fort Sullivan in Passamaquoddy Bay. To these were
later added Fort Trumbull at New London, Fort Delaware near Wilmington, Fort Severn at Annapolis, Fort Washington on the Potomac, Fortress
Monroe at the entrance to Chesapeake Bay, Fort Macon at Beaufort, North
Carolina, Fort Pulaski in Savannah Harbor, and additional forts at New
York. Many of these new defenses replaced earlier fortifications. Similar
posts were constructed on the Gulf coast to protect Pensacola Harbor,
Mobile Bay, and the mouth of the Mississippi. These fortifications were in
an almost continual state of repair and alteration, and some were only irregu-
larly garrisoned.

The danger from foreign intrigue in the West was largely removed by
the Louisiana Purchase of 1803, but Louisiana was foreign territory to be
occupied, and the initial occupation was largely military. American troops
occupied New Orleans on December 20, 1803, and from that time on the
city served intermittently as a garrison for troops. Early in 1804 the army

moved into other strategic locations in the new territory, meeting no resistance but on the lookout for trouble. Such centers as Natchitoches, Attakapas, and Opelousas in present-day Louisiana were sites of army garrisons for four or five years or longer. Farther north in the Purchase, American troops moved into Arkansas Post near the mouth of the Arkansas River and New Madrid on the Mississippi near the mouth of the Ohio. In 1805 they established Fort Belle Fontaine on the south bank of the Missouri River, four miles from its junction with the Mississippi, a post which served as headquarters for the Middle West until the erection of Jefferson Barracks in 1826. The expedition of Lewis and Clark, sent out to explore the vast Louisiana region, resulted in no military establishments, but in 1808 Fort Osage was built on the Missouri River near the western boundary of present-day Missouri for protection of the government trading house there. It served as the farthest outpost of American authority for more than a decade.

The army had begun to move, too, in the Old Northwest—to protect the government factories and to maintain order among the Indian tribes. Thus in 1803 troops built Fort Dearborn on the site of the future city of Chicago, and in 1808 they established Fort Madison on the west bank of the Mississippi in the present state of Iowa. These posts indicated the intention of the United States to oppose the British traders who overran the area and who threatened American authority over the Indians.[1] And in 1811 Fort Harrison was established on the east bank of the Wabash River at Terre Haute, as protection against the threatened attacks of Tecumseh and the Prophet.

By the beginning of the War of 1812, the small American army, which had an authorized strength of fewer than 10,000 men, was drawn in a thin line around the periphery of the nation. The artillery posts of the seacoast were inadequate protection against foreign enemies; the posts manned along the Canadian border were small and weak, and they easily succumbed to British and Indian attack; and the frontier outposts in the Indian country hardly formed an impressive cordon.

[1]The government trading factories in large part were located where there was a garrison of regular troops, or posts were established at the site of factories for their protection. Of the twenty-eight factories established under the factory system from 1795 to 1822, twenty-two had a military post in the vicinity, and frequently the factory was designated by the name of the fort: Coleraine, Fort Wilkinson, Fort Hawkins, Fort Mitchell, Tellico, Hiwassee, Fort Wayne, Detroit, Chicago (Fort Dearborn), Belle Fontaine, Natchitoches, Sulphur Fork (Cantonment Taylor), Arkansas Post, Fort Osage, Fort Madison, Mackinac, Green Bay (Fort Howard), Prairie du Chien (Fort Crawford), Fort Edwards, and Fort Armstrong. The government Indian agencies also were frequently established in the shadow of a military post or were the reason for the location of such forts.

The War of 1812 itself erased a good many of the marks of American control in the West. Indians massacred the troops of Fort Dearborn as they attempted to evacuate the post in 1812. The garrison at Fort Madison fled to St. Louis before the threatening savages. Fort Mackinac fell to the British, and Fort Shelby, which the Americans had hastily constructed at Prairie du Chien in June, 1814, was taken by the British in July. The Indians had largely supported the British, on whom they depended for trade, and at the end of the war, although the Treaty of Ghent reasserted American claims to the Northwest, the United States was forced to begin anew to make its authority felt in the region of the Lakes and the upper Mississippi. The Indians and the British traders, who were still distributing British flags and British medals on American soil, had to be made aware that the United States now expected to assert her authority in fact over the area.

The War Department began to move immediately. Following the urging of Lewis Cass, newly appointed governor of Michigan Territory, it made plans to block the channels through which the British traders moved into the Mississippi and Missouri territory from Canada. Re-establishment of the post at Chicago was undertaken, a post at Green Bay (Fort Howard) was approved, and troops began to move up the Mississippi. The year 1816 thus saw, besides the reopening of Fort Dearborn and the establishment of Fort Howard, the building of three new posts on the upper Mississippi—Fort Edwards at present-day Warsaw, Illinois, Fort Armstrong on Rock Island, and Fort Crawford at Prairie du Chien.

The map in Plate 1 shows the distribution of the troops of the regular army in 1817. The concentration of the troops along the St. Lawrence boundary and in the South in the vicinity of Mobile and New Orleans reflects a residue from the deployments of the war. But the fanning out of troops into the Northwest is clearly evident. Fort Osage was still the farthest outpost, but the region of the upper Mississippi and Great Lakes was well provided with small garrisons.

Not satisfied with the line of posts from Green Bay to Prairie du Chien and Rock Island, the War Department proposed in addition to advance up both the Mississippi and the Missouri, in order to counteract the influence of the British settlement of Lord Selkirk on the Red River of the North, which was thought to be attempting to establish British control over the Indians of the Northwest. According to the plans of Secretary of War John C. Calhoun, a two-forked movement would be undertaken. One body of troops would proceed up the Mississippi River. Another group would ascend the Missouri River to the Mandan Village (near present-day Bismarck), or even as far as the mouth of the Yellowstone River, to establish a second post.

A third post at the head of navigation on the Minnesota River would form a link between the two.

The grandiose scheme fell far short of fulfillment, for the expedition sent up the Missouri was held back by transportation difficulties and ran into the snag of congressional opposition to heavy expenditures. But the troops did advance as far as Council Bluffs, where in 1819 they established the post of Fort Atkinson, which served as control over the Missouri River Valley until Fort Leavenworth replaced it in 1827. On the Mississippi the plans of Calhoun met a better fate. Fort Snelling, established at the con-

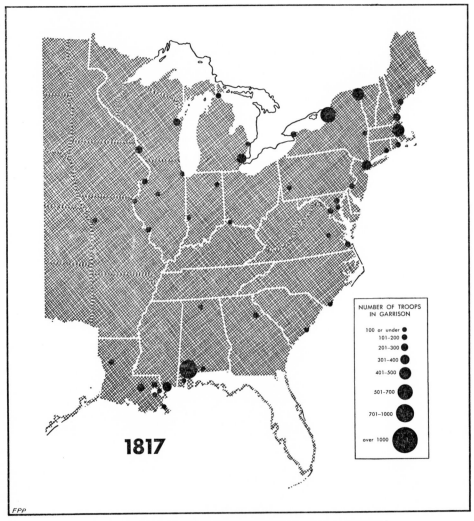

PLATE 1: DISTRIBUTION OF REGULAR ARMY TROOPS

6

fluence of the Minnesota and the Mississippi in the fall of 1819, developed into one of the key military outposts in the West and figured in nearly all plans for frontier defense until the Civil War. Calhoun had high hopes for the success of these military posts. If they were adequately garrisoned, he argued, the Northwest would be safe for American fur traders, and the fur trade, so long dominated by the British, would fall into American hands.

A similar advance, though less dramatic, took place in the Southwest. As the first removal treaty with eastern Indians was concluded in 1817, Fort Smith was established on the Arkansas River, at what is now the western

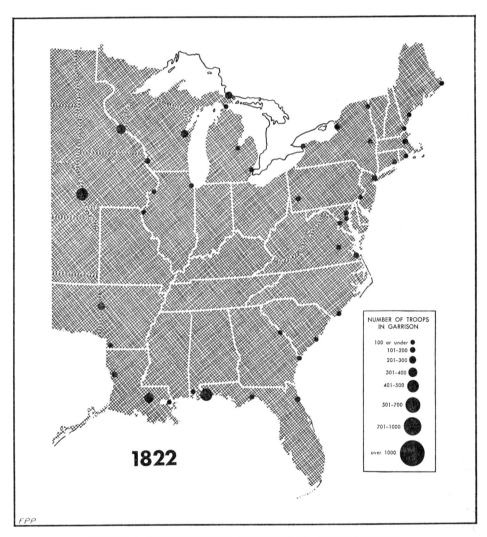

PLATE 2: DISTRIBUTION OF REGULAR ARMY TROOPS

7

boundary of Arkansas; it maintained peace as the eastern Indians moved into an area once held by other Indians. And in 1822, another permanent post—Fort Jesup—was established in Louisiana midway between the Red and Sabine rivers, to keep a watchful eye on the Spanish border.

The military frontier of 1822 is shown on Plate 2. The influence of American military power was expanding, and Indians in the area east of the Mississippi no longer presented a major problem.

The War Department did not always follow a consistent frontier defense policy. It had too few troops to meet its needs, for authorized strength of the army had been reduced to 6,000 men in 1821, and it had to make the best possible use of those that were available. Calhoun advocated a line of exterior posts along the Indian frontier. As settlement advanced, older posts could be abandoned at the interior and their garrisons used to man newer posts on the perimeter. In deciding what posts should be maintained and which abandoned, however, Calhoun admitted that he had "to choose between two evils; and to select the arrangement which is not absolutely good of itself, but which has the fewest objections."[2] The smallness of the military establishment made such a decision necessary, and Calhoun's successors faced a similar dilemma. In 1826 this exterior line in the Northwest embraced Sault Ste. Marie (where Fort Brady had been established in 1822), Green Bay, the mouth of the Minnesota, Prairie du Chien, and Council Bluffs. On the southern end of the frontier, the pattern was completed by Forts Jesup and Smith, to which had been added Forts Gibson and Towson in 1824. The two latter posts, located in what is now eastern Oklahoma, were designed to keep order among the Indians of the Plains and those others moving in from east of the Mississippi.

Calhoun and his successor, James Barbour, believed that the troops should be concentrated in a few frontier centers rather than dispersed in numerous small units. A few imposing garrisons, they believed, would not only impress the Indians but aid in the maintenance of discipline among the soldiers. In accordance with this plan, they concentrated forces at Jefferson Barracks, established a few miles below St. Louis in 1826, which became a central depot for troops and supplies for much of the West.

In 1830 the defense system followed a fairly simple arrangement (Plate 3). Small fortifications were maintained along the Atlantic coast, along the frontier of the Great Lakes, and at the mouth of the Mississippi. In the West there was a concentration of troops at Jefferson Barracks and small

[2]Calhoun to Lewis Cass, July 2, 1823, in J. Franklin Jameson, ed., *Correspondence of John C. Calhoun (Annual Report of the American Historical Association for the Year 1899, Part II, Washington, 1900)*, 148.

garrisons at selected points along the Indian border. A line of posts marked the Fox-Wisconsin waterway between the Lakes and the Mississippi: Fort Howard, Fort Crawford, and Fort Winnebago, a new fort built at the portage between the two rivers in 1828.

New plans were continually being drawn up in the War Department, although they did not drastically change frontier defense. In 1836 Secretary of War Lewis Cass proposed the creation of a great military road in the West which would form a sort of cordon joining the military posts. "It is my opinion," he reported, "that, by opening a proper communication from

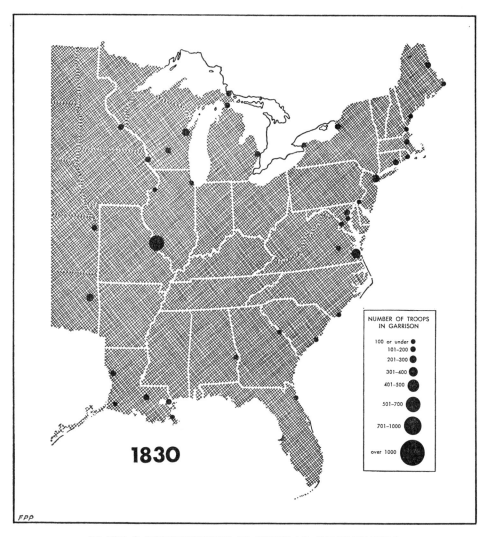

PLATE 3: DISTRIBUTION OF REGULAR ARMY TROOPS

9

some place upon the Red River, not far from Fort Towson, passing west of the ceded country in Arkansas, Missouri, and Michigan, to the right bank of the Mississippi, above the mouth of the Des Moines, and below the St. Peter's [Minnesota River], and by the establishment of proper posts along this communication, better protection will be afforded to the frontiers than in any other manner."[3]

Cass's successor, Joel R. Poinsett, objected to the idea of an exterior cordon, insisting instead that the lines of communication should run from interior to exterior, not along the edge of the Indian country. He set up a scheme of forts to implement his plan. General Edmund P. Gaines submitted a similar plan in 1838, and two years later a board of officers submitted yet another detailed plan for the distribution of the forts in the West. But the planning of the War Department and military officials was interrupted by three events, which in large part determined the actual distribution of the available military manpower.

The first of these was Indian Removal. The idea of an exchange of land with the eastern Indians, giving them lands in the West as a means of freeing the regions east of the Mississippi of Indian title, has been attributed to Thomas Jefferson. Little was accomplished in persuading the Indians to accept the removal idea, however, until after the War of 1812, when increasing pressure of the whites on Indian lands forced renewed consideration of the scheme by the federal government. In 1817 a group of Choctaws accepted land in Arkansas in exchange for their holdings in Mississippi and Alabama, but nothing more was done until the citizens of Georgia began to force the removal of the Cherokees. In 1825 President James Monroe strongly urged the removal plan, pledging the Indians that the government of the United States would protect them in their new homes, where they would be free of state interference. And in that year treaties with the western tribes provided land for the eastern Indians. In 1830, the Jacksonians passed a Removal Bill which authorized the government to carry out plans for wholesale removal. Armed with this legislation, the War Department negotiated treaties with the southern tribes and started their movement to the area set aside for them west of Arkansas and Missouri. Army posts there were garrisoned to prevent conflict between the incoming Indians and the Indians of the Plains and to prevent encroachment of the whites upon the Indian lands. Plate 4 (1839) shows the concentration of troops in this southwest area, at Forts Jesup, Towson, Gibson, Smith, and Leavenworth.

The Seminole War, which came as a direct result of the Indian Removal program, also determined the concentration of troops. The Seminole Indians

[3]Report of Cass, February 19, 1836, *American State Papers: Military Affairs*, 4:150–151.

in Florida strongly objected to removal; attempts to remove them caused a series of outbreaks which soon covered Florida and southeastern Georgia with military installations and drained into the Florida war most of the troops from the posts on the eastern seaboard. The Seminole War posts were temporary if not ephemeral affairs, small blockhouses or camps established to meet the emergency in a given area, but a few forts in Florida acquired a more or less permanent status—posts like Fort Brooke, established at Tampa in 1824, Fort Marion at St. Augustine, and Fort King, set up in 1827.

While troubled with the Seminole difficulties in the South, the United

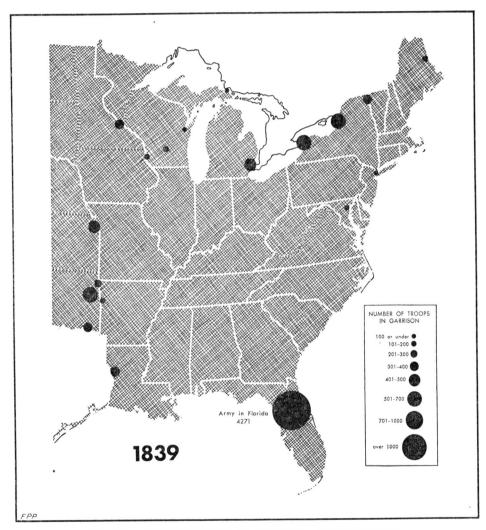

NUMBER OF TROOPS
IN GARRISON

100 or under
101–200
201–300
301–400
401–500
501–700
701–1000
over 1000

Army in Florida
4271

1839

FPP

PLATE 4: DISTRIBUTION OF REGULAR ARMY TROOPS

11

States also faced a military problem in the North—the so-called Patriot War of 1838–1840. There occurred in those years one of the periodic outbreaks of agitation for the invasion of Canada on the part of self-styled patriots, to free her from British rule and perhaps annex her to the United States. As armed groups gathered along the frontier at Detroit and at the New York border, military commanders sought to prevent mischief-makers from embroiling the United States in a full-scale war with England. Troops concentrated at Detroit, Niagara, Oswego, and Plattsburgh to maintain order and protect American interests.

Most of the remaining troops at the end of the decade were on the Indian frontier in the Northwest, where Forts Brady, Howard, Winnebago, Crawford, and Snelling still had their regular complement of troops.

As the Seminole difficulties receded and the patriots' attempts came to nothing, the distribution of troops returned to a more normal pattern. Men regarrisoned the Atlantic posts, and the forts along the St. Lawrence-Great Lakes frontier were reduced to their usual small garrisons. Military attention was once more focused on the West, where there was a continual probing into the Indian country. One of the spots of advance was the present state of Iowa, in which the Indians were gradually being pushed back to make room for advancing settlers. As a result of the Black Hawk War a narrow wedge of land west of the Mississippi was freed of its Indian title, and to keep order between Indians and whites in the area the army built a small dragoon post near the mouth of the Des Moines River in 1834. Six years later Fort Atkinson was built on the Turkey River in the northeast corner of Iowa to guard the Winnebagos, who had been moved to a reservation in that region. After a new treaty in 1842 opened up another section of rich land to white settlers, Fort Des Moines was built in central Iowa to prevent white encroachments until the Indians had withdrawn.

In the Southwest at the same time new posts made their appearance. Soldiers built Fort Washita in 1842 near the Red River west of Fort Towson to protect the emigrating eastern Indians from the wilder tribes of the Plains. In the same year Fort Scott was built in eastern Kansas, just west of the Missouri line, to serve as a link in the military road that ran from Fort Leavenworth to Fort Gibson. The distribution of these forces is shown on Plate 5 (1843).

The Mexican War seriously disrupted this arrangement. Even before the outbreak of actual hostilities, troops in large number departed for Texas, leaving the regular posts with skeletal garrisons or with no troops at all. Forts Crawford, Winnebago, and Howard in Wisconsin were evacuated, and other posts held only a handful of troops, although some were manned by volunteer troops, who served on the old frontiers until the regulars returned.

The Mexican War itself prompted the establishment of a few posts

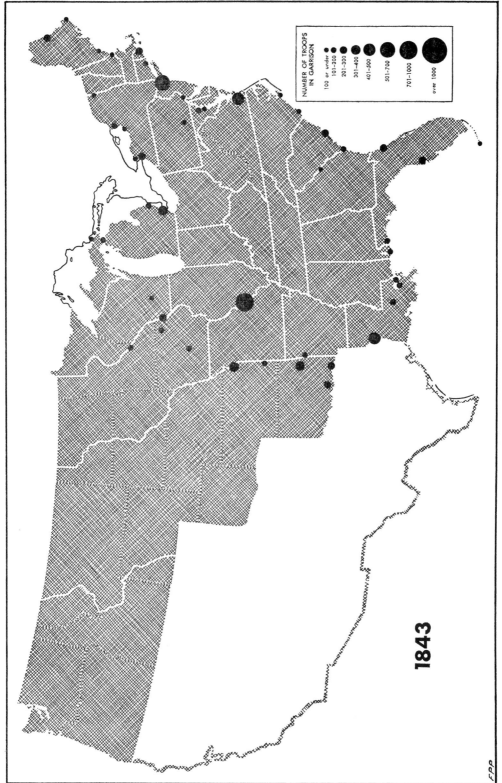

1843

PLATE 5: DISTRIBUTION OF REGULAR ARMY TROOPS

NUMBER OF TROOPS IN GARRISON

100 or under
101–200
201–300
301–400
401–500
501–700
701–1000
over 1000

FPP

which continued to serve the military frontier after the fighting had ceased. In October, 1845, troops occupied Austin and San Antonio, which became more or less regular stations for soldiers from that date on, and Corpus Christi was occupied in the same year. In March, 1845, Fort Polk was established at Point Isabel, Texas, and at the same time Fort Brown was built at Brownsville.

As the war moved west, new posts fell into American hands in New Mexico and California. Colonel Stephen Watts Kearny occupied Santa Fe in August, 1846, and began construction of Fort Marcy there in September. Posts were established at Taos in October, 1847, at Albuquerque in the next month, and at Las Vegas, New Mexico, in February, 1848. In California, United States troops occupied the Presidio of Monterey in January, 1847, and in April established a post at the Presidio of San Francisco.

The Mexican War, followed by the cession of New Mexico and California to the United States, was a great turning point in the western military frontier. The newly acquired areas opened up a vast region to American settlement and exploitation. The westward movement of whites to Texas, the Rio Grande Valley in New Mexico, California, and Oregon called for increased military protection from federal troops. But problems of establishing and maintaining the frontier outposts were multiplied, for the posts were no longer on the edge of settled areas, easily reached by the river system of the eastern United States. Scattered now at vast distances from the sources of supply and in remote areas where few local supplies could be obtained, the posts seriously drained the War Department's energies.

In Texas alone, between the signing of the Treaty of Guadalupe Hidalgo on February 2, 1848, and the end of 1849, a dozen new military posts were established to protect the frontier from Indian incursions and to protect the trails that crossed Texas toward the Far West. Along the southern Rio Grande the army established Fort Ringgold in October, 1848, and Forts McIntosh and Duncan in March, 1849, while at the western tip of the state El Paso was occupied in February, 1848, and a post was established at San Elizario, below on the Rio Grande, in September, 1849. Stretching north and south through the middle of Texas was a string of outposts established in late 1848 and 1849—from Fort Worth on the Trinity in the north to Fort Inge near present-day Uvalde and Fort Merrill on the Nueces in the south. Forts Graham, Gates, Croghan, Martin Scott, and Lincoln formed the connecting links from north to south. At the same time new posts appeared along the upper Rio Grande in New Mexico, while in California Fort Yuma was built at the confluence of the Colorado and Gila rivers.

The Mexican Cession was balanced to the north by the acquisition of a clear title to the Oregon country south of the forty-ninth parallel. Movement of emigrants to Oregon had been steady throughout the 1840's, and

14

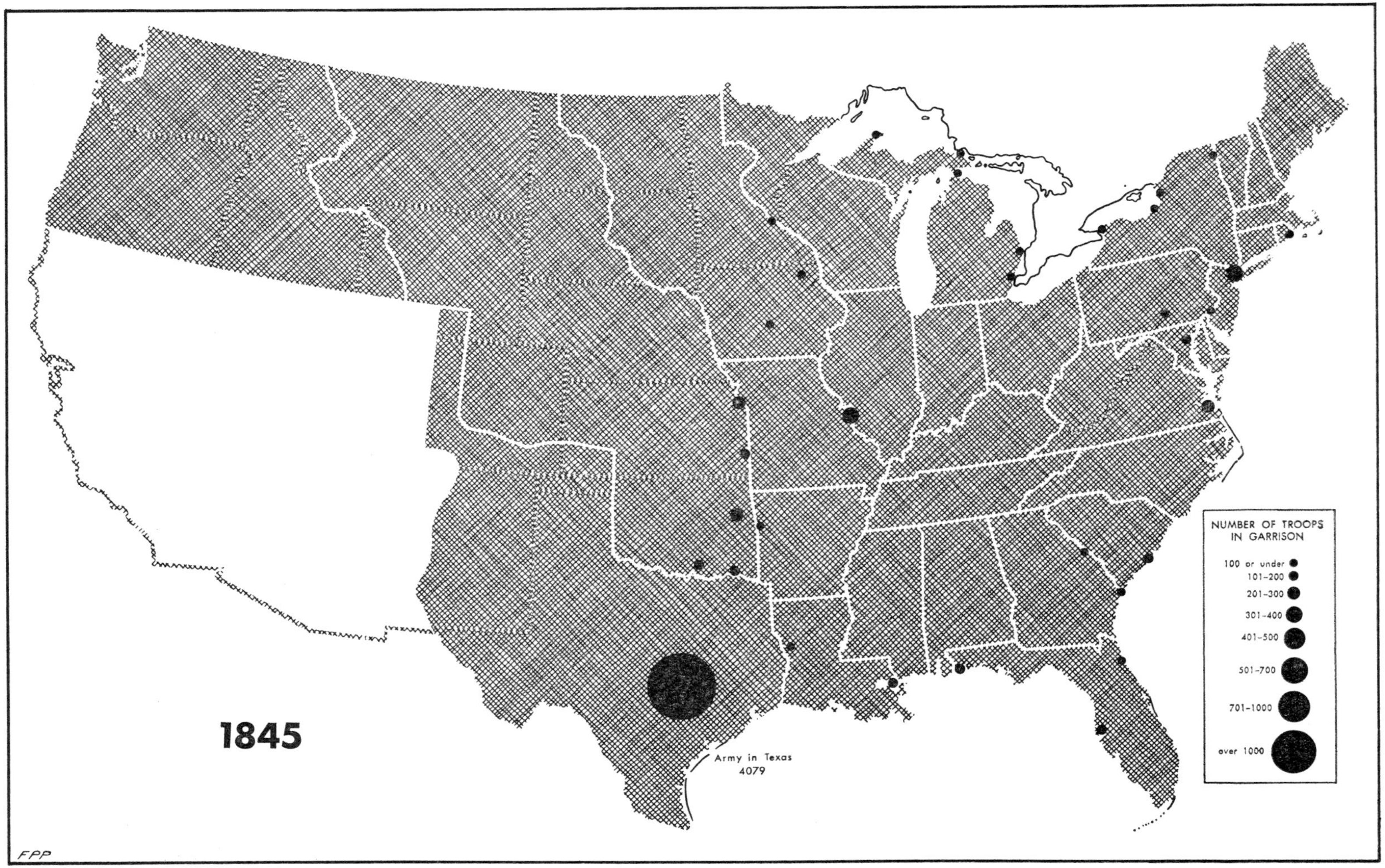
NUMBER OF TROOPS IN GARRISON
100 or under
101-200
201-300
301-400
401-500
501-700
701-1000
over 1000
Army in Texas
4079
1845
FPP

PLATE 6: DISTRIBUTION OF REGULAR ARMY TROOPS

settlements in the Columbia River area had begun. To protect these citizens, troops were placed on the Columbia, where Vancouver Barracks was established at the site of the Hudson's Bay Company post in May, 1849, Camp Astoria at the mouth of the river, and Fort Dalles at the gorge of the river in May, 1850. Additional troops guarded the Oregon Trail, from Missouri westward. In May, 1848, Fort Kearny was established on the south bank of the Platte to protect the emigrants, and in June, 1849, United States troops occupied the old trading posts of Fort Laramie on the North Platte in what is now eastern Wyoming. Both of these forts became key points on the Trail. Farther to the west a camp called Cantonment Loring was established on the Snake River near Fort Hall, but this post was considered unnecessary and the troops were withdrawn in May, 1850.

The spread of Americans into the Pacific Northwest and into the Southwest was accompanied by minor advances on other parts of the Indian frontier. In Minnesota, a new military post, Fort Ripley, was built in April, 1849, on the upper Mississippi to control the Winnebagos who had been moved into the area. In Iowa, Fort Dodge was built on the upper Des Moines River as protection for the settlers against the Sioux. In Oklahoma, a temporary Camp Arbuckle was established near the Canadian River to protect travelers on the road from Fort Smith to Santa Fe from Indian depredations. And in Florida, fresh disturbances among the Seminoles caused the establishment of new posts in 1849 and 1850.

By 1850 (Plate 7) the army had shifted its main effort to the area west of the ninety-eighth meridian. The tiny coastal fortifications and the posts along the Great Lakes maintained their vigil, but the western half of the continent had become the scene of military activity. This activity steadily increased as settlers, miners, and emigrants stirred up Indian hostility.

During the decade of the 1850's continual Indian troubles forced the expansion of the military frontier and the multiplication of posts both in the Southwest and in the Pacific Northwest, as points of contact between Indians and whites called for particular attention. In Texas, the inner chain of forts established in 1848 and 1849 was joined by a supplementary line of defense when the Texas tribes brought pressure against the inner line. The Secretary of War in 1851 ordered additional troops into Texas to set up a series of new forts. In the summer of 1851 Fort Belknap on the Red Fork of the Brazos River was established, and in November a post which took the nickname "Phantom Hill" was built on the Clear Fork of the Brazos. Farther to the south Forts McKavett, Terrett, and Clark were located on the same general line in 1852. Other Texas posts were established at specific points for Indian control. Camp Cooper in Throckmorton County was established to protect the reservation Indians stationed there in 1856, and Camp Colorado was built in the same year in Coleman County. Farther

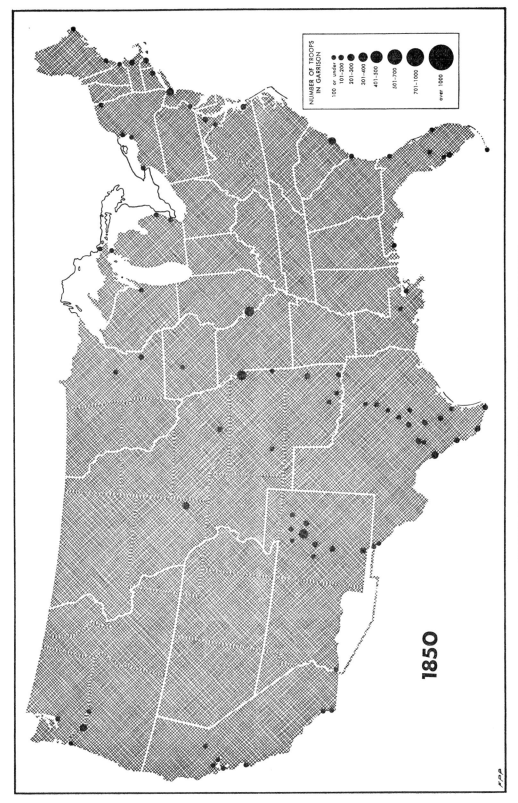

1850

NUMBER OF TROOPS
IN GARRISON

100 or under
101–200
201–300
301–400
401–500
501–700
701–1000
over 1000

PLATE 7: DISTRIBUTION OF REGULAR ARMY TROOPS

to the west Fort Lancaster on the Pecos was built in 1855, and in the Big Bend country Forts Davis, Stockton, and Quitman guarded California-bound emigrants.

In the Territory of New Mexico there was a less definite line of defense, but the depredations of the Indians on the settlers and miners called for additional installations of troops. The army built Forts Fillmore and Conrad along the Rio Grande in 1851 and Fort Thorn in 1853, and stationed troops at Los Lunas in 1852. Meanwhile Fort Defiance was established in 1851 in the heart of the Navaho country, just west of the present boundary of New Mexico, and the miners in the Santa Rita copper mines were protected by Fort Webster, built in 1852. In 1851 Fort Union was established about one hundred miles northeast of Santa Fe, to hold in check the northern tribes of Apaches and Utes and to serve as a central supply depot for the other posts in New Mexico. In 1852 Cantonment Burgwin was built north of Taos, and in 1854 Fort Craig was added to the posts along the Rio Grande, but the Indians did not stay peaceful. When the Mescalero and Jicarilla Apaches took to the warpath, troops built Fort Stanton on the Bonita River for the protection of the southeastern region of the Territory, while in the newly acquired Gadsden Purchase to the west they established Fort Buchanan in 1856 and Fort Breckinridge in 1860. North of the present state of New Mexico, but within New Mexico Territory according to its boundaries of that day, Fort Massachusetts (celebrated as the first army post in Colorado) was established in 1852 on Ute Creek, as protection against the Utes and Apaches. The fort was replaced by Fort Garland a few miles to the south in 1858.

The influx of Americans into California after the discovery of gold in 1848 and the acquisition of the territory at the end of the Mexican War caused widespread tension between the newcomers and the Indians in the area. The Americans seemed determined to grab everything in the territory for themselves, and the Indians were often driven to hostility in their attempt to preserve their lands and their identity. The soldiers not only had to protect the settlers and the emigrants from Indian depredations, but eventually had to protect the Indians as well from the ruthlessness of the whites. The War Department ultimately dotted California with military installations—forts defending the settlements on the coast, posts in the mining country to protect the miners, and garrisons along the routes of communication to protect the large numbers of people going to and from the mines.

In 1849 garrisons were established at San Diego and at Benicia at the western end of Suisun Bay, and in the same year Fort Far West was located at a strategic point on Bear Creek, to guard the emigrant routes and the wagon roads to the mines, which crossed at that spot. The miners in the San Joaquin Valley were protected by Fort Miller, established in May, 1851. In 1852 Fort Reading was built in the northern Sacramento Valley and farther to the north Fort Jones was established on the Scott River. At the southern end of the great valley Fort Tejon was established in 1854 to command the pass of that name. To control the Mohave and Paiute Indians along the lower Colorado, Fort Mohave was established in 1859.

When Indian scares in northwestern California brought calls for more troops, the War Department responded by establishing a number of small posts along the coast and in the valleys of the coastal range. One of these was Fort Humboldt, at the mouth of the Humboldt River, garrisoned in 1853; another was Fort Bragg, built on the coast south of Cape Mendocino in 1857. Fort Crook was added in the Pit River country in 1857. Further Indian alarms led to the establishment of Fort Ter-Waw on the Klamath Indian reservation in the same year, and a year later, when a mass uprising of the Indians was rumored, the War Department established Fort Gaston in the Hoopa Valley and Camp Wright in Mendocino County.

The chain of California posts extended into what is now the State of Oregon, where similar Indian threats and outbreaks terrified the white inhabitants. Fort Orford was established ten miles south of Cape Blanco in September, 1851, and Fort Lane, in the mountains just north of the California line, was established in 1853. In 1856 Fort Umpqua was located on the north side of the Umpqua River near its mouth. North in the Willamette Valley, Forts Hoskins and Yamhill were established in 1856 to keep order among the Indians placed on reservations.

During the same period of the mid-'fifties Indian disturbances in present-day Washington drew the attention of the military to the Pacific Northwest. The movement of settlers and miners into the region irritated the tribes and in 1855 a general outbreak, known as the Yakima War, brought American troops into the region and resulted in the establishment of a number of significant military posts. The army built Fort Cascades at the cascades of the Columbia above Fort Vancouver in 1855, and in 1856 established Fort Walla Walla as a center of military force in the southeastern corner of the Territory and Fort Simcoe in the Simcoe Valley as a bastion against the hostile Yakimas.

As miners moved to the north, posts appeared in 1856 on Bellingham Bay, sixteen miles south of the mouth of the Fraser River, and at Port Townsend at the entrance to Puget Sound. At the southern extremity of Puget Sound, Fort Steilacoom stood guard beginning in August, 1849.

The years 1857 and 1858 brought a heavy concentration of troops into the Utah country as a result of the Mormon War. The famous trading post, Fort Bridger, in what is now the southwestern corner of Wyoming, was destroyed by the Mormons when the United States troops approached. The site was leased to the United States, and Fort Bridger was rebuilt as a military post. In the summer of 1858 the troops built Camp Floyd (later called Fort Crittenden) midway between Salt Lake City and Provo, as a center of American authority until the tensions between the Mormons and their hostile neighbors had ceased. Two years later, when the Indians in the Carson Valley in western Nevada went on the warpath, the troops moved into that region to restore the peace; there they built Fort Churchill on the Carson River about twenty-five miles east of Virginia City.

Other changes, too, were made. Fort Ridgely at the Sioux reservation along the Minnesota River was established in 1853, as the frontier of settlement pushed across the Mississippi into Minnesota. In Kansas, Fort Riley was established in 1853 at the junction of the Smoky Hill and Republican forks of the Kansas River, and in 1859 Fort Larned was built in western Kansas on the right bank of the Pawnee River, near its confluence with the Arkansas, in order to protect the Santa Fe Trail. The hostilities of the Kiowa called for a concentration of troops in that area in 1860. Along the Missouri River in Dakota, also, military posts made their appearance. The trading posts of Fort Pierre and Fort Lookout were temporarily occupied as military posts from 1855 to 1857, and in 1856 Fort Randall was built as a base of supplies and as a protection for settlers against hostile Indians. On the border of Minnesota, directly west from Fort Ripley, Fort Abercrombie was established in 1858 at the head of navigation of the Red River of the North. In Oklahoma, Fort Cobb was established on the Washita River in October, 1859.

This rapid expansion of military installations caused much concern and necessitated careful planning in the War Department. Secretary of War John B. Floyd, in his annual report of December, 1857, spoke of the need to garrison "68 forts of a large and permanent character, so far, at least, as it is possible to supply men for the purpose; and to occupy 70 posts less permanently established, where the presence of a force is absolutely required."[4] The tremendous extent of this undertaking was set forth by Floyd:

> The external boundary of our country, requiring throughout a more or less vigilant military supervision, is 11,000 miles in length, presenting every variety of climate and temperature, from the inclement cold of our Canada frontier to the tropical regions of southern Texas. But the occu-

[4]Report of the Secretary of War, December 5, 1857, Sen. Ex. Doc. No. 11, 35 Cong., 1 sess., serial 920, p. 3.

pation of this long line of frontier is a trifling difficulty in comparison with that of protecting the double line of Indian frontier, extending from the Lake of the Woods to the banks of the Rio Grande, on the east side of the Rocky Mountains, and from beyond the river Oregon [the Columbia] on the British frontier to the head of the Gulf of California, on the western slope of those mountains. Superadded to these lines, requiring to be occupied, are the great lines of intercommunication between the valley of the Mississippi and the Pacific ocean, which imperatively demand that protection which only the United States troops can furnish.[5]

Floyd scoffed, in his report of 1859, at the use of the term "peace establishment" to describe this army scattered over an area of three million square miles. "All the incidents pertaining to an active war establishment characterize our service throughout the year," he asserted, "excepting only the casualties upon the battle field; and these, in our service, are far from being few or insignificant."[6] The work of the troops, the long marches, the amount of heavy fatigue duty, the privation and hardship the soldiers were forced to endure, were not exceeded in any service, he maintained, and not equalled in any other peace establishment.

The exterior defensive lines of which the Secretary of War spoke were of secondary importance in this warlike peace establishment on the eve of the Civil War, for the American army in the 1850's was distinctly a western frontier army (Plate 8). The artillery posts along the coast had all but lost their garrisons, as the more imminent dangers of the West called for the use of the available troops in that part of the nation.

The Civil War, with its thousands of troops and its drawn-out campaigns, diverted attention from the Indian frontier, but it did not remove the Indian dangers nor the need for army garrisons in the Indian country. While the fighting was going on in the South, the posts in the West (often with volunteer troops in place of the United States regulars) carried on their essential function. As new needs arose, new posts were built and garrisoned.

The secession of the Southern States created a critical problem for the posts within their borders. General David Twiggs, commanding in Texas, surrendered all the federal property under his command to the Confederates, and the regular troops marched out of the posts in April and May, 1861, either leaving the forts unmanned or turning them over to Southern troops. The troops in Indian Territory abandoned their posts and marched to Fort Leavenworth.

---

[5]*Ibid.*

[6]Report of the Secretary of War, December 1, 1859, Sen. *Ex.* Doc. No. 2, 36 Cong., 1 sess., serial 1024, p. 3.

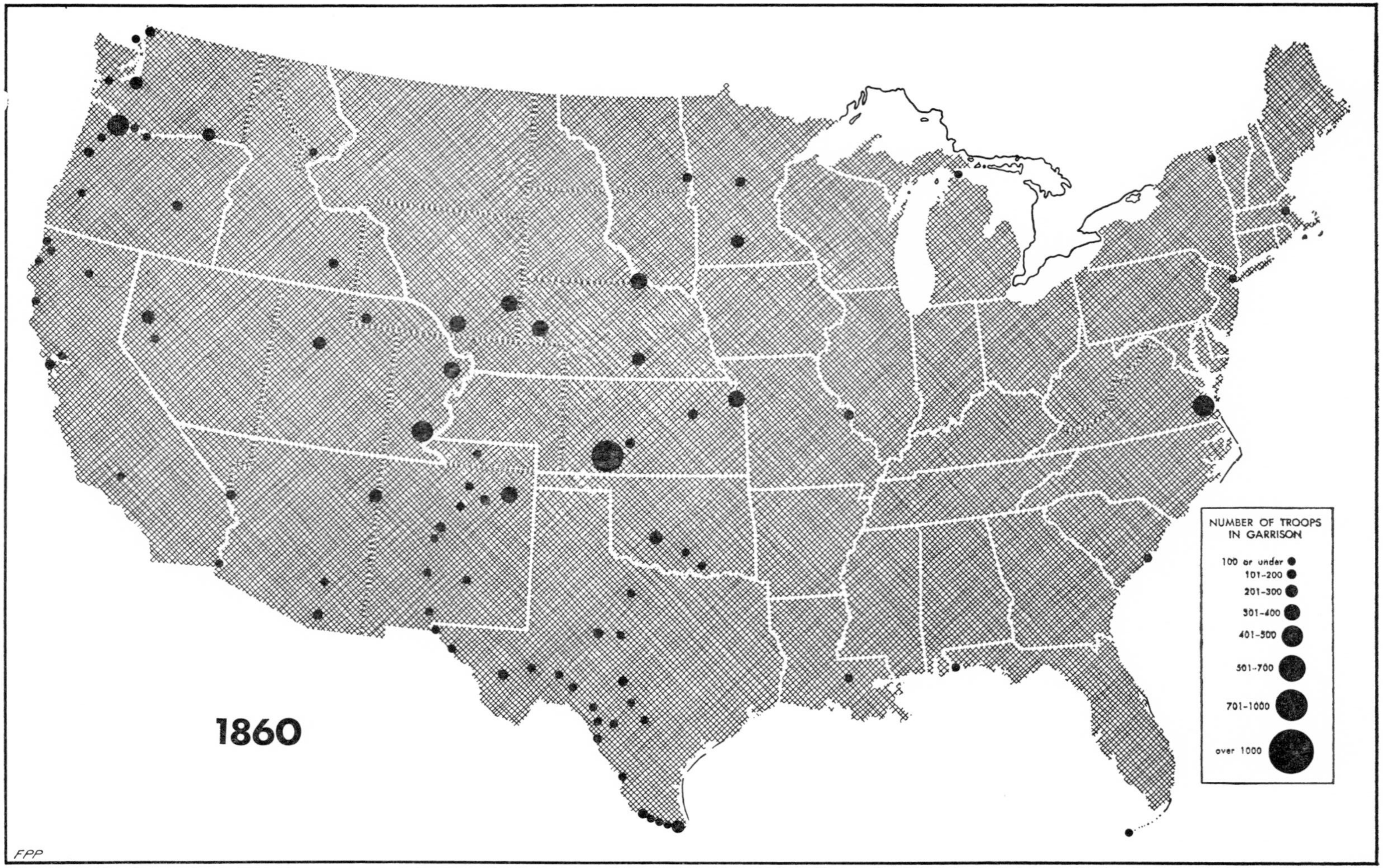

NUMBER OF TROOPS
IN GARRISON

100 or under
101-200
201-300
301-400
401-500
501-700
701-1000
over 1000

1860

PLATE 8: DISTRIBUTION OF REGULAR ARMY TROOPS

FPP

In the Territory of New Mexico, the federal forces were consolidated in order to meet the Southern threat. The centers of defense were to be Forts Fillmore and Craig on the Rio Grande, Fort Union guarding the supply lines from Fort Leavenworth, and Forts Stanton and Garland. In June and July, 1861, Fort McLane at the copper mines, Fort Breckinridge, and Fort Buchanan were abandoned. The Confederate invasion of the Rio Grande Valley forced the evacuation of Fort Fillmore, and Fort Stanton was abandoned when news came of the surrender of the troops leaving Fort Fillmore. The Confederacy soon controlled Santa Fe and most of the towns of the Territory. The victory was short-lived, however, for the aggressive action of Colorado volunteers and then of California volunteers forced the Southern troops out of the Territory.

During the Civil War the Indian problem did not lie dormant. The Indians, sensing that the preoccupation of the Union with the Civil War gave them a new opportunity to assert their claims and grievances, created disturbances that necessitated the erection of new posts.

In California, as the miners continued their encroachments on the Indian country and as the mining activities stimulated the influx of stockmen and agricultural pioneers, the Indians' hostility increased. The depredations called for new military posts, which were often begun and manned by California volunteers but as soon as possible turned over to the troops of the regular army. In March, 1862, Fort Baker was established near the Mad River in northwestern California to check the Indians. Camp Lincoln was established in June of that year at Crescent City. To protect miners in the Owens River Valley, Camp Independence was built in 1862, and Camp Babbitt was built at the same time near Visalia. As mining activity spread to new areas, so too did the military establishments. In 1865 Fort Bidwell was built in the extreme northeastern corner of the state.

Along the coast, too, the Civil War years saw the extension of military installations. The San Francisco area was strengthened with the establishment of Fort Point (later designated Fort Winfield Scott) in 1861 and by Fort Mason and the post on Angel Island in 1863. And in 1862 the army built Drum Barracks just south of Los Angeles. These fortifications were part of the coastal defenses of the nation, but their existence strengthened in general the military forces in California, and troops from the coastal forts could be called upon to take part in Indian control if the need arose.

In New Mexico and Arizona, Indian depredations kept the troops occupied after the retreat of the Confederate forces. In May, 1862, a fort was established at Tucson, which had become an important mining center, and in July a detachment of California volunteers established Fort Bowie at Apache Pass in the Chiricahua Mountains, to protect a spring at the site and to guard the road to Tucson. Fort Wingate was established in the

Navaho country about twenty miles southwest of Mount Taylor in New Mexico in October, 1862, then was moved later in the decade to a new site sixty-five miles to the west. In the next month Fort Sumner was established on the left bank of the Pecos River at Bosque Redondo to guard Apache and Navaho prisoners. And to the north, on the Canadian River, Fort Bascom was built in August, 1863, to keep under control the Comanche, Kiowa, and other tribes of the region of the Canadian and Red rivers.

As the decade advanced the War Department established Fort Whipple near Prescott, Arizona, Fort Goodwin near the Gila River in southeastern Arizona, and Fort McDowell on the west bank of the Verde River northeast of Phoenix. In October, 1865, the site of old Fort Breckinridge was reoccupied and designated Fort Grant, though the post was moved in 1872 to a new site at the foot of Mount Graham. Thus continued the general coverage of Arizona with military posts that was to last beyond the end of the century.

The second year of the Civil War was marked by the serious Sioux outbreak in Minnesota. The Indians, irritated by delays in the arrival of annuities, disturbed by the increasing encroachments of the whites into their region, and well aware that the military forces of the state had been weakened by the call of the regular troops to the battle areas in the South, rose up against the settlers in the Minnesota River Valley. Thus began an Indian war of considerable dimension, though it has been much overshadowed by the war to save the Union. The whites struck back quickly at the Sioux, and the war extended to the west of Minnesota as the army campaigned against the Indians in the Missouri River Valley of Dakota Territory. The Department of the Northwest, under General John Pope, was set up to handle the difficulties on the northwestern frontier. As the campaigns against the Sioux progressed, new military forts were established. After defeating the hostiles, the expedition moving up the Missouri in 1863 under the command of General Alfred H. Sully established a fort bearing his name on the east bank of the Missouri near present-day Pierre, South Dakota. The site proved to be unsatisfactory, however, and in 1865 the post was moved to a new location about thirty miles above the original establishment.

In 1864, when the campaign moved further up the Missouri, Fort Rice was established about forty miles south of present Bismarck. As General Sully moved northwest through Dakota Territory he garrisoned the fur trading posts at Fort Union and Fort Berthold. A reservation was set up on the Missouri in present-day South Dakota for the Indians who had been captured in the war, and Fort Thompson was built there for their protection.

The active campaigns against the hostiles thus began the military occupation of the upper Missouri area, but other developments as well contributed to this movement of troops. The discovery of gold in Idaho and Montana in the early 1860's brought the usual flood of miners into the region in search of easy fortunes. There was a rush of miners and emigrants to Fort Benton, a trader's establishment on the upper Missouri, which became a jumping-off place for the mines. In order to keep open the routes of travel to the mining region—both the overland trails and the Missouri River—new forts were called for. In 1866, Fort Buford replaced Fort Union on the Missouri near the mouth of the Yellowstone, and Fort Stevenson was built in 1867 between Fort Buford and Fort Rice, replacing Fort Berthold, whose garrison moved to the new post. A number of posts were established at the same time in eastern Dakota Territory to keep check on the Sioux. Fort Sisseton (first called Fort Wadsworth) was established at the head of the Coteau des Prairies in 1864, Forts James and Dakota in southeastern Dakota in 1865, and Fort Ransom on the Sheyenne River and Fort Totten at Devils Lake in 1867.

The mining frontier in Montana was approached not only from the east across Dakota and up the Missouri River, but from the south as well. A favorite route was the Bozeman Trail, which moved north from Fort Laramie on the North Platte, along the Powder River into Montana Territory. The road traversed treasured hunting grounds of the Sioux, and the federal government undertook to protect the miners by a series of military posts running north from Fort Laramie. In 1865 Fort Reno was built on the Powder River about one hundred eighty miles northwest of Fort Laramie, and in the summer of 1866 Fort Phil Kearny, which became the principal post on the Bozeman Trail, was established on the Piney Fork of the Powder River in the foothills of the Big Horn Mountains. At the top of the trail Fort C. F. Smith was built in August, 1866, in southern Montana, where the Bozeman Trail crossed the Big Horn River. To these were added Fort Fetterman, established on the North Platte about eighty miles west of Fort Laramie, in 1867, and Fort Ellis on the East Gallatin River east of the present city of Bozeman, Montana, in the same year.

In Montana other posts were also built immediately after the Civil War for the protection of the miners and the routes to the mines. Camp Cooke on the Missouri and Fort Shaw on the Sun River, near the Great Falls of the Missouri, were built in 1866 and 1867 as a continuation of the line of posts along the Missouri in Dakota. In 1869 the trading post of Fort Benton was garrisoned by regular troops, and Fort Logan was built near Diamond City to protect that spot and neighboring mining camps from Indian depredations.

In Kansas and eastern Colorado, meanwhile, other Indian disturbances and dangers caused the multiplication of posts in that central area. Fort

Zarah was established in September, 1864, near the Arkansas River in central Kansas, to furnish a base of operations against the Kiowa and Comanche Indians. At the same time Fort Harker (first called Fort Ellsworth) was built on the north bank of the Smoky Hill River near the crossing of the old Santa Fe stage road. Where the Santa Fe Trail crossed the Arkansas, near present-day Dodge City, Fort Dodge was established in 1865 and used as a base of operations against the Arapaho and Cheyenne Indians. Fort Wallace was established on the South Fork of the Smoky Hill in October, 1865, and Fort Reynolds on the Arkansas about twenty miles east of Pueblo, in 1867.

The immediate post-Civil War years also witnessed the springing up of small posts in the mining regions of northern Nevada, southeastern Oregon, and southwestern Idaho. In 1863 Fort Boise was established in the Boise River Valley to protect emigrants from the Shoshoni Indians. In 1865 Camp Lyon was established on the north fork of the Jordan River on the southwestern border of Idaho, and in the following year Camp Three Forks Owyhee was established nearby on the south fork of the Owyhee River near the junction of the three branches. In northern Nevada, on the east bank of the Quinn River, Fort McDermit was established in August, 1865, and a little to the west Camp McGarry was set up at Summit Springs in October. At the northern end of the Ruby Range, a few miles south of the Humboldt River, Fort Halleck appeared in 1867. In 1866 three short-lived forts were built in southern Oregon—Camps Warner, Alvord, and C. F. Smith—to protect emigrants and guard the mining regions. In the following year Fort Harney, a post that guarded eastern Oregon until 1880, was established farther north.

In Texas after the Civil War, the problem of Indian control reverted to the United States troops. A number of the posts that had been evacuated at the beginning of the War were now regarrisoned, and new forts were established, forming a chain of defense across western Texas from Fort Richardson, built in 1867 on a tributary of the Trinity River to protect emigrants and the cattle trails, to Fort Davis on the south, which was reoccupied in the same year to protect the trails and to act as a base for operations against the hostile Apaches. Between these posts Fort Griffin in 1867 replaced Fort Belknap in protecting the settlements against the Comanche and Kiowa Indians, and Fort Concho was established at the end of the year at the junction of the Concho and North Concho rivers. Fort Stockton was re-established in July. The distribution of troops for 1867 is shown on Plate 9.

It is clear from the map, however, that the defense of the western frontier was only part of the problem facing the War Department. The concentration of troops in present-day Kansas, Wyoming, and Dakota, and in the Southwest, was matched by the numerous garrisons in the South, stationed there in occupation during Reconstruction. These latter garrisons were not

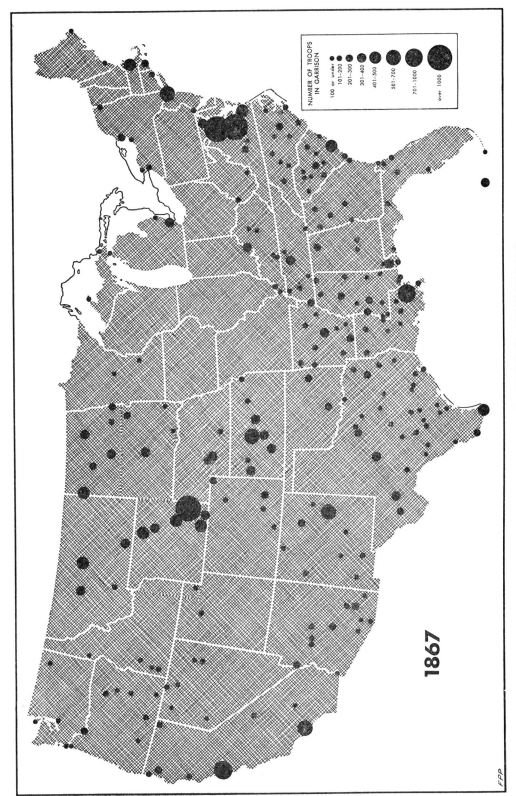

1867

PLATE 9: DISTRIBUTION OF REGULAR ARMY TROOPS

NUMBER OF TROOPS
IN GARRISON

100 or under
101–200
201–300
301–400
401–500
501–700
701–1000
over 1000

part of the military frontier, nor were they formally set up as military forts. But they were a problem for the War Department in deploying the available troops, and they must be included in the picture of troop distribution in the years immediately after the Civil War.

Between 1867 and the end of the decade few significant changes were made in the military frontier, although as the troops were pulled out of the South, the Indian frontier in the West became again the focal point of army interest. One important change, however, was the withdrawal of the garrisons from the posts along the Bozeman Trail. The Sioux, who had so violently resisted the introduction of the military posts in their favorite hunting grounds of the Powder River Valley, forced the United States government to retreat. By a treaty signed in 1868, the United States agreed to abandon the posts it had established so shortly before. Forts Reno, Phil Kearny, and C. F. Smith disappeared, and the land they had guarded was once more the domain of the Indians.

The government policy of placing the subdued Indians on reservations made it necessary for military troops to be stationed nearby to keep order and to protect the reservation Indians from the wild Indians who did not wish to submit to the ordered life of farmers. In 1870 the army established military garrisons at the Whetstone, Grand River, Cheyenne River, Lower Brulé, and Crow Creek agencies, all of which were located along the Missouri River in Dakota Territory. Three of these stations were turned into regular forts—Fort Hale at Lower Brulé Agency, Fort Bennett at Cheyenne River Agency, and Fort Yates at Standing Rock, where the Grand River Agency had been relocated.

Increasing Indian difficulties on the southern Great Plains caused the expansion of army activity into western Oklahoma, where Fort Supply was established in November, 1868, at the confluence of the two streams that formed the North Fork of the Canadian River. In March of the next year Fort Sill was established near the foot of the Wichita Mountains. These posts served as bases of operations against the Kiowa, Comanche, and other hostiles of the Plains and held sizable garrisons while the Indian dangers continued.

In Arizona a sprinkling of new establishments appeared. Camp Hualpai was established near Aztec Pass about forty miles northeast of Prescott in May, 1869. Camp Crittenden was built in 1868 at the site of old Fort Buchanan in southern Arizona, and in the same year Camp Colorado was established on the Colorado River Indian Reservation about forty miles north of La Paz. In 1870 Fort Apache was established on the White Mountain River to protect nearby settlements from Apache raids.

In Wyoming, too, there was a general widening of the military frontier.

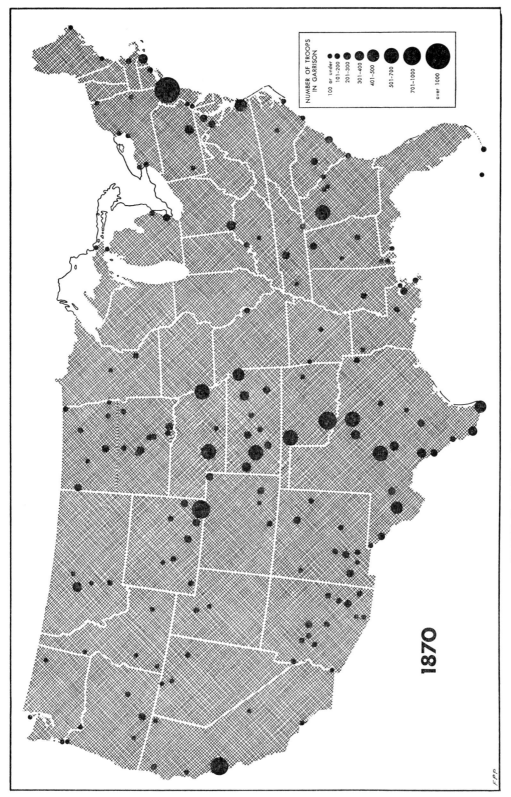

1870

PLATE 10: DISTRIBUTION OF REGULAR ARMY TROOPS

NUMBER OF TROOPS
IN GARRISON

100 or under
101–200
201–300
301–400
401–500
501–700
701–1000
over 1000

F.P.P.

Fort D. A. Russell was established in 1867 at present Cheyenne to protect the Union Pacific Railroad, and in the following year Fort Fred Steele was established near the present city of Rawlins to protect the line near its crossing of the North Platte River. In 1869, to fulfill the terms of a treaty with the Shoshoni and Bannock Indians for their protection from the Sioux, Cheyenne, and other hostile Indians, a military post was established in the Wind River Valley. Originally located on the Popo Agie River at the site of present-day Lander, the post was first called Camp Augur. Its name was changed to Camp Brown and then to Fort Washakie and its location moved to a site on the South Fork of the Little Wind River. In 1870 Camp Stambaugh was established near South Pass as protection to the miners who came into the region. These developments are shown on Plate 10 (1870).

The 1870's were another decade of Indian wars. The treaty of 1868 with the Sioux had provided for reservations for the tribes west of the Missouri and had stipulated that the Powder River Valley in Wyoming and the territory north of the North Platte in Nebraska would be reserved as hunting grounds for certain tribes. The peace that followed the signing of the treaty, however, did not last long. The movement west of the Northern Pacific Railroad was looked upon by the Indians as a violation of their reservations, and troops had to be detailed to accompany survey crews in western Dakota. In 1872 Fort Seward was established at the railroad crossing of the James River at present Jamestown, and Fort Abraham Lincoln (first called Fort McKeen) was established near present Bismarck to protect the construction crews on the road.

The Sioux reservations in Dakota, which the government had promised to protect against white intrusion, were soon invaded. In 1874 General George A. Custer made a reconnaissance expedition into the Black Hills and came out with reports of golden riches in the area. This was too much for the gold seekers, who gathered at points along the Missouri and in Nebraska to outfit for illegal excursions into gold country. The troops of the Missouri River posts did what they could to discourage the miners, but soon the government withdrew its military opposition to the gold seekers, and miners by the thousands invaded the area. The Indians were convinced that they would have to fight to preserve their lands.

Meanwhile the Sioux in the Powder River country and in western Dakota Territory continued to be hostile toward the United States and toward the tribes that had settled on the reservations. The government declared that Agency Indians who were not on the reservations by January 31, 1876, were to be considered hostiles, and when the ultimatum was not met, the army prepared for action. Soon the army found most of the Sioux and Cheyenne warriors arrayed against it, and steps were taken to begin their subjugation.

30

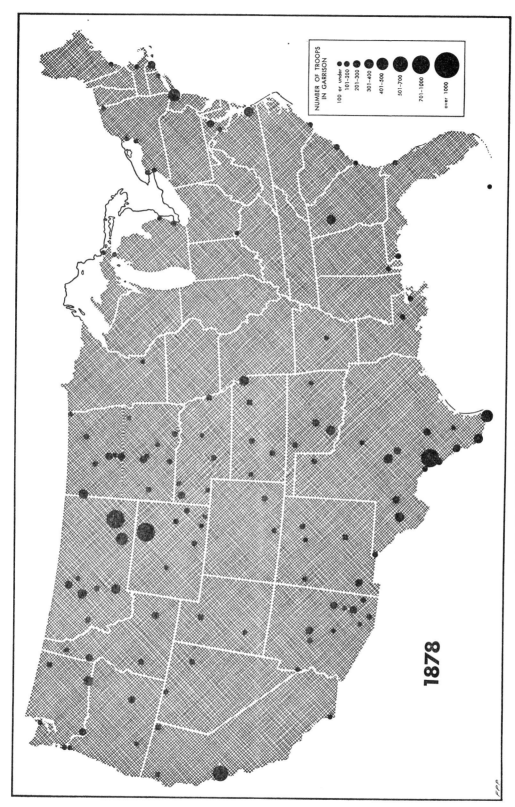

1878

PLATE 11: DISTRIBUTION OF REGULAR ARMY TROOPS

NUMBER OF TROOPS
IN GARRISON

100 or under
101–200
201–300
301–400
401–500
501–700
701–1000
over 1000

Three columns of troops began to move against the Indians in Montana, and it was in this campaign that the "massacre" of General Custer's troops at the Little Big Horn occurred. This victory did the Indians little good, for reinforcements were rushed into the Indian country, and the Sioux chiefs were relentlessly pursued until they were captured or driven into Canada. The defenses of the West were strengthened by the erection of new permanent fortifications in the region where the Indians' troubles were centered. In 1876, Congress appropriated money for two new posts on the Yellowstone. Fort Keogh was built at the mouth of the Tongue River, at present Miles City, Montana, in 1876, and in the following year Fort Custer was established at the junction of the Big Horn and the Little Big Horn rivers. Meanwhile a new post called Fort McKinney was built in the Powder River Valley near the site of old Fort Reno. These forts were heavily garrisoned until the Indian troubles died away. At the same time Fort Missoula was established in the Flathead country near the present city of Missoula, and Fort Meade was established in the Black Hills in 1878.

The Sioux warriors in the northwestern corner of Nebraska also called for careful watching, and the federal government sent troops into the area to protect the agencies and to keep order among the restless Indians. Fort Robinson was established on the White River at the Red Cloud Agency in March, 1874, and Camp Sheridan was located at the Spotted Tail Agency in the same region.

Along the Oklahoma-Texas border the Red River War of 1874 was the last major struggle, and additional posts were established in the area to serve as bases of operation. In 1874 Fort Reno was located on the North Fork of the Canadian River, near the Cheyenne and Arapaho Indian Agency, and in 1875 a cantonment was established farther up the same river, which never got an official name but was referred to as Cantonment on the North Fork of the Canadian River. To aid in the opening of a cattle route which would avoid the settlements in Indian Territory and Kansas, Fort Elliott was established in the Texas Panhandle in 1875. Farther south in Texas the great difficulties lay along the Rio Grande, where marauding Indians on the border caused much concern. The posts on the river itself were well garrisoned, and a heavy concentration of troops was centered at Fort Clark.

Plate 11 (1878) shows the general picture of troop distribution at the end of the major Indian fighting in the West. From that point on there were few new posts in the West of major significance. Only in Montana, where the Sioux were still not secure on reservations, did important posts appear. Here Fort Assinniboine, near the present city of Havre, was established in 1879, and for some time was heavily garrisoned. Fort Maginnis was located near Lewistown in 1880, and in the same year Camp Poplar River was established near the Missouri River in the eastern section of the state.

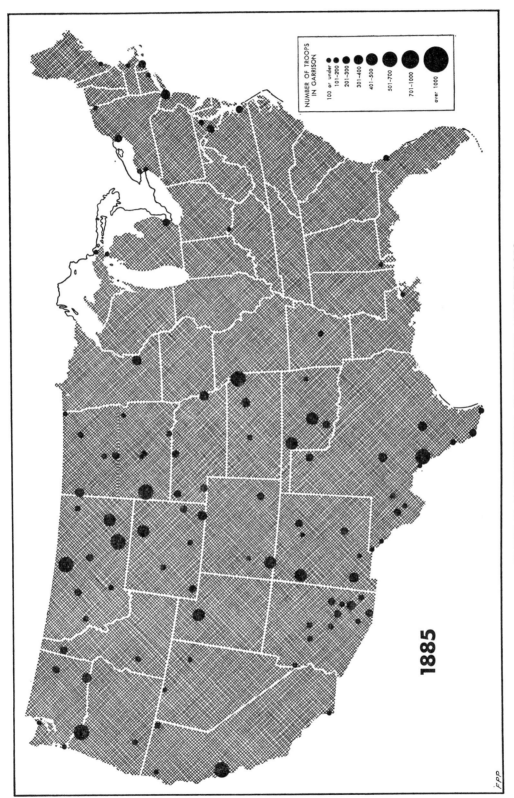

1885

PLATE 12: DISTRIBUTION OF REGULAR ARMY TROOPS

NUMBER OF TROOPS
IN GARRISON

100 or under
101-200
201-300
301-400
401-500
501-700
701-1000
over 1000

Only isolated dangers necessitated new posts in other regions of the nation. Fort Niobrara was established in northern Nebraska in 1880, and in the same year Fort Spokane was located near the junction of the Spokane and Columbia rivers in eastern Washington.

In general the movement was retrenchment rather than expansion. The tribes were placed on reservations where they were dependent upon government supplies for their subsistence. Some Indian raids along the Canadian border kept troops in the northern posts, but the Indian frontier disappeared quickly in the 1880's. The Northern Pacific was completed in 1883, and the Great Northern, too, moved into the West. The posts along the Missouri River no longer served a useful purpose as the settlers swarmed into the region, and one by one they passed out of existence. What was true along the upper Missouri was true in other parts of the West as well. Everywhere there was consolidation of troops and abandonment of the smaller posts.

Secretary of War Robert T. Lincoln noted at the end of 1884 that "the Army has enjoyed almost complete rest from active field operations," and he remarked about the "unprecedented quiet among the Indians, there having been reported during the year no disturbance to cause the firing of a single musket."[7] This Indian quiet, the rapid extension of the railroads which made it possible to transport troops quickly to areas where they were needed, and the increase of western settlement made it advisable to abandon many outposts. The troops were concentrated at larger permanent posts as quickly as quarters could be provided, and the outlying installations were turned over to the Department of the Interior. The Secretary of War rejoiced at the economy and improved conditions for discipline and instruction of the troops which this concentration afforded.

Plate 12 (1885) shows the beginning of the end. The military distribution was still dictated by frontier conditions, and Indian troubles still cropped up. Fort Duchesne in eastern Utah was established in 1886 to keep order among the Utes, and 1886 was a busy year for the troops in Arizona pursuing and finally capturing Geronimo and his band. But consolidation was going on apace, and if new posts appeared in the West, Indians were not the reason for their establishment. Camps Medicine Butte and Pilot Butte in western Wyoming were set up in 1885 to control anti-Chinese rioting along the construction route of the Union Pacific, and Fort Logan at Denver was established in 1887 as the result of pressure from civic-minded citizens who thought that a military post would be good for the business of the region.

It is customary to mark the close of the Indian conflicts in the West

[7]Report of the Secretary of War, November 21, 1884, *House Ex. Doc.* No. 1, Part 2, 48 Cong., 2 sess., serial 2277, p. 5.

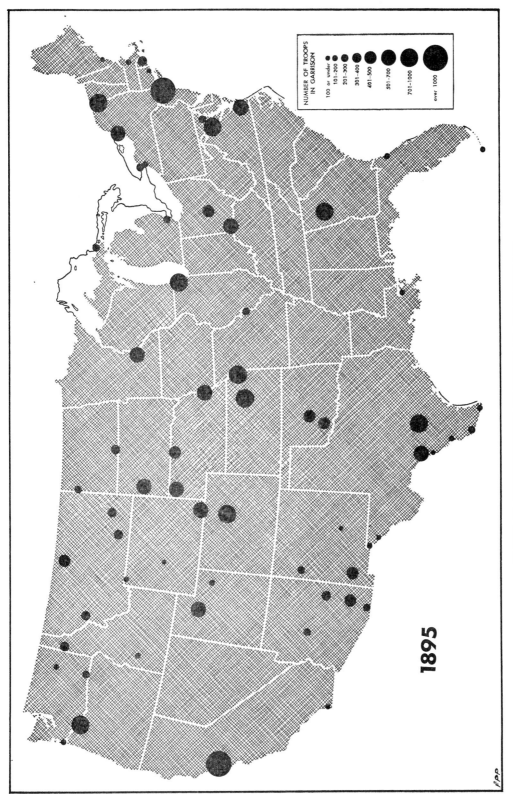

1895

NUMBER OF TROOPS
IN GARRISON

100 or under
101–200
201–300
301–400
401–500
501–700
701–1000
over 1000

FPP

PLATE 13: DISTRIBUTION OF REGULAR ARMY TROOPS

with the battle of Wounded Knee in 1890. Five years after that event the distribution of military troops no longer reflected frontier needs. In 1891 the Secretary of War declared that a quarter of the posts which had been occupied in 1889 had since been given up, and ten or twelve more were set for abandonment as soon as suitable shelter for the troops could be found at other garrisons. By 1892 the War Department believed that the Indian wars were about at an end. "In the march of population and civilization westward," the annual report declared, "that which was so long known as the frontier has disappeared." In that year ninety-six posts were reported, thirty-three of them located east of the Mississippi. At the end of 1894 the number of posts had been reduced to eighty, and the next year saw another small reduction. It was then simply a matter of housing the troops of the peacetime army, and all sections of the country wanted to be considered. New posts like Fort Sheridan, north of Chicago, and Fort McPherson at Atlanta were just as important as Fort Riley or Fort Sill.

Plate 13 shows the distribution of troops in 1895. Although some small forts in the Indian areas were retained, especially to guard reservations, the troops were spread more or less equally over the whole United States.

MAPS

The maps on the following pages show the locations of the military posts listed in the Catalog. If there was more than one post at a single site or locality, only one of them is named on the maps. The base map is the Map of the Landforms of the United States, by Erwin Raisz, prepared originally to accompany Wallace W. Atwood, *The Physiographic Provinces of North America* (Ginn and Company, Boston, 1940).

Fort Wilkins 1844–70

Fort Brady 1822–

Fort Mackinac 1796–1894

Fort Howard 1816–52

Fort Niagara 1796–

Fort Porter 1863–

Fort Saginaw 1822–24

Fort Gratiot 1814–79

Fort Sheridan 1887–

Detroit 1796–

Fort Dearborn 1803–36

Fort Miami 1796–97

Fort Defiance 1794–97

Fort Wayne 1794–1819

Fort Adams 1794–95

Fort McIntosh 1778–91

Fort St. Marys 1794–96

Fort Recovery 1793–96

Loramie's 1794–98

Pittsburgh 1777–

Fort Steuben 1786–96

Fort Greenville 1793–97

Columbus Barracks 1875–

Fort Jefferson 1791–96

Fort Harrison 1811–18

Fort St. Clair 1791–96

Fort Hamilton 1791–97

Fort Harmar 1785–90

Fort Washington 1789–1804

Fort Knox 1787–1816

Newport Barracks 1803–94

Fort Finney 1786–93

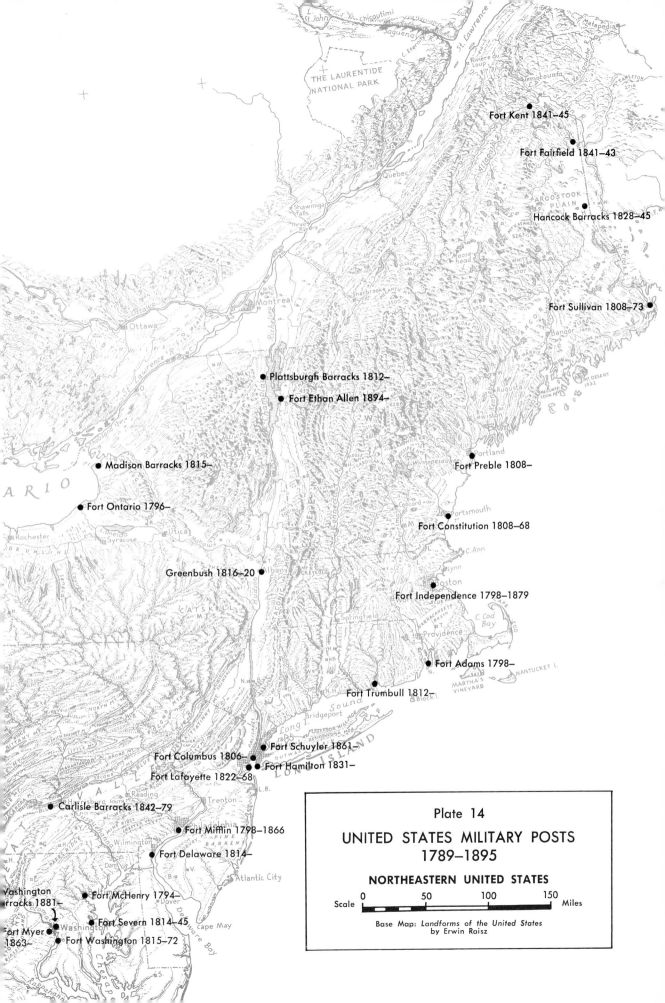

Fort Kent 1841–45

Fort Fairfield 1841–43

Hancock Barracks 1828–45

Fort Sullivan 1808–73

Plattsburgh Barracks 1812–

Fort Ethan Allen 1894–

Madison Barracks 1815–

Fort Preble 1808–

Fort Ontario 1796–

Fort Constitution 1808–68

Greenbush 1816–20

Fort Independence 1798–1879

Fort Adams 1798–

Fort Trumbull 1812–

Fort Schuyler 1861–

Fort Columbus 1806–

Fort Hamilton 1831–

Fort Lafayette 1822–68

Carlisle Barracks 1842–79

Fort Mifflin 1798–1866

Fort Delaware 1814–

Washington Barracks 1881–

Fort McHenry 1794–

Fort Severn 1814–45

Fort Myer 1863–

Fort Washington 1815–72

Plate 14

UNITED STATES MILITARY POSTS
1789–1895

NORTHEASTERN UNITED STATES

Scale 0   50   100   150 Miles

Base Map: *Landforms of the United States*
by Erwin Raisz

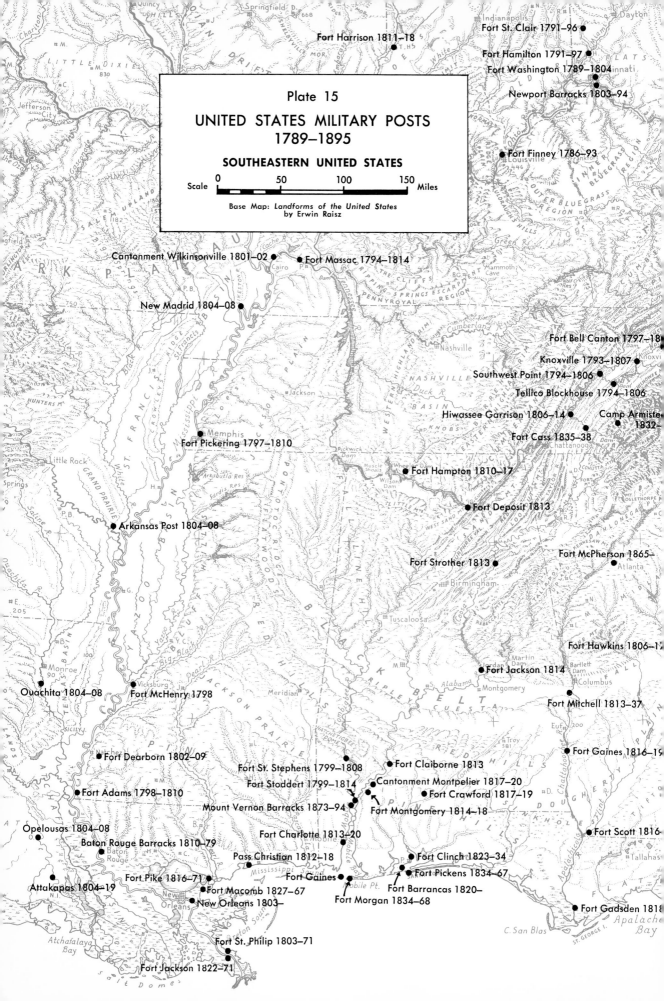

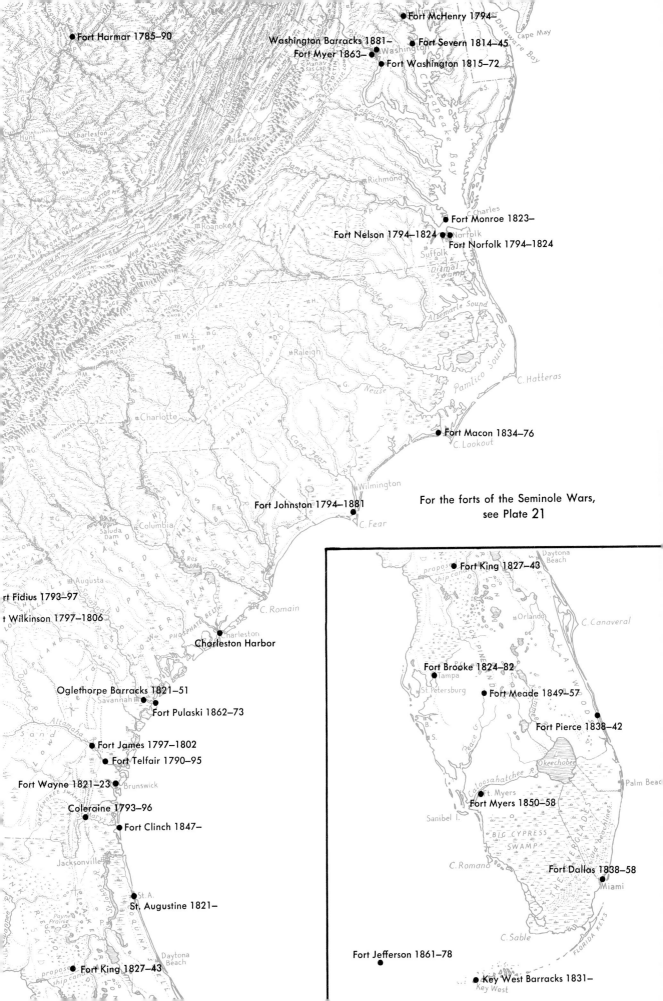

Fort Harmar 1785–90

Fort McHenry 1794–

Washington Barracks 1881–
Fort Myer 1863–
Fort Severn 1814–45
Fort Washington 1815–72

Fort Monroe 1823–

Fort Nelson 1794–1824
Fort Norfolk 1794–1824

Fort Macon 1834–76

Fort Johnston 1794–1881

For the forts of the Seminole Wars,
see Plate 21

Fort King 1827–43

rt Fidius 1793–97

t Wilkinson 1797–1806

Charleston Harbor

Fort Brooke 1824–82

Oglethorpe Barracks 1821–51

Fort Meade 1849–57

Fort Pulaski 1862–73

Fort Pierce 1838–42

Fort James 1797–1802

Fort Telfair 1790–95

Fort Wayne 1821–23

Fort Myers 1850–58

Coleraine 1793–96

Fort Clinch 1847–

St. Augustine 1821–

Fort Dallas 1838–58

Fort Jefferson 1861–78

Fort King 1827–43

Key West Barracks 1831–

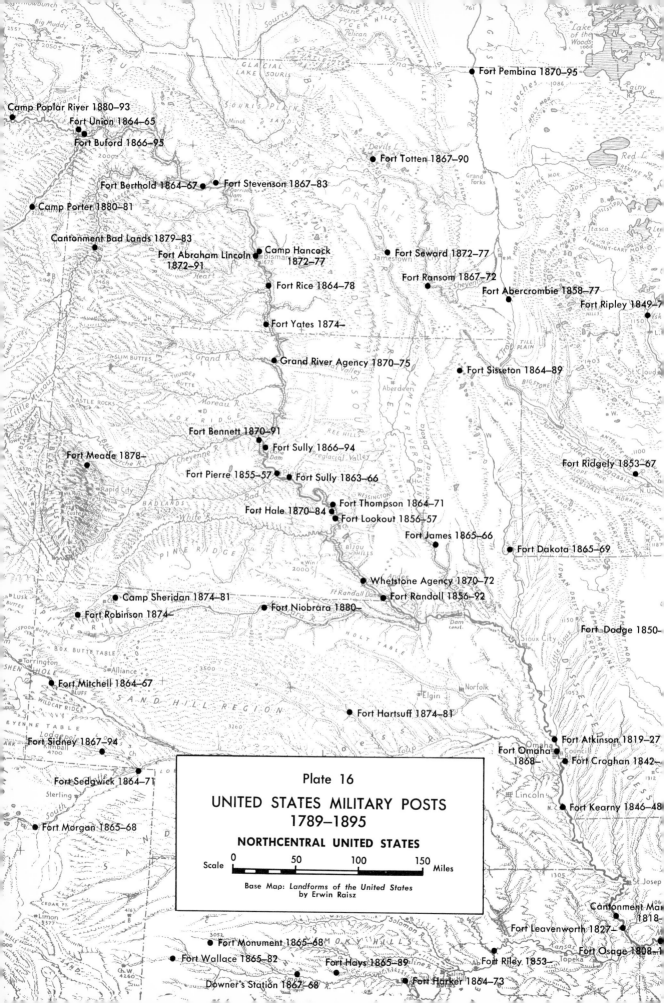

Camp Poplar River 1880–93
Fort Union 1864–65
Fort Buford 1866–95
Fort Pembina 1870–95
Fort Totten 1867–90
Fort Berthold 1864–67   Fort Stevenson 1867–83
Camp Porter 1880–81
Cantonment Bad Lands 1879–83
Fort Abraham Lincoln 1872–91   Camp Hancock 1872–77   Fort Seward 1872–77
Fort Ransom 1867–72
Fort Rice 1864–78   Fort Abercrombie 1858–77
Fort Yates 1874–   Fort Ripley 1849–7
Grand River Agency 1870–75   Fort Sisseton 1864–89
Fort Bennett 1870–91
Fort Sully 1866–94   Fort Ridgely 1853–67
Fort Meade 1878–
Fort Pierre 1855–57   Fort Sully 1863–66
Fort Thompson 1864–71
Fort Hale 1870–84   Fort Lookout 1856–57
Fort James 1865–66
Fort Dakota 1865–69
Whetstone Agency 1870–72
Camp Sheridan 1874–81   Fort Randall 1856–92
Fort Robinson 1874–   Fort Niobrara 1880–
Fort Dodge 1850–
Fort Mitchell 1864–67
Fort Hartsuff 1874–81
Fort Atkinson 1819–27
Fort Sidney 1867–94   Fort Omaha 1868–   Fort Croghan 1842–
Fort Sedgwick 1864–71
Fort Kearny 1846–48
Fort Morgan 1865–68

Plate 16
UNITED STATES MILITARY POSTS
1789–1895
NORTHCENTRAL UNITED STATES
Scale 0   50   100   150 Miles
Base Map: Landforms of the United States
by Erwin Raisz

Cantonment Ma 1818–
Fort Leavenworth 1827–
Fort Osage 1808–1
Fort Monument 1865–68
Fort Wallace 1865–82   Fort Hays 1865–89   Fort Riley 1853–
Downer's Station 1867–68   Fort Harker 1864–73

Fort Wilkins 1844–70

Fort Brady 1822–

Fort Mackinac 1796–1894

Fort Snelling 1819–

Fort Howard 1816–52

Fort Saginaw 1822–24

Fort Winnebago 1828–45

Fort Atkinson 1840–49

Fort Crawford 1816–56

Detroit 1796–

Fort Sheridan 1887–

Fort Miami 1796–97

Chicago

Fort Dearborn 1803–36

Fort Defiance 1794–97

Fort Wayne 1794–1819

Fort Armstrong 1816–36

t Des Moines 1843–46

Fort Adams 1794–95

Fort St. Marys 1794–96

Fort Recovery 1793–96

Loramie's 1794–98

Fort Sanford 1842–43

Fort Clark 1813–17

Fort Greenville 1793–97

Fort Madison 1808–13

Fort Jefferson 1791–96

Fort Des Moines 1834–37

Fort St. Clair 1791–96

Fort Edwards 1816–24

Fort Hamilton 1791–97

Cincinnati

Fort Harrison 1811–18

Fort Washington 1789–1804

Newport Barracks 1803–94

Fort Belle Fontaine 1805–26

Fort Knox 1787–1816

St. Louis

Jefferson Barracks 1826–

Fort Finney 1786–93

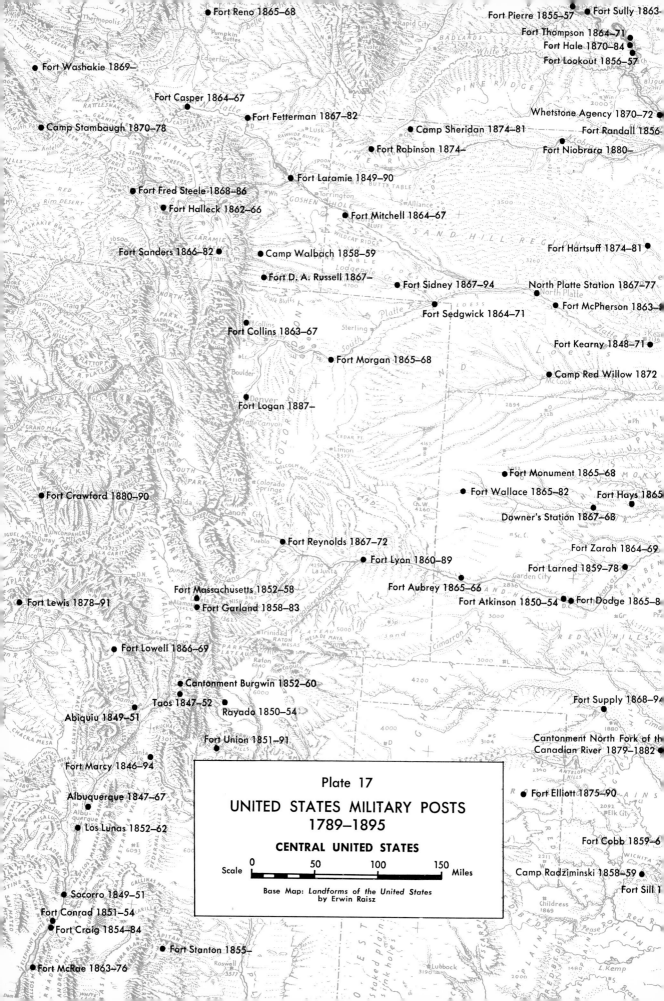

Fort Reno 1865–68

Fort Pierre 1855–57   Fort Sully 1863–

Fort Thompson 1864–71

Fort Hale 1870–84

Fort Lookout 1856–57

Fort Washakie 1869–

Fort Casper 1864–67

Whetstone Agency 1870–72

Fort Fetterman 1867–82

Camp Sheridan 1874–81   Fort Randall 1856

Camp Stambaugh 1870–78

Fort Robinson 1874–   Fort Niobrara 1880–

Fort Laramie 1849–90

Fort Fred Steele 1868–86

Fort Halleck 1862–66

Fort Mitchell 1864–67

Fort Hartsuff 1874–81

Fort Sanders 1866–82   Camp Walbach 1858–59

Fort D. A. Russell 1867–   Fort Sidney 1867–94   North Platte Station 1867–77

Fort McPherson 1863–

Fort Collins 1863–67   Fort Sedgwick 1864–71

Fort Kearny 1848–71

Fort Morgan 1865–68   Camp Red Willow 1872

Fort Logan 1887–

Fort Monument 1865–68

Fort Crawford 1880–90   Fort Wallace 1865–82   Fort Hays 1865

Downer's Station 1867–68

Fort Reynolds 1867–72   Fort Zarah 1864–69

Fort Lyon 1860–89   Fort Larned 1859–78

Fort Aubrey 1865–66

Fort Lewis 1878–91   Fort Massachusetts 1852–58   Fort Atkinson 1850–54   Fort Dodge 1865–8

Fort Garland 1858–83

Fort Lowell 1866–69

Cantonment Burgwin 1852–60   Fort Supply 1868–9

Taos 1847–52

Abiquiu 1849–51   Rayado 1850–54

Fort Union 1851–91   Cantonment North Fork of the Canadian River 1879–1882

Fort Marcy 1846–94

Albuquerque 1847–67   Fort Elliott 1875–90

Los Lunas 1852–62

Fort Cobb 1859–6

Socorro 1849–51   Camp Radziminski 1858–59

Fort Conrad 1851–54   Fort Sill 1

Fort Craig 1854–84

Fort Stanton 1855–

Fort McRae 1863–76

Plate 17
UNITED STATES MILITARY POSTS
1789–1895

CENTRAL UNITED STATES

Scale   0   50   100   150   Miles

Base Map: Landforms of the United States
by Erwin Raisz

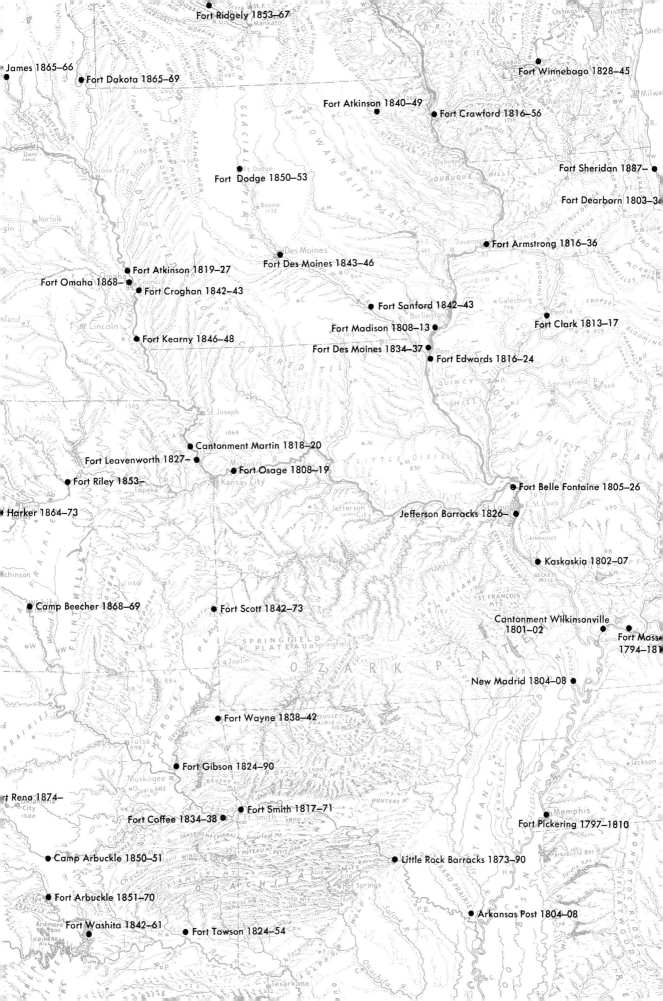

James 1865–66
Fort Dakota 1865–69
Fort Ridgely 1853–67
Fort Winnebago 1828–45
Fort Atkinson 1840–49
Fort Crawford 1816–56
Fort Sheridan 1887–
Fort Dodge 1850–53
Fort Dearborn 1803–3(
Fort Armstrong 1816–36
Fort Des Moines 1843–46
Fort Atkinson 1819–27
Fort Omaha 1868–
Fort Croghan 1842–43
Fort Sanford 1842–43
Fort Clark 1813–17
Fort Madison 1808–13
Fort Des Moines 1834–37
Fort Kearny 1846–48
Fort Edwards 1816–24
Cantonment Martin 1818–20
Fort Leavenworth 1827–
Fort Osage 1808–19
Fort Belle Fontaine 1805–26
Fort Riley 1853–
Harker 1864–73
Jefferson Barracks 1826–
Kaskaskia 1802–07
Camp Beecher 1868–69
Fort Scott 1842–73
Cantonment Wilkinsonville 1801–02
Fort Mass
1794–181
New Madrid 1804–08
Fort Wayne 1838–42
Fort Gibson 1824–90
t Reno 1874–
Fort Smith 1817–71
Fort Coffee 1834–38
Fort Pickering 1797–1810
Camp Arbuckle 1850–51
Little Rock Barracks 1873–90
Fort Arbuckle 1851–70
Fort Washita 1842–61
Fort Towson 1824–54
Arkansas Post 1804–08

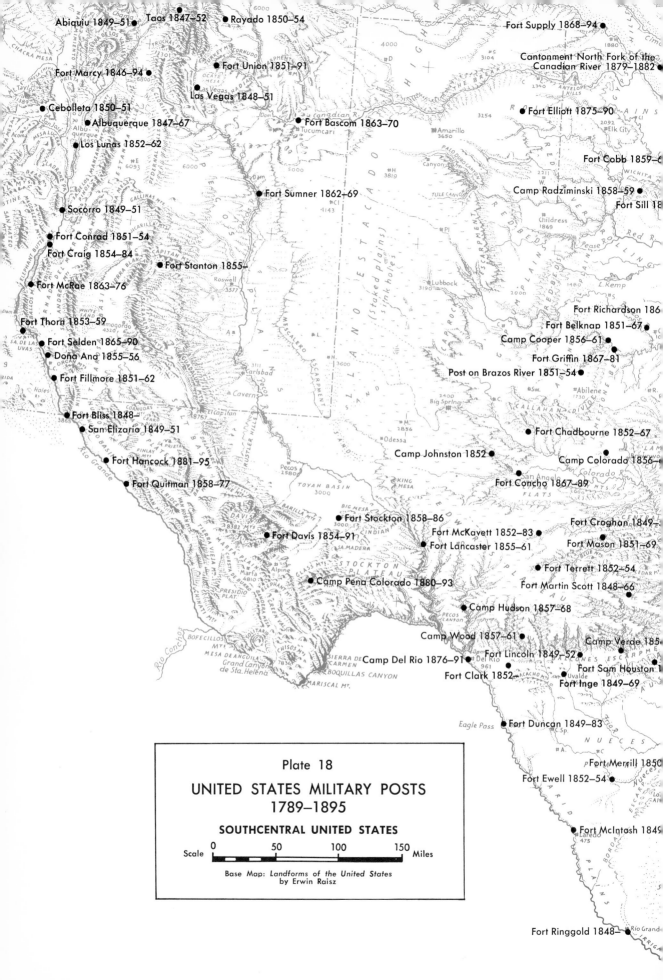

Abiquiu 1849–51 •   Taos 1847–52 •   Rayado 1850–54 •

Fort Supply 1868–94 •

Cantonment North Fork of the
Canadian River 1879–1882

Fort Marcy 1846–94 •   • Fort Union 1851–91

Las Vegas 1848–51 •

• Fort Elliott 1875–90

Cebolleta 1850–51 •
• Albuquerque 1847–67
• Fort Bascom 1863–70

Fort Cobb 1859–

Los Lunas 1852–62 •

Camp Radziminski 1858–59 •

• Fort Sumner 1862–69

Fort Sill 18

Socorro 1849–51 •

• Fort Conrad 1851–54
Fort Craig 1854–84 •

Fort Stanton 1855– •

Fort McRae 1863–76 •

Fort Richardson 186

Fort Thorn 1853–59 •

Fort Belknap 1851–67 •
Camp Cooper 1856–61 •

Fort Selden 1865–90 •
Doña Ana 1855–56 •

Fort Griffin 1867–81 •

• Fort Fillmore 1851–62

Post on Brazos River 1851–54 •

Fort Bliss 1848– •
San Elizario 1849–51 •

Fort Chadbourne 1852–67 •

Fort Hancock 1881–95 •

Camp Johnston 1852 •

Camp Colorado 1856–

Fort Quitman 1858–77 •

Fort Concho 1867–89 •

Fort Stockton 1858–86 •

Fort McKavett 1852–83 •

Fort Croghan 1849–

Fort Davis 1854–91 •

Fort Lancaster 1855–61 •

Fort Mason 1851–69 •

Fort Terrett 1852–54 •

Camp Pena Colorado 1880–93 •

Fort Martin Scott 1848–66 •

Camp Hudson 1857–68 •

Camp Wood 1857–61 •

Camp Verde 185

Camp Del Rio 1876–91 •

Fort Lincoln 1849–52 •

Fort Sam Houston 1

Fort Clark 1852– •

Fort Inge 1849–69

Fort Duncan 1849–83 •

Fort Merrill 1850

Fort Ewell 1852–54 •

Plate 18

UNITED STATES MILITARY POSTS
1789–1895

SOUTHCENTRAL UNITED STATES

Scale   0   50   100   150   Miles

Base Map: *Landforms of the United States*
by Erwin Raisz

Fort McIntosh 1849

Fort Ringgold 1848–

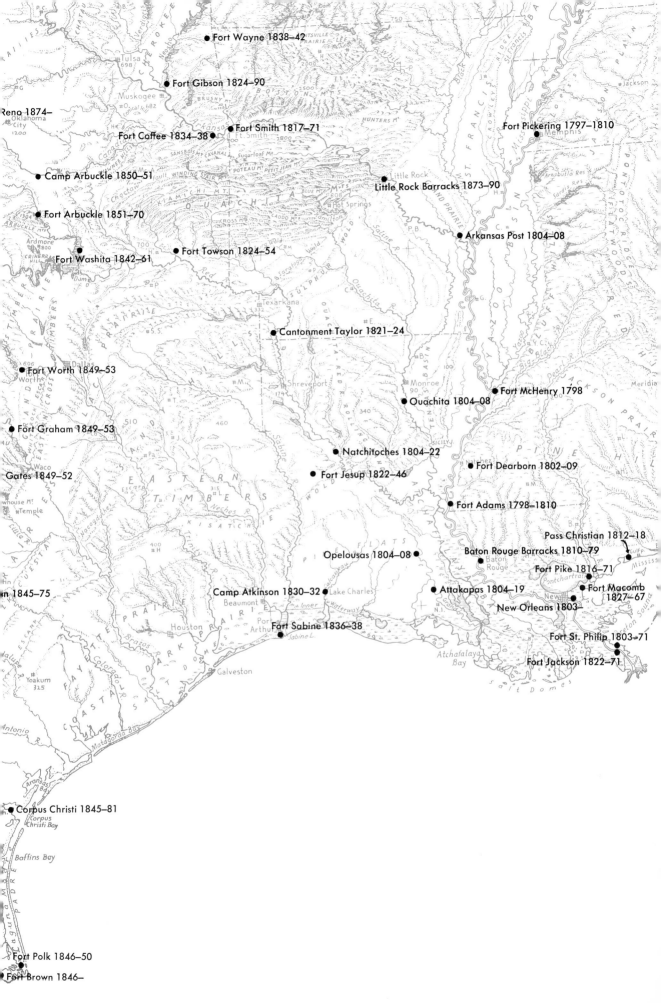

Fort Wayne 1838–42

Fort Gibson 1824–90

Reno 1874–

Fort Smith 1817–71

Fort Coffee 1834–38

Fort Pickering 1797–1810

Camp Arbuckle 1850–51

Little Rock Barracks 1873–90

Fort Arbuckle 1851–70

Arkansas Post 1804–08

Fort Washita 1842–61

Fort Towson 1824–54

Cantonment Taylor 1821–24

Fort Worth 1849–53

Fort McHenry 1798

Ouachita 1804–08

Fort Graham 1849–53

Natchitoches 1804–22

Gates 1849–52

Fort Jesup 1822–46

Fort Dearborn 1802–09

Fort Adams 1798–1810

Pass Christian 1812–18

Opelousas 1804–08

Baton Rouge Barracks 1810–79

Fort Pike 1816–71

Fort Macomb 1827–67

Attakapas 1804–19

New Orleans 1803

Camp Atkinson 1830–32

1845–75

Fort Sabine 1836–38

Fort St. Philip 1803–71

Fort Jackson 1822–71

Corpus Christi 1845–81

Fort Polk 1846–50

Fort Brown 1846–

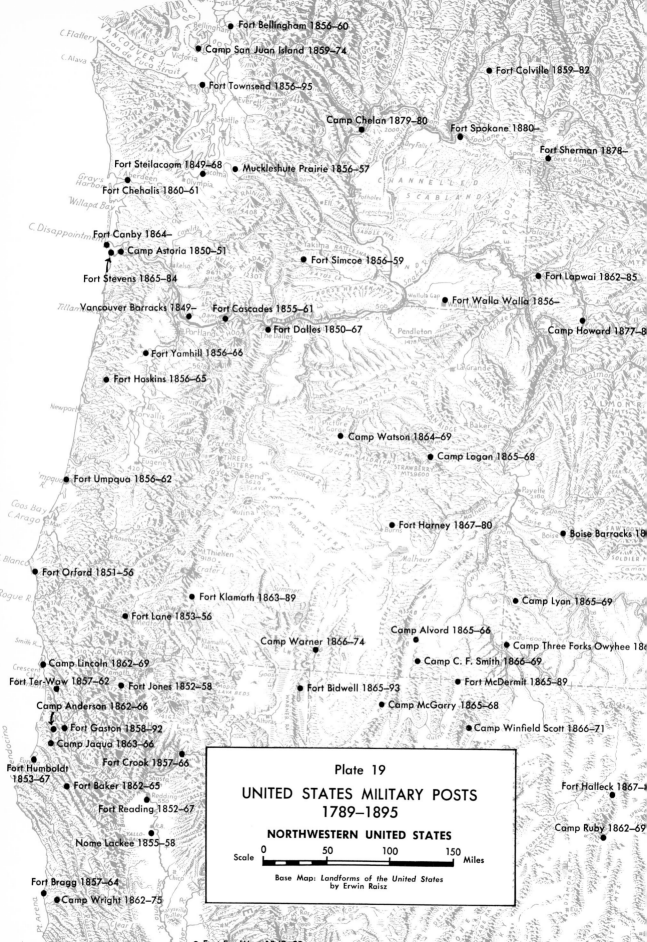

Fort Bellingham 1856–60
Camp San Juan Island 1859–74
Fort Colville 1859–82
Fort Townsend 1856–95
Camp Chelan 1879–80
Fort Spokane 1880–
Fort Sherman 1878–
Fort Steilacoom 1849–68
Muckleshute Prairie 1856–57
Fort Chehalis 1860–61
Fort Canby 1864–
Camp Astoria 1850–51
Fort Simcoe 1856–59
Fort Lapwai 1862–85
Fort Stevens 1865–84
Vancouver Barracks 1849–
Fort Cascades 1855–61
Fort Walla Walla 1856–
Fort Dalles 1850–67
Camp Howard 1877–8
Fort Yamhill 1856–66
Fort Hoskins 1856–65
Camp Watson 1864–69
Camp Logan 1865–68
Fort Umpqua 1856–62
Fort Harney 1867–80
Boise Barracks 18
Fort Orford 1851–56
Fort Klamath 1863–89
Camp Lyon 1865–69
Fort Lane 1853–56
Camp Alvord 1865–66
Camp Warner 1866–74
Camp Three Forks Owyhee 18
Camp Lincoln 1862–69
Camp C. F. Smith 1866–69
Fort Ter-Waw 1857–62
Fort Jones 1852–58
Fort Bidwell 1865–93
Fort McDermit 1865–89
Camp Anderson 1862–66
Camp McGarry 1865–68
Fort Gaston 1858–92
Camp Jaqua 1863–66
Camp Winfield Scott 1866–71
Fort Crook 1857–66
Fort Humboldt 1853–67
Fort Halleck 1867–1
Fort Baker 1862–65
Fort Reading 1852–67
Camp Ruby 1862–69
Nome Lackee 1855–58
Fort Bragg 1857–64
Camp Wright 1862–75
Fort Far West 1849–52

Plate 19

UNITED STATES MILITARY POSTS
1789–1895

NORTHWESTERN UNITED STATES

Scale 0   50   100   150 Miles

Base Map: *Landforms of the United States*
by Erwin Raisz

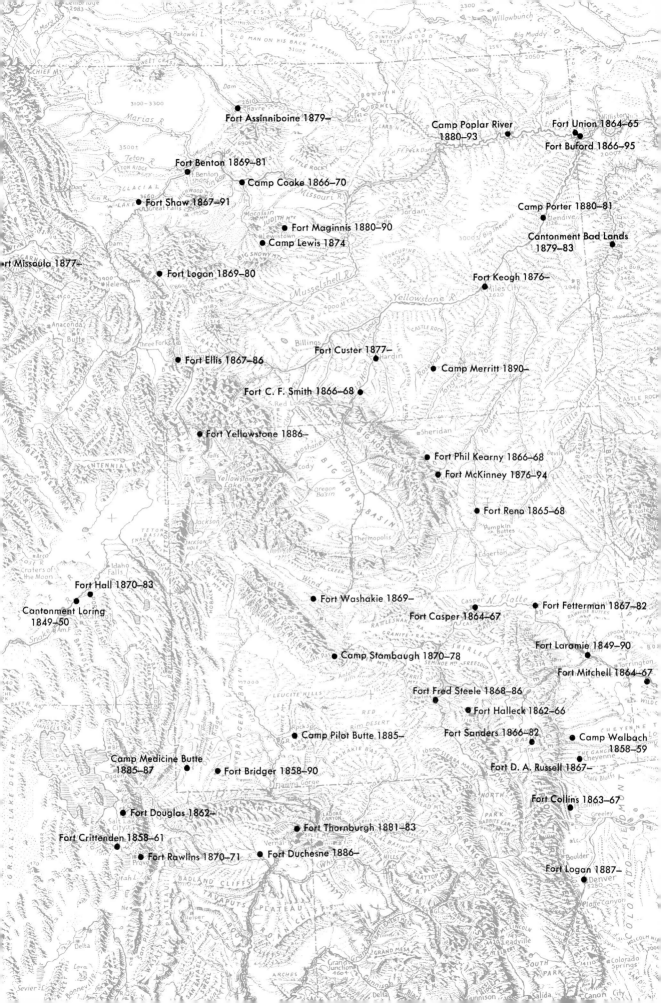

Fort Assinniboine 1879–

Camp Poplar River 1880–93

Fort Union 1864–65

Fort Buford 1866–95

Fort Benton 1869–81

Camp Coake 1866–70

Camp Porter 1880–81

Fort Shaw 1867–91

Fort Maginnis 1880–90

Cantonment Bad Lands 1879–83

Camp Lewis 1874

rt Missoula 1877–

Fort Logan 1869–80

Fort Keogh 1876–

Fort Ellis 1867–86

Fort Custer 1877–

Camp Merritt 1890–

Fort C. F. Smith 1866–68

Fort Yellowstone 1886–

Fort Phil Kearny 1866–68

Fort McKinney 1876–94

Fort Reno 1865–68

Fort Hall 1870–83

Fort Washakie 1869–

Fort Fetterman 1867–82

Cantonment Loring 1849–50

Fort Casper 1864–67

Fort Laramie 1849–90

Camp Stambaugh 1870–78

Fort Mitchell 1864–67

Fort Fred Steele 1868–86

Fort Halleck 1862–66

Camp Pilot Butte 1885–

Fort Sanders 1866–82

Camp Walbach 1858–59

Camp Medicine Butte 1885–87

Fort Bridger 1858–90

Fort D. A. Russell 1867–

Fort Collins 1863–67

Fort Douglas 1862–

Fort Thornburgh 1881–83

Fort Crittenden 1858–61

Fort Logan 1887–

Fort Rawlins 1870–71

Fort Duchesne 1886–

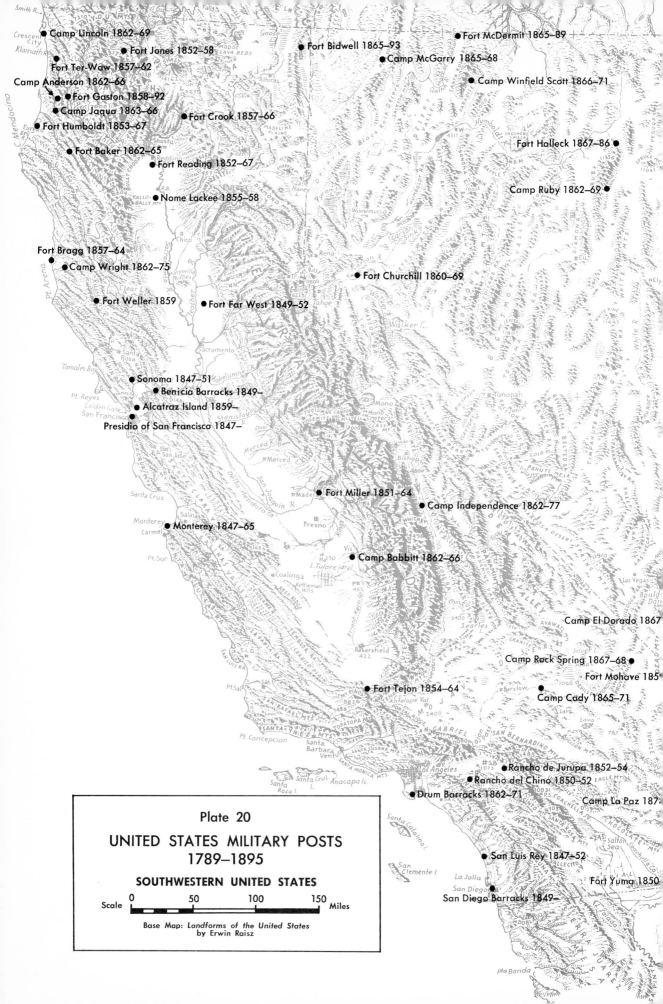

Camp Lincoln 1862–69
Fort Jones 1852–58
Fort Ter-Waw 1857–62
Camp Anderson 1862–66
Fort Gaston 1858–92
Camp Jaqua 1863–66
Fort Humboldt 1853–67
Fort Baker 1862–65
Fort Reading 1852–67
Nome Lackee 1855–58
Fort Crook 1857–66

Fort Bidwell 1865–93
Camp McGarry 1865–68
Camp Winfield Scott 1866–71
Fort McDermit 1865–89
Fort Halleck 1867–86
Camp Ruby 1862–69

Fort Bragg 1857–64
Camp Wright 1862–75
Fort Weller 1859
Fort Far West 1849–52
Fort Churchill 1860–69

Sonoma 1847–51
Benicia Barracks 1849–
Alcatraz Island 1859–
Presidio of San Francisco 1847–

Fort Miller 1851–64
Camp Independence 1862–77

Monterey 1847–65

Camp Babbitt 1862–66

Camp El Dorado 1867

Camp Rock Spring 1867–68
Fort Mohave 185
Camp Cady 1865–71

Fort Tejon 1854–64

Rancho de Jurupa 1852–54
Rancho del Chino 1850–52
Drum Barracks 1862–71
Camp La Paz 187

San Luis Rey 1847–52
Fort Yuma 1850

San Diego Barracks 1849–

Plate 20

UNITED STATES MILITARY POSTS
1789–1895

SOUTHWESTERN UNITED STATES

Scale   0   50   100   150   Miles

Base Map: Landforms of the United States
by Erwin Raisz

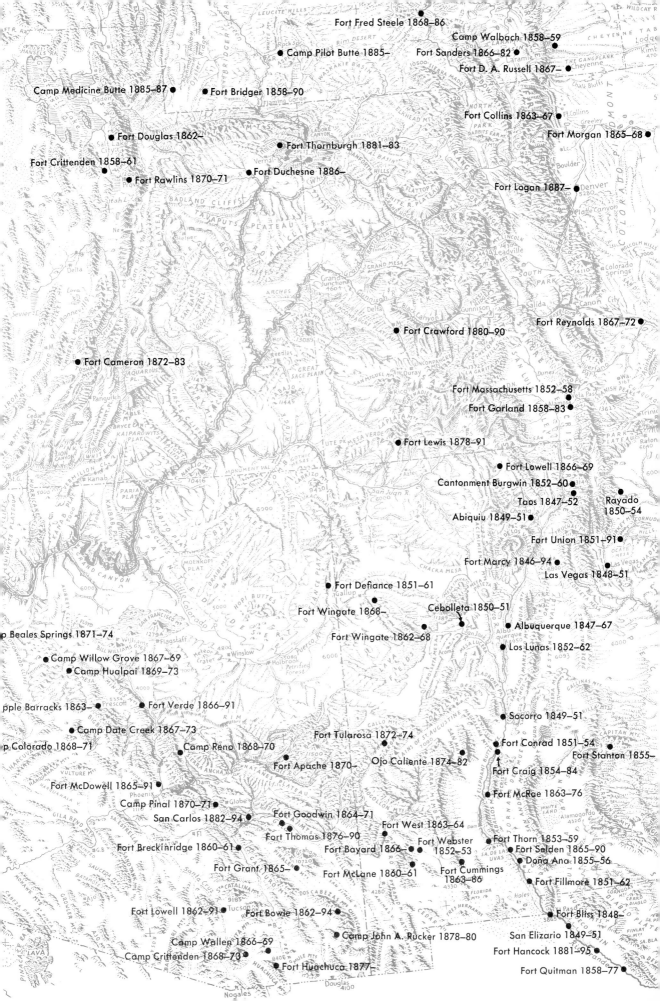

Fort Fred Steele 1868–86

Camp Walbach 1858–59

Camp Pilot Butte 1885– Fort Sanders 1866–82

Fort D. A. Russell 1867–

Camp Medicine Butte 1885–87 Fort Bridger 1858–90

Fort Collins 1863–67

Fort Morgan 1865–68

Fort Douglas 1862–

Fort Crittenden 1858–61 Fort Thornburgh 1881–83

Fort Rawlins 1870–71 Fort Duchesne 1886–

Fort Logan 1887–

Fort Cameron 1872–83

Fort Crawford 1880–90 Fort Reynolds 1867–72

Fort Massachusetts 1852–58

Fort Garland 1858–83

Fort Lewis 1878–91

Fort Lowell 1866–69

Cantonment Burgwin 1852–60

Taos 1847–52 Rayado 1850–54

Abiquiu 1849–51

Fort Union 1851–91

Fort Marcy 1846–94 Las Vegas 1848–51

Fort Defiance 1851–61

Fort Wingate 1868– Cebolleta 1850–51

Albuquerque 1847–67

Fort Wingate 1862–68 Los Lunas 1852–62

p Beales Springs 1871–74

Camp Willow Grove 1867–69

Camp Hualpai 1869–73

pple Barracks 1863– Fort Verde 1866–91 Socorro 1849–51

Camp Date Creek 1867–73 Fort Tularosa 1872–74 Fort Conrad 1851–54

p Colorado 1868–71 Camp Reno 1868–70 Fort Stanton 1855–

Fort Apache 1870– Ojo Caliente 1874–82 Fort Craig 1854–84

Fort McDowell 1865–91

Camp Pinal 1870–71 Fort McRae 1863–76

San Carlos 1882–94 Fort Goodwin 1864–71

Fort West 1863–64 Fort Thorn 1853–59

Fort Thomas 1876–90 Fort Webster Fort Selden 1865–90

Fort Breckinridge 1860–61 Fort Bayard 1866– 1852–53 Doña Ana 1855–56

Fort Grant 1865– Fort Cummings Fort Fillmore 1851–62

Fort McLane 1860–61 1863–86

Fort Lowell 1862–91 Fort Bliss 1848–

Fort Bowie 1862–94 San Elizario 1849–51

Camp John A. Rucker 1878–80

Camp Wallen 1866–69 Fort Hancock 1881–95

Camp Crittenden 1868–73

Fort Huachuca 1877– Fort Quitman 1858–77

A CATALOG OF THE

MILITARY POSTS OF THE UNITED STATES

1789 - 1895

A

FORT ABERCROMBIE [North Dakota, 1858–1877]. Fort Abercrombie was built on the west bank of the Red River of the North at the approximate head of navigation, about twelve miles north of the present city of Wahpeton, North Dakota, in the vicinity of a place known as Graham's Point, Minnesota. The post was set up on August 28, 1858, then abandoned in 1859, but reoccupied in 1860. Troops were finally withdrawn on October 23, 1877.   [141, 256]

POST OF ABIQUIU [New Mexico, 1849–1851]. A temporary camp was established on the Rio Chama, about forty-five miles northwest of Santa Fe in April, 1849, by the "Santa Fe Guards," a volunteer company. The post was abandoned by them in October, 1849, but it was reoccupied on January 29, 1850, by United States troops, who garrisoned the post until November 5, 1851.

FORT ABRAHAM LINCOLN [North Dakota, 1872–1891]. On June 14, 1872, a temporary camp named Fort McKeen was built on the west bank of the Missouri River near the present site of Bismarck, North Dakota, to protect the construction crews of the Northern Pacific Railroad. On August 15, 1872, the post was moved to a new site about five miles away, and on November 19, 1872, it was renamed Fort Abraham Lincoln. It was abandoned on July 22, 1891.   [156]

FORT ADAMS [Mississippi, 1798–1810]. Fort Adams was established on October 5, 1798, at Loftus Heights, on the left bank of the Mississippi River at what was then the extreme southwestern corner of United States territory. Four miles to the east of the fort, Cantonment Columbian Spring was established in 1807, probably to care for large numbers of troops which the fort itself could not accommodate. Both the fort and the cantonment were abandoned in 1810.

CAMP ADAMS [Missouri]. See Jefferson Barracks.

FORT ADAMS [Ohio, 1794–1796]. Fort Adams was established in June, 1794, on the left bank of the St. Marys River, about twenty-five miles north of Fort Recovery. The post was abandoned in the spring of 1796.

FORT ADAMS [Rhode Island, 1798–]. Fort Adams was built on Brenton Point, Newport Harbor, at the entrance to Narragansett Bay. Its earliest use after the Revolutionary War was in 1798. After that date it was garrisoned more or less regularly, although sometimes it fell under the jurisdiction of nearby Fort Wolcott.

FORT ADAMS [Tennessee]. See Fort Pickering.

POST OF ALBUQUERQUE [New Mexico, 1847–1867]. The military post at Albuquerque was occupied by United States troops on November 17, 1847. It was abandoned in August, 1867.

ALCATRAZ ISLAND [California, 1859—]. One of the fortifications of San Francisco Bay, Alcatraz Island was occupied by troops on December 30, 1859.

CAMP ALERT [Kansas]. See Fort Larned.

FORT ALLEN [Vermont]. See Fort Ethan Allen.

CAMP ALVORD [Oregon, 1865–1866]. Camp Alvord was established on September 5, 1865, near Alvord Lake in southeastern Oregon, to protect travelers. It was abandoned on May 25, 1866.

CAMP ANDERSON [California, 1862–1866]. Fort Anderson was established on March 22, 1862, on Redwood Creek, eighteen miles from Fort Gaston. It was abandoned in August or September, 1862, but in February, 1864, the site was reoccupied and called Camp Anderson. The post was abandoned in the fall of 1866.

POST OF ANGEL ISLAND [California, 1863—]. A post was established on Angel Island in San Francisco Bay on September 12, 1863. It was first called Camp Reynolds, but after 1866 was known as Post of Angel

Island, until it was renamed Fort McDowell on April 4, 1900.

FORT APACHE [Arizona, 1870—]. A post, designated as Camp Ord, was established on the White Mountain River in Apache County, Arizona, on May 16, 1870, to protect nearby settlements from Apache raids. On August 1, 1870, the post was renamed Camp Mogollon and on September 12, 1870, Camp Thomas. On February 2, 1871, the post was designated Camp Apache and on April 5, 1879, was finally named Fort Apache.

CAMP ARBUCKLE [Oklahoma, 1850–1851]. On August 22, 1850, a post was established on the road from Fort Smith to Santa Fe, about a mile from the Canadian River, to protect travelers from Indian depredations. The post, named Camp Arbuckle, was abandoned on April 17, 1851, and the troops moved to a new site near the Washita River to build Fort Arbuckle.

FORT ARBUCKLE [Oklahoma, 1851–1870]. Located four miles south of the Washita River, seventy-six miles northwest of its confluence with the Red River, near the present city of Davis, Oklahoma, Fort Arbuckle was established on April 19, 1851, to protect the Chickasaw Indians from the wild Indians of the Plains and to aid California-bound travelers. It was occupied by the Confederacy in May, 1861, and reoccupied by United States troops in November, 1866. The post was finally abandoned on June 24, 1870.   **[218]**

FORT ARIVAYPA [Arizona]. See Fort Breckinridge.

ARKANSAS POST [Arkansas, 1804–1808]. After the acquisition of Louisiana, United States military troops occupied the Spanish post known as Arkansas Post, located near the mouth of the Arkansas River. The post was occupied from 1804 to about 1808.

CAMP ARMISTEAD [Tennessee, 1832–1835]. Camp Armistead, on the west bank of the Tellico River in the Cherokee Nation, about fifty miles south of Knoxville, was established on June 30, 1832. It was abandoned on March 3, 1835.

FORT ARMSTRONG [Illinois, 1816–1836]. Fort Armstrong was established on the southern end of Rock Island in May, 1816, as part of the chain of defenses in the Northwest erected after the War of 1812. The post was abandoned in May, 1836.

[137, 228, 230]

FORT ASSINNIBOINE [Montana, 1879—]. Fort Assinniboine, authorized by Congress on June 18, 1878, to protect the citizens of Montana from the hostile incursions of the Sioux, was established in the Milk River country near the present city of Havre, Montana, in May, 1879. It had a large garrison throughout the rest of the frontier period.

CAMP ASTORIA [Oregon, 1850–1851]. Camp Astoria was a temporary camp established on May 31, 1850, on the south bank of the Columbia River ten miles from its mouth, near the city of Astoria, Oregon. The post was abandoned on October 11, 1851.

FORT ATKINSON [Iowa, 1840–1849]. Fort Atkinson, on the Turkey River at the present town of Fort Atkinson, Iowa, was established on May 31, 1840, to keep order among the Winnebago Indians, who had been moved into the area. The post was abandoned on February 24, 1849, since the Winnebagos had been moved to a new reservation in

north central Minnesota.   [142, 202]

FORT ATKINSON [Kansas, 1850–1854]. Fort Atkinson, just west of the present city of Dodge City, Kansas, was established on August 8, 1850, near the crossing of the Arkansas River by the Santa Fe Trail. The post was abandoned on October 2, 1854.

CAMP ATKINSON [Louisiana, 1830–1832]. Camp Atkinson was located on the Calcasieu River, near the present town of Lake Charles, Louisiana. It was established in April or May, 1830, and was abandoned on January 2, 1832.

FORT ATKINSON [Nebraska, 1819–1827]. This post, on the west bank of the Missouri River, a short distance above the present city of Omaha, Nebraska, was established in September, 1819, as a result of the "Yellowstone Expedition" sent up the Missouri in that year. The post was built first on the river bottom and called Camp and then Cantonment Missouri. In 1820 it was moved two miles south to the top of the bluff and was designated Cantonment Council Bluffs. It was named Fort Atkinson in 1821. At one time the largest and most advanced of all the frontier posts, it was abandoned in June, 1827, being replaced as guardian of that area by Fort Leavenworth.

[187, 188, 189, 285, 286]

POST AT ATTAKAPAS [Louisiana, 1804–1819]. When the United States occupied the Louisiana Purchase a garrison was established at Attakapas, Louisiana. The post was regularly garrisoned from 1804 to 1808 and there were troops stationed there again in 1818 and 1819.

FORT AUBREY [Kansas, 1865–1866]. Fort Aubrey was established in September, 1865, on the Arkansas River, about fifty miles east of Fort Lyon, and near the present town of Syracuse, Kansas. The post was abandoned on April 15, 1866.

CAMP AUGUR [Wyoming]. See Fort Washakie.

POST AT AUSTIN [Texas, 1845–1875]. This locality was first occupied by United States troops in October, 1845, and was maintained as a post until 1854. In 1865 the city was again garrisoned, and in 1866 a site on the left bank of the Colorado River, a mile west of the city, was selected for the post. The post was abandoned in August, 1875.

B

CAMP BABBITT [California, 1862–1866]. Camp Babbitt was established on June 24, 1862, near Visalia, California. It was abandoned on August 9, 1866.

CANTONMENT BAD LANDS [North Dakota, 1879–1883]. Cantonment Bad Lands was established on November 10, 1879, on the west bank of the Little Missouri River in Billings County, North Dakota, to protect the workmen employed in the construction of the Northern Pacific Railroad. The post was abandoned on May 4, 1883.

FORT BAKER [California, 1862–1865]. Fort Baker was established on March 23, 1862, near the Mad River, to keep the Indians of that vicinity in check. The post was abandoned in July, 1865.

CAMP BAKER [Montana]. See Fort Logan [Montana].

CAMP BARBOUR [California]. See Fort Miller.

FORT BARRANCAS [Florida, 1820–]. Built originally by the Spanish at the west side of the entrance to Pensacola Harbor,

Fort Barrancas was first occupied by United States troops on October 21, 1820. The fort was a naval reserve from 1825 to 1844, and in 1861 was seized by Confederate forces. In 1862 it was recaptured by United States troops. The fort itself was not regularly used after the Civil War, the troops being garrisoned at nearby Barrancas Barracks.

FORT BASCOM [New Mexico, 1863–1870]. Fort Bascom, located on the east bank of the Canadian River in San Miguel County, New Mexico, was established on August 15, 1863. Its garrison helped control the Comanche, Kiowa, and other Indians of the Canadian and Red River region. The post was occupied until December, 1870, when the troops and stores were transferred to Fort Union.

[151, 262]

BATON ROUGE BARRACKS [Louisiana, 1810–1879]. The Spanish town and fort of Baton Rouge were occupied by United States troops on December 10, 1810, and buildings were erected for the garrison. In 1819 a tract of land was purchased and shortly afterward construction of an arsenal and barracks was commenced. From January, 1861, to May, 1862, the post was occupied by Confederate forces, and on June 6, 1879, the garrison was finally withdrawn.

FORT BAYARD [New Mexico, 1866–]. Fort Bayard was established on August 21, 1866, northeast of the present Silver City, New Mexico, at the base of the Santa Rita Mountains. It was built to protect the miners in the region from the Apache Indians.

CAMP BEALES SPRINGS [Arizona, 1871–1874]. Located about forty miles east of Fort Mohave on the Mohave road, this post was established on March 25, 1871, during Indian troubles in the Southwest. It was abandoned in April, 1874.

POST OF BEAVER [Utah]. See Fort Cameron.

CAMP BEECHER [Kansas, 1868–1869]. A post was established on June 11, 1868, on the Little Arkansas River a short distance from its confluence with the Arkansas, about a mile from present Wichita, as part of the line of defense in Kansas, especially against the Cheyennes. The camp was first known as Camp Davidson, but its name was changed to Camp Beecher about November, 1868. The post was abandoned in October, 1869. **[102]**

FORT BELKNAP [Texas, 1851–1867]. To overawe the hostile Indians in the Red River area, Fort Belknap was established on June 13, 1851, on the north bank of the Salt Fork of the Brazos River, near the present city of Graham, Texas. The original site was ten miles above the junction of the Salt Fork with the Clear Fork of the Brazos, but in November, 1851, the site was moved two miles down river. The post was abandoned on February 23, 1859, but it was temporarily reoccupied in the spring and summer of

1867, the troops leaving to establish Fort Griffin on July 29, 1867. **[94, 229]**

FORT BELL CANTON [Tennessee, 1797–1800]. To protect the Cherokee lands from white encroachment, Fort Bell Canton was established on the Holston River in 1797. The post was abandoned by 1800.

FORT BELLE FONTAINE [Missouri, 1805–1826]. Fort or Cantonment Belle Fontaine was established in the fall of 1805 on the south bank of the Missouri River four miles from its junction with the Mississippi. The post was first located on the bottom lands along the river but four years later was transferred to the bluff. The post served as military headquarters for the Middle West until the erection of Jefferson Barracks in 1826. **[160, 226]**

FORT BELLINGHAM [Washington, 1856–1860]. This post was established on August 26, 1856, on Bellingham Bay, about sixteen miles south of the mouth of the Fraser River. It was abandoned on April 28, 1860.

BENICIA BARRACKS [California, 1849–]. In April, 1849, a depot for the Quartermaster's Department was established at Benicia, California, at the western end of Suisun Bay. In 1852 the post was designated Benicia Barracks and with the exception of short intervals served continuously as a military post.

FORT BENNETT [South Dakota, 1870–1891]. This post was established on May 17, 1870, on the west bank of the Missouri River, seven miles above Fort Sully, for the purpose of controlling the Indians at the Cheyenne Agency. Until December 30, 1878, it was designated the Post at Cheyenne Agency; then it was renamed Fort Bennett. On November 17, 1891, the garrison was withdrawn and the post abandoned. The site is now inundated by Oahe Reservoir. **[80]**

FORT BENTON [Montana, 1869–1881]. Fort Benton, on the left bank of the Missouri River at the head of navigation about forty miles below the Great Falls of the Missouri, was occupied by United States troops on October 17, 1869. Prior to that time it had been a post of the American Fur Company, first called Fort Lewis and then named Fort Benton in honor of Senator Thomas Hart Benton. The military post was abandoned on May 31, 1881.

FORT BERTHOLD [North Dakota, 1864–1867]. In 1864 troops were sent to protect the trading outpost of Fort Berthold, located on the north bank of the Missouri River about thirty miles below the mouth of the Little Missouri River, on a site now inundated by Garrison Reservoir. In 1865 a military post was formally established there. The post was abandoned in 1867.

FORT BIDWELL [California, 1865–1893]. Fort Bidwell was established on July 17, 1865, in the extreme northeast corner of California. The name was changed to Camp Bidwell on August 31, 1866, and on April 5, 1879, the designation Fort Bidwell was restored. The post was occupied until October 21, 1893.

BIG HORN POST [Montana]. See Fort Custer.

FORT BLISS [Texas, 1848–]. During Indian troubles in the Southwest after the Mexican War a detachment of United States troops arrived at El Paso on February 11, 1848, and remained in camp there without setting up a permanent garrison. On September 14, 1849, the Military Post of El Paso was established, but the troops were withdrawn to Fort Fillmore on August 17, 1851. On January 11, 1854, troops again garrisoned the site, and on March 8, 1854, the post name was changed to Fort Bliss. This post was located on the left bank of the Rio Grande, a mile and a half above El Paso. From 1861 to 1865 the United States troops were withdrawn. In 1868 a new site was chosen northeast of the original camp, and the name Camp Concordia was given to the new installation from March 1, 1868, to March 23, 1869, when the name Fort Bliss was restored. In October, 1893, still another new location was occupied, which has continued as the site of the post.

[143, 249, 270]

BOISE BARRACKS [Idaho, 1863–]. On June 28, 1863, detachments of Oregon Cavalry and Washington Infantry established a post in the Boise River Valley near present-day Boise, Idaho, to protect emigrant trains against Shoshoni Indians. The post was first called Camp Boise, then designated as Fort Boise. On April 5, 1879, the name was changed to Boise Barracks.

FORT BOWIE [Arizona, 1862–1894]. A post was established on July 28, 1862, by a detachment of California Volunteers, at Apache Pass in the Chiricahua Mountains, on the road from Tucson, Arizona, to Mesilla, New Mexico. It was designed to guard the road and to protect a spring at the site. The post returns refer to the post as Fort Bowie until January, 1867, when they changed to Camp Bowie. On April 5, 1879, the post was officially designated Fort Bowie.

FORT BOWYER [Alabama]. See Fort Morgan [Alabama].

FORT BRADY [Michigan, 1822–]. A post was established on the Sault Ste. Marie on the south bank of the river about fifteen miles from Lake Superior on July 6, 1882. It had various designations—Post at Sault Ste. Marie, Post at St. Marys, and Cantonment Brady—until it was named Fort Brady in 1825. During the Mexican War the post was manned by Michigan Volunteers and from 1857 to 1866 was unoccupied.

FORT BRAGG [California, 1857–1864]. Fort Bragg (also called Camp Bragg) was established on June 11, 1857, about fifty miles south of Cape Mendocino, at the present town of Fort Bragg, California. The post was abandoned in the fall of 1864.   **[68]**

POST ON BRAZOS RIVER [Texas, 1851–1854]. During Indian troubles in the Southwest a post was established on November 14, 1851, on the Clear Fork of the Brazos River, about fifteen miles north of the present city of Abilene, Texas. It was part of the line of forts erected to protect the trails to the California gold fields. The post was also called Fort Phantom Hill, but this was never an official designation. The post was abandoned on April 6, 1854.   **[244]**

FORT BRECKINRIDGE [Arizona, 1860–1861]. A post was established on May 8, 1860, at the confluence of the San Pedro River and the Arivaipa River, named Fort Arivaypa. On August 6, 1860, the name was changed to Fort Breckinridge. The post was destroyed by fire and abandoned on July 10, 1861. The site was temporarily reoccupied by California Volunteers from May to October, 1862, under the name of Fort Stanford. In 1865 a new post, Camp Grant, was established on the same site.

FORT BRIDGER [Wyoming, 1858–1890]. Fort Bridger, originally a frontier trading post located on Black's Fork of the Green

River in the southwest corner of the present state of Wyoming, was rebuilt as a United States military post in the summer of 1858, by the troops sent to settle the Mormon troubles. The post was occupied until November 6, 1890.   **[103, 132]**

FORT BROOKE [Florida, 1824–1882]. A military post at the head of Tampa Bay near the mouth of the Hillsborough River was occupied on January 20, 1824, to protect the Seminole Indians in the area from outside elements. Until 1835 the post was reported as Cantonment Brooke and thereafter as Fort Brooke. It was one of the principal posts during the Seminole War and was occupied regularly until 1860. After the Civil War it was a seasonal camp for the garrison at Key West and was finally abandoned in December, 1882.   **[109, 110]**

FORT BROWN [Texas, 1846—]. A military camp was established on the left bank of the Rio Grande at present Brownsville, Texas, opposite the Mexican city of Matamoras, on March 28, 1846. At first called Fort Taylor, its name was changed to Fort Brown on May 17, 1846. In March, 1861, the fort was abandoned to the Confederacy, but it was reoccupied in July, 1865.   **[255]**

CAMP BROWN [Wyoming]. See Fort Washakie.

FORT BUCHANAN [Arizona, 1856–1861]. To protect the Santa Cruz Valley, Fort Buchanan was established on November 17, 1856, on the Sonoita River southeast of Tucson, Arizona. It was abandoned on July 23, 1861, but Camp Crittenden was built in the same locality in 1868.

BUFFALO BARRACKS [New York, 1839–1845]. Buffalo Barracks, located in the northern portion of Buffalo, New York, was established on May 6, 1839, and abandoned on September 30, 1845.

FORT BUFORD [North Dakota, 1866–1895]. Fort Buford was established on June 13, 1866, on the left bank of the Missouri River near the mouth of the Yellowstone, as part of a plan for a chain of military posts between Fort Leavenworth and the Columbia River. The post played an active part in settling Indian troubles and in es-

tablishing the Indians upon reservations. It was occupied continuously until its abandonment in 1895.

FORT BUFORD [Wyoming]. See Fort Sanders.

CANTONMENT BURGWIN [New Mexico, 1852–1860]. Cantonment Burgwin was established about nine miles north of Taos, New Mexico, near the Rio Grande, on August 14, 1852. It was abandoned on May 18, 1860.

C

FORT C. F. SMITH [Montana, 1866–1868]. Fort C. F. Smith was established on August 12, 1866, on the Big Horn River in southern Montana, at the crossing of the Bozeman Trail. By agreement with the Sioux, the post was abandoned on July 29, 1868.

CAMP C. F. SMITH [Oregon, 1866–1869]. Camp C. F. Smith was established in southeastern Oregon near the Pueblo Mines in April or May, 1866. Most of the troops were withdrawn on July 23, 1869, leaving behind only a small detachment.

CAMP CADY [California, 1865–1871]. Camp Cady, located on the north bank of the Mohave River, was established in March, 1865, to protect the wagon trails of the region. The post was abandoned on April 24, 1871.   **[280]**

FORT CALHOUN [Nebraska]. See Fort Atkinson [Nebraska].

FORT CAMERON [Utah, 1872–1883]. A post was established two miles east of Beaver, Utah, on May 25, 1872, for better enforcement of the laws in the Mormon territory. The post was originally called the Post of Beaver or Beaver Canyon, but on June 30, 1874, the name was changed to Fort Cameron. The post was abandoned on May 1, 1883.

FORT CANBY [Arizona, 1863–1864]. Fort Canby was established in the summer of 1863 by Colonel Kit Carson on the site of Fort Defiance as a base of operations against the Navaho Indians. It was abandoned on October 20, 1864.

FORT CANBY [Washington, 1864—]. On April 5, 1864, a post was occupied on the north side of the mouth of the Columbia River and named Fort Cape Disappointment. Its name was changed on January 28, 1875, to Fort Canby.

FORT CAPE DISAPPOINTMENT [Washington]. See Fort Canby [Washington].

CARLISLE BARRACKS [Pennsylvania, 1842–1879]. Carlisle, Pennsylvania, was the site of a pre-Revolutionary War military post, which in the early nineteenth century was used as a headquarters and as a training school. Carlisle Barracks seems to have been first used as a regular garrison for troops in November, 1842, and the post was used as a recruiting center and a cavalry training school. In 1879 the post was discontinued.

FORT CASCADES [Washington, 1855–1861]. Fort Cascades was established on September 30, 1855, on the north bank of the Columbia River as protection against threatened Indian attacks. It was abandoned on November 6, 1861.

FORT CASPER [Wyoming, 1864–1867]. A post was built at the location of the Platte River bridge by volunteer troops in 1864. On September 28, 1865, the post was named Fort Casper. (This is the spelling on most of the official records, although the officer for whom the post was named spelled his name Caspar.) The post was occupied until October 19, 1867. **[168, 216]**

FORT CASS [Tennessee, 1835–1838]. Fort Cass, at Calhoun, Tennessee, was established about April, 1835. It was abandoned on December 12, 1838.

POST AT CEBOLLETA [New Mexico, 1850–1851]. A post was established in September, 1850, at Cebolleta, New Mexico, about forty miles west of Albuquerque. It was evacuated in October, 1851.

CAMP CENTER [Kansas]. See Fort Riley.

FORT CHADBOURNE [Texas, 1852–1867]. Fort Chadbourne, established on October 28, 1852, was located on Oak Creek, thirty miles above its junction with the Colorado River at the present city of Fort Chadbourne, Texas, to protect the area from Indian depredations. The troops were withdrawn on March 23, 1861, and the post was reoccupied on May 25, 1867. The post was finally abandoned in December, 1867.

CHARLESTON HARBOR [South Caro-

lina]. The defense works at Charleston Harbor were generally reported together, and it is not possible to distinguish accurately the various installations and the dates when they were garrisoned. Included were such defense works as Fort Johnson, Castle Pinckney, Fort Moultrie, and Fort Sumter. **[88, 243]**

FORT CHARLOTTE [Alabama, 1813–1820]. The Spanish post, Fort Charlotte, located at the city of Mobile, Alabama, was surrendered to American forces in April, 1813. The post was occupied until about 1820.

FORT CHEHALIS [Washington, 1860–1861]. Fort Chehalis was established at the mouth of the Chehalis River, Grays Harbor, Washington, on February 11, 1860. It was abandoned on June 19, 1861.

CAMP CHELAN [Washington, 1879–1880]. A post called Camp Chelan was established on September 2, 1879, on the Columbia River at Lake Chelan. It was abandoned on October 13, 1880, and the troops were sent to Camp Spokane.

CAMP NEAR CHEYENNE AGENCY [Oklahoma]. See Fort Reno [Oklahoma].

POST AT CHEYENNE AGENCY [South Dakota]. See Fort Bennett.

FORT CHILDS [Nebraska]. See Fort Kearny.

FORT CHURCHILL [Nevada, 1860–1869]. When Indian tribes of the Carson Valley took to the warpath, a military post called Fort Churchill was built on the north side of the Carson River about twenty-five miles east of Virginia City. Its purpose was to protect the main routes and the mining camps and outlying ranches in the area. The post was established on July 20, 1860, and abandoned on September 29, 1869.   **[223]**

FORT CLAIBORNE [Alabama, 1813]. Fort Claiborne was established in 1813 on the Alabama River, at the site of the present town of Claiborne, Alabama. It had only a temporary existence.

FORT CLAIBORNE [Louisiana]. See Natchitoches.

FORT CLARK [Illinois, 1813–1817]. Fort Clark was built on the right bank of the Illinois River, at the site of Peoria, Illinois, in 1813. It was garrisoned for a few years after the War of 1812, probably until 1817. It was completely destroyed by the Indians in 1819.

FORT CLARK [Missouri]. See Fort Osage.

FORT CLARK [Texas, 1852—]. A post was established near the village of Brackettville, Texas, on June 29, 1852, to protect the border area against Indian depredations. The post was first called Fort Riley but on July 15, 1852, was designated Fort Clark. It was abandoned on March 19, 1861, then was reoccupied on December 12, 1866. It was an important link in the border defenses against hostile tribes, who frequently crossed the border from Mexico.

FORT CLARKE [Iowa]. See Fort Dodge [Iowa].

FORT CLAY [Wyoming]. See Platte Bridge Station.

FORT CLINCH [Florida, 1823–1834]. A Fort Clinch located three miles from Pensa-

cola, Florida, was established in 1823, and abandoned on October 21, 1834.

FORT CLINCH [Florida, 1847—]. A Fort Clinch, located at Fernandina, Florida, near the mouth of the St. Marys River, was a coastal defense begun in 1847. It was not regularly garrisoned.

FORT COBB [Oklahoma, 1859–1869]. Fort Cobb was established on October 1, 1859, on the Washita River at the present town of Fort Cobb, Oklahoma. The post was evacuated on May 5, 1861, but it was reoccupied after the Civil War in November, 1868, and served as a center for the control of the Kiowa and Comanche Indians. It was finally abandoned on March 12, 1869, in favor of Fort Sill.   **[295]**

FORT COEUR D'ALENE [Idaho]. See Fort Sherman.

FORT COFFEE [Oklahoma, 1834–1838]. Fort Coffee was established on the right bank of the Arkansas River, about a dozen miles west of the present Arkansas boundary, on June 17, 1834. It was an important post during the removal of the Indians, and was abandoned on October 19, 1838.

POST AT COLERAINE [Georgia, 1793–1796]. A garrison was established in about 1793 at Coleraine, on the St. Marys River in Georgia, and maintained there until about 1796.

FORT COLLINS [Colorado, 1863–1867]. Fort Collins (originally called Camp Collins) was established in the fall of 1863 on the Cache la Poudre River at Laporte, Colorado, to protect the station of the overland stage route and to protect emigrant trains and settlers from Indian depredations. Because of floods, the post was moved in August, 1864, to the site of the present city of Fort Collins, Colorado. The post was abandoned in the spring of 1867.   **[261]**

CAMP COLORADO [Arizona]. See Fort Mohave.

CAMP COLORADO [Arizona, 1868–1871]. Camp Colorado was established on the Colorado River Indian Reservation about forty miles north of La Paz, Arizona, on November 25, 1868. The troops were withdrawn and the post abandoned in April, 1871.

CAMP COLORADO [Texas, 1856–1861]. Camp Colorado was established on August 2, 1856, six miles north of the Colorado River on the road between Fort Belknap and Fort Mason to protect settlers on the frontier from hostile Indians. In July, 1857, it was moved to a new site on Jim Ned Creek, twenty-two miles north. The post was abandoned on February 26, 1861.   **[119, 120]**

COLUMBIA BARRACKS [Washington]. See Vancouver Barracks.

CANTONMENT COLUMBIAN SPRING [Mississippi]. See Fort Adams [Mississippi].

FORT COLUMBUS [New York, 1806—]. Fort Columbus, one of the defenses of New York Harbor, was begun on Governors Island in 1806, replacing Fort Jay. It was irregularly garrisoned.

COLUMBUS BARRACKS [Ohio, 1875—]. This post, at Columbus, Ohio, was established as Columbus Arsenal in 1863. By orders of September 24, 1875, the post was changed to a recruiting depot and was designated Columbus Barracks.

FORT COLVILLE [Washington, 1859–1882]. Fort Colville was established on June 20, 1859, in the Colville Valley because of Indian troubles. It was located on Mill Creek, a few miles north of the present city of Colville, Washington. The post was abandoned on November 1, 1882.   **[292]**

FORT CONCHO [Texas, 1867–1889]. A post was established on December 4, 1867, at the junction of the Concho and North Concho rivers, at the present San Angelo, Texas. It was first called Camp Hatch and then Camp Kelley; in March, 1868, the name was changed to Fort Concho. The post was strategically located at the junction of lines of communication and served as a base of operations against hostile Indians. It was abandoned on June 20, 1889. **[104, 118, 169]**

CAMP CONCORDIA [Texas]. See Fort Bliss.

FORT CONNOR [Wyoming]. See Fort Reno [Wyoming].

FORT CONRAD [New Mexico, 1851–1854]. This post was established on September 8, 1851, on the west bank of the Rio Grande near Valverde, New Mexico. The post was abandoned on March 31, 1854, and the troops moved south a few miles to garrison Fort Craig.   **[263]**

FORT CONSTITUTION [New Hampshire, 1808–1868]. Fort Constitution was erected in 1808 at the entrance to Portsmouth Harbor, three miles east of the city. It was irregularly garrisoned until May, 1868.

CAMP COOKE [Montana, 1866–1870]. Camp Cooke was established on July 11, 1866, on the south bank of the Missouri River at the mouth of the Judith River, as the first permanent military camp in Montana. The post was garrisoned until March 31, 1870.

CAMP COOPER [Texas, 1856–1861]. Camp Cooper was established on January 2, 1856, on the Clear Fork of the Brazos River in Throckmorton County, Texas, to protect the reservation Indians living there. The post was abandoned on February 21, 1861. **[112]**

POST OF CORPUS CHRISTI [Texas, 1845–1881]. Corpus Christi, Texas, was occupied by United States troops in 1845 and 1846. A post was garrisoned again from October, 1850, to January, 1852, from March 13, 1869, to May 9, 1870, and from May 29, 1880, to May 4, 1881.

FORT COTTONWOOD [Nebraska]. See Fort McPherson [Nebraska].

POST AT COTTONWOOD SPRINGS [Nebraska]. See Fort McPherson [Nebraska].

CANTONMENT COUNCIL BLUFFS [Nebraska]. See Fort Atkinson [Nebraska].

FORT CRAIG [New Mexico, 1854–1884]. Fort Craig was established on March 31, 1854, when Fort Conrad was abandoned. It was located on the west bank of the Rio Grande, at the entrance of the Jornado del Muerto, as protection against the Apaches. It was abandoned in September, 1884. **[264]**

FORT CRAWFORD [Alabama, 1817–1819]. Fort Crawford, located at the site of the present town of Brewton, Alabama, was established in 1817 and maintained until 1819.

FORT CRAWFORD [Colorado, 1880–1890]. A military post was established on the west bank of the Uncompahgre River, about eight miles south of the present city of Montrose, Colorado, in June, 1880, after an uprising in 1879. The post was originally known as the Cantonment on the Uncompahgre, but on December 15, 1886, its designation was changed to Fort Crawford. The post was abandoned on September 23, 1890. **[224]**

CAMP CRAWFORD [Texas]. See Fort McIntosh.

FORT CRAWFORD [Wisconsin, 1816–1856]. Fort Crawford was established at Prairie du Chien, on the left bank of the Mississippi about two miles above the mouth of the Wisconsin River, in June, 1816, as part of the movement into the Northwest after the War of 1812. On December 16, 1830, the troops were moved to new barracks on higher ground south of the original site. The post was temporarily abandoned in 1826–1827 and for a few months in 1845, and from June, 1846, to September, 1848, the regular troops were replaced by volunteers. The post was abandoned again on April 29, 1849, reoccupied on October 19, 1855, and permanently abandoned on June 9, 1856.

[203, 204, 250]

CAMP CRITTENDEN [Arizona, 1868–1873]. Camp Crittenden was established on March 4, 1868, at the former site of Fort Buchanan at the headwaters of the Sonoita in present Santa Cruz County, to protect the settlers of the area. The post was abandoned on June 1, 1873.

CRITTENDEN

FORT CRITTENDEN [Utah, 1858–1861]. A post was established about midway between Salt Lake City and Provo, Utah, on August 24, 1858. The post was first called Camp Floyd, but on February 6, 1861, its name was changed to Fort Crittenden. The fort was abandoned on July 27, 1861.

FORT CROGHAN [Iowa, 1842–1843]. A post was established on May 31, 1842, near the Council Bluffs on the east bank of the Missouri River. It was first called Camp Fenwick, but its name was changed to Fort Croghan about November, 1842. The post was abandoned on September 5, 1843.

FORT CROGHAN [Texas, 1849–1853]. Fort Croghan was established on March 18, 1849, on the north bank of Hamilton Creek, about ten miles from its junction with the Colorado River. The post was abandoned in December, 1853.

FORT CROOK [California, 1857–1866]. Fort Crook was established on July 1, 1857, on Fall River in the Pit River country. It was abandoned in May, 1866.

CUSTER

FORT CROOK [Nebraska]. See Fort Omaha.

FORT CROSS [North Dakota]. See Fort Seward.

POST AT CROW CREEK AGENCY [South Dakota]. See Fort Thompson.

FORT CUMMINGS [New Mexico, 1863–1886]. Fort Cummings was located at Cooks Springs, northwest of present-day Deming, New Mexico, on October 2, 1863, to control the Apaches and to guard the trails to California. The post was abandoned in August, 1873, and reoccupied in 1880. The troops finally withdrew on October 3, 1886.

FORT CUSTER [Montana, 1877—]. On July 4, 1877, a military post named Big Horn Post or Big Horn Barracks was established on the right bank of the Big Horn River about a mile and a half above its junction with the Little Big Horn. It was part of the movement of troops into the region after the Custer massacre. The name was changed to Fort Custer on November 8, 1877.

D-E

FORT D. A. RUSSELL [Wyoming, 1867—]. A post was situated at present-day Cheyenne, Wyoming, on the line of the Union Pacific Railroad where the railroad would cross Crow Creek. It was established on July 21, 1867, and was first called Post on Crow Creek. On July 31, 1867, the post was designated Fort D. A. Russell. It was renamed Fort Francis E. Warren in 1929.   **[192]**

FORT DAKOTA [South Dakota, 1865–1869]. Fort Dakota was established on May 1, 1865, on the left bank of the Big Sioux River, at the present city of Sioux Falls, South Dakota. It was first garrisoned by volunteer troops, but regular army troops arrived on June 8, 1866, and remained until June 18, 1869, when the post was abandoned.

FORT DALLAS [Florida, 1838–1858]. Fort Dallas was established by army troops in February, 1838, at the mouth of the Miami River at the inner shore of Biscayne Bay. The post was repeatedly abandoned and then reoccupied until July 10, 1858, when the troops were withdrawn for the last time.

FORT DALLES [Oregon, 1850–1867]. A post was established on the south bank of the Columbia River at the dalles of the Columbia on May 21, 1850. It was first called Camp Drum, but its name was changed to Fort Dalles in June, 1853. The post was an important outpost and supply base during the Indian wars of the 1850's. It was finally abandoned in June, 1867.

CAMP DATE CREEK [Arizona, 1867–1873]. A post, called Camp McPherson, was established on May 11, 1867, on the south bank of Date Creek about fifty miles southwest of Prescott, Arizona, near the site of a temporary post occupied on Date Creek in the summer of 1866. The post was named Camp Date Creek on November 23, 1868. It was abandoned on August 30, 1873.

CAMP DAVIDSON [Kansas]. See Camp Beecher.

FORT DAVIS [Texas, 1854–1891]. This post was established on October 7, 1854, near the sources of the Limpia River, to defend the overland trail from hostile Indians. The post was abandoned on April 13, 1861, but it was reoccupied on June 29, 1867, and served as a point of departure for expeditions against the Apaches. The post was abandoned on July 31, 1891.   **[251]**

70

CAMP DAVIS [Wyoming]. See Platte Bridge Station.

FORT DEARBORN [Illinois, 1803–1836]. Fort Dearborn was established on August 17, 1803, at the site of present Chicago, Illinois. It was destroyed in 1812 but reoccupied in June, 1816. It was not occupied from October, 1823, to October, 1828, and for other short periods. The post was finally abandoned in December, 1836.   **[238, 284]**

FORT DEARBORN [Mississippi, 1802–1809]. As a protection against the Choctaw Indians, Fort Dearborn was established in 1802 near Washington, the seat of government of Mississippi Territory. The post was abandoned about 1809.

FORT DEFIANCE [Arizona, 1851–1861]. Fort Defiance was established on September 18, 1851, at the mouth of Bonita Canyon in the Navaho country. The post was abandoned on April 25, 1861, but the site was reoccupied as Fort Canby in 1863–1864.   **[258]**

FORT DEFIANCE [Ohio, 1794–1797]. Fort Defiance was begun on August 9, 1794, at the junction of the Maumee and the Auglaize rivers, at the site of present Defiance, Ohio. The post was abandoned at the end of 1797.

FORT DELAWARE [Delaware, 1814–]. Construction of a fortification was begun on Pea Patch Island in the Delaware River in 1814, and the post was officially designated Fort Delaware in orders of April 18, 1833. The post was irregularly garrisoned, becoming important in wartime as a guardian of the Delaware River.   **[248, 291]**

CAMP DEL RIO [Texas, 1876–1891]. A post was established on September 6, 1876, near the town of Del Rio, Texas, for the protection of the Rio Grande frontier. It was first called Post of San Felipe, but on March 18, 1881, the name was changed to Camp Del Rio. The post was garrisoned until May 8, 1891.

POST NEAR DENVER [Colorado]. See Fort Logan [Colorado].

FORT DEPOSIT [Alabama, 1813]. Fort Deposit, located on the Tennessee River at the site of the present city of Fort Deposit, Alabama, was established by General Andrew Jackson in 1813. It was not continued after the War of 1812.

FORT DES MOINES [Iowa, 1834–1837]. The first Fort Des Moines (also called Camp Des Moines) was established on September 25, 1834, at the mouth of the Des Moines River at the site of the present city of Keokuk, Iowa. The post was abandoned on June 1, 1837.   **[144, 153, 271]**

FORT DES MOINES [Iowa, 1843–1846]. The second Fort Des Moines was established on May 20, 1843, at the fork of the Des Moines and Raccoon rivers, at the present city of Des Moines, Iowa. It was founded to protect the lands of the Indians from white encroachment until the Indians moved west according to treaty stipulations. On March 12, 1846, the troops were withdrawn for the Mexican War, and the post was abandoned.   **[96, 145, 153, 271]**

POST AT DETROIT [Michigan, 1796–]. Detroit was an old military center and in 1796 the post was surrendered to the United States by the British. It served as headquarters for the troops in the Northwest after the War of 1812. Various names (including Fort Shelby) were applied to the post at Detroit, and various sites were occupied. In 1838 the designation Detroit Barracks was adopted. This post was abandoned in June, 1851, but a military establishment was maintained at Detroit Arsenal. Fort Wayne, on a new site on the Detroit River, was occupied in 1861.

[181, 184, 214, 234]

CAMP DEVIN [Arizona]. See Camp Hualpai.

FORT DIAMOND [New York]. See Fort Lafayette.

FORT DODGE [Iowa, 1850–1853]. A post was established on August 2, 1850, on the Des Moines River at the site of the present town of Fort Dodge, Iowa, to protect the region from Indian depredations. It was originally called Fort Clarke, but the designation was changed to Fort Dodge on June 25, 1851. The post was abandoned June 2, 1853.   **[146]**

FORT DODGE [Kansas, 1865–1882]. Fort Dodge was located on the left bank of the Arkansas River on the Santa Fe Trail, near the present Dodge City, Kansas. A military camp had been established there in 1864, but the fort was not formally established until the arrival of Wisconsin Volunteers on September 9, 1865. The post guarded travelers on the Santa Fe Trail and was an important center of operations against the hostile Arapaho and Cheyenne Indians. It was abandoned on October 2, 1882.

POST AT DOÑA ANA [New Mexico, 1855–1856]. A post at Doña Ana, New Mexico, in the Rio Grande Valley fifty miles above El Paso, was garrisoned from August, 1855, to February, 1856. The troops acted as escort to the government's Pacific railroad survey.

FORT DOUGLAS [Utah, 1862–]. A post was established on October 26, 1862, at the base of the Wasatch Range about three miles east of Salt Lake City, to protect the overland mail route and to control the Mormons in the vicinity. The post was first called Camp Douglas, but on December 30, 1878, the designation was changed to Fort Douglas.

DOWNER'S STATION [Kansas, 1867–1868]. This outpost on the Smoky Hill route to the Colorado gold fields, about fifty miles west of Fort Hays, was established as a military post on May 30, 1867. It was abandoned on May 28, 1868.

DRUM BARRACKS [California, 1862–1871]. This post was established in January, 1862, one mile from Wilmington, California, now part of Los Angeles. Until December, 1863, the returns designated the post as Camp Drum, thereafter as Drum Barracks. The post was abandoned on November 7, 1871.

CAMP DRUM [Oregon]. See Fort Dalles.

FORT DUCHESNE [Utah, 1886–]. Fort Duchesne was established on August 20, 1886, on the right bank of the Uinta River, eight miles above its junction with the Duchesne River in northeastern Utah, for control of the Ute Indians.

FORT DUNCAN [Texas, 1849–1883]. A post was established on March 27, 1849, at Eagle Pass, on the east bank of the Rio Grande, one-half mile from the river, at what was considered one of the most commanding positions on the frontier. It was first called Camp at Eagle Pass or Camp on the Rio Grande, but on November 14, 1849, it was officially named Fort Duncan. The post was abandoned on July 11, 1859, reoccupied on March 8, 1860, then evacuated again on March 20, 1861. After the Civil War it was reoccupied on March 23, 1868, and finally abandoned on August 31, 1883. On April 1, 1886, a subpost of Fort Clark was established on the site of Fort Duncan, known as Camp at Eagle Pass, which maintained law and order along the border until after World War I.   [121]

CAMP AT EAGLE PASS [Texas]. See Fort Duncan.

FORT EDWARDS [Illinois, 1816–1824]. Fort Edwards was established in September, 1816, on the east bank of the Mississippi River, opposite the mouth of the Des Moines River, at the present city of Warsaw, Illinois, as security against the Potawatomi Indians. The post was irregularly garrisoned and was finally abandoned in July, 1824. [79]

CAMP EL DORADO [Nevada, 1867]. Camp El Dorado was established on the right bank of the Colorado River, near the mouth of El Dorado Canyon on January 15, 1867. The post was abandoned on August 24, 1867.

FORT ELLIOTT [Texas, 1875–1890]. To aid in opening up a route for Texas cattle to the north which would avoid the settlements in the Indian Territory and Kansas, a temporary camp was first established on the North Fork of the Red River in the Texas pan-

handle in September, 1874. In February, 1875, Cantonment North Fork of the Red River was established on the site. A new site for the cantonment, on Sweetwater Creek, was occupied on June 5, 1875, known as Cantonment on the Sweetwater. The post was designated Fort Elliott on February 21, 1876. The last troops left the post on October 20, 1890.   [113]

FORT ELLIS [Montana, 1867–1886]. Fort Ellis was established on the left bank of the East Gallatin River east of the present city of Bozeman, Montana, on August 27, 1867, for protection against the Indians. It was abandoned on August 31, 1886.

FORT ELLSWORTH [Kansas]. See Fort Harker.

POST OF EL PASO [Texas]. See Fort Bliss.

FORT ETHAN ALLEN [Vermont, 1894—]. Fort Ethan Allen was first occupied on September 28, 1894, although it had been named by orders of March 13, 1893. It was located near Burlington, Vermont.   [269]

FORT EWELL [Texas, 1852–1854]. Fort Ewell was established at the southern bend of the Nueces River at the junction of the San Antonio and Laredo road, on May 18, 1852. It was abandoned on October 3, 1854, and the troops were transferred to Fort McIntosh.

73

F-G-H

FORT FAIRFIELD [Maine, 1841–1843]. Because of the boundary dispute which resulted in the so-called "Aroostook War," Fort Fairfield was established on September 10, 1841, on the south bank of the Aroostook River, six miles from its confluence with the St. John River. The post was abandoned on September 2, 1843.

FORT FAR WEST [California, 1849–1852]. A post was established on September 28, 1849, on Bear Creek, near the present city of Marysville, California. It occupied a strategic position guarding emigrant routes and wagon roads to the mines. The post was reported as Camp Far West until 1851, then as Fort Far West. It was abandoned on May 4, 1852.

FORT FAUNTLEROY [New Mexico]. See Fort Lyon [New Mexico].

FORT FAYETTE [Pennsylvania]. See Forts at Pittsburgh.

FORT FENWICK [Iowa]. See Fort Croghan [Iowa].

FORT FETTERMAN [Wyoming, 1867– 1882]. Fort Fetterman was established on July 19, 1867, on the North Platte River, at the mouth of La Prele Creek, about eighty miles northwest of Fort Laramie near present-day Douglas, Wyoming. It was abandoned on May 20, 1882.

FORT FIDIUS [Georgia, 1793–1797]. For the protection of the Georgia frontier, Fort Fidius was established in 1793 on the north bank of the Oconee River. The post was abandoned about 1797.

FORT FILLMORE [New Mexico, 1851– 1862]. This post was established on September 23, 1851, on the east bank of the Rio Grande near Mesilla, about forty miles above El Paso. On July 26, 1861, it was evacuated, and from August 11 to November 13, 1862, it was briefly reoccupied by Union forces. **[114, 265]**

FORT FINNEY [Kentucky, 1786–1793]. A post called Fort Finney was established on the north bank of the Ohio River near the mouth of the Miami River in November, 1785. In August, 1786, this post was evacuated and the garrison moved down the river to the falls of the Ohio, at present-day Louisville, Kentucky, where another fort with the same name was established. Troops were reported at the site as late as 1793.

FORT FLETCHER [Kansas]. See Fort Hays.

FORT FLOYD [New Mexico]. See Fort McLane.

CAMP FLOYD [Utah]. See Fort Crittenden [Utah].

FORT FOOTE [Maryland, 1863–1878]. This post was located on the east bank of the Potomac about eight miles below Washington and was part of the defenses of Washington. Construction was begun in the spring of 1863 and the post was officially named Fort Foote on September 17 of that year. The post was discontinued on November 10, 1878.

FORT FRANCIS E. WARREN [Wyoming]. See Fort D. A. Russell.

FORT FRANKLIN [Pennsylvania]. See Forts at Pittsburgh.

FORT FRED STEELE [Wyoming, 1868–1886]. To protect the line of the Union Pacific Railroad near its crossing of the North Platte River, troops were stationed along the line in the spring of 1868. On June 15, 1868, a military post was officially established on the west bank of the North Platte near the present city of Rawlins, Wyoming. The post was abandoned on November 3, 1886.

FORT GADSDEN [Florida, 1818–1821]. During his invasion of Florida, Andrew Jackson established Fort Gadsden on the east bank of the Apalachicola River in March,

1818. The post was abandoned in July, 1821.

FORT GAINES [Alabama]. Fort Gaines was built on the eastern point of Dauphin Island at the entrance to Mobile Bay in 1822. It does not seem to have been regularly garrisoned. In January, 1861, it was seized by Alabama troops and was held by the Confederacy until August 8, 1864.

FORT GAINES [Georgia, 1816–1819]. In 1816 Fort Gaines was established on the Chattahoochee River near the Creek boundary. A few troops were maintained at the post until 1819.

FORT GAINES [Minnesota]. See Fort Ripley.

FORT GARLAND [Colorado, 1858–1883]. Fort Garland was a new post garrisoned on June 24, 1858, by troops from abandoned Fort Massachusetts, which had been located about six miles to the north. The primary purpose of the fort was to protect the settlers of the San Luis Valley and to guard from the Utes and the Apaches the roads running south to Taos. The post was abandoned on November 30, 1883. **[225]**

FORT GASTON [California, 1858–1892]. A post was established on December 4, 1858, on the west bank of the Trinity River about fourteen miles above its junction with the Klamath River in the Hoopa Valley Indian Reservation, as protection against Indian depredations. The post was first called Fort Gaston; the name was changed to Camp Gaston on January 1, 1867, and back to Fort Gaston on April 5, 1879. The post was abandoned on June 26, 1892.

FORT GATES [Texas, 1849–1852]. Fort Gates was established on the north bank of the Leon River, a tributary of the Brazos, on October 26, 1849. It was abandoned in March, 1852.

FORT GEORGE H. THOMAS [North Dakota]. See Fort Pembina.

FORT GIBSON [Oklahoma, 1824–1890]. Fort Gibson (called Cantonment Gibson in the early years) was established in April, 1824, on the east bank of the Neosho or Grand River two and one-half miles above its confluence with the Arkansas River. The fort protected the routes of travel and controlled the Cherokee and Osage Indians. It was abandoned in 1857 and reoccupied on April 5, 1863, by volunteer troops, who were replaced by regulars on February 18, 1866. The post was finally abandoned on September 22, 1890.   **[139, 140]**

FORT GOODWIN [Arizona, 1864–1871]. Fort Goodwin was established on June 21, 1864, two and one-half miles south of the Gila River in southeastern Arizona. The post returns designate the post as Camp Goodwin beginning in December, 1866. The post was abandoned on March 14, 1871.

FORT GRAHAM [Texas, 1849–1853]. This post was established on March 27, 1849, on the east bank of the Brazos River in Hill County, Texas. On the first returns the post was designated Camp Thornton. It was abandoned on November 9, 1853.

POST AT GRAND RIVER AGENCY [South Dakota, 1870–1875]. A military post was established at the Grand River Agency, on the west bank of the Missouri at the confluence of the Grand River, in May, 1870. The site was abandoned on June 6, 1875.

FORT GRANT [Arizona, 1865—]. On Octo-

ber 31, 1865, the site of abandoned Fort Breckinridge at the junction of the San Pedro River and the Arivaipa River was occupied. The post was first called Camp on San Pedro River, but on January 8, 1866, it was designated Fort Grant. Beginning in February, 1867, the designation Camp Grant was used. At the end of 1872 a new site at the foot of Mount Graham, about seventy miles southeast of the original post, was occupied. The first troops arrived at the site, which was known as New Camp Grant, on December 19, 1872. On March 31, 1873, the old post was discontinued and the new post called simply Camp Grant. On April 5, 1879, the name was changed again to Fort Grant.

FORT GRATIOT [Michigan, 1814–1879]. Fort Gratiot, on the west bank of the St. Clair River one-half mile from the outlet of Lake Huron, was established on May 14, 1814. The post was abandoned in 1821, but it was re-established in 1828 because of unrest among the Indians in Wisconsin. Periodically unoccupied, the fort was finally abandoned about June 1, 1879.   **[183]**

CANTONMENT AT GREENBUSH [New York, 1816–1820]. A garrison was maintained after the War of 1812 until about 1820 at Greenbush, now part of a suburb of Albany, New York.

FORT GREENE [Georgia, 1794–1804]. Fort Greene was built on Cockspur Island at the mouth of the Savannah River in 1794. It was destroyed by the ocean in 1804.

FORT GREENVILLE [Ohio, 1793–1797]. Fort Greenville was established in September, 1793, on a branch of the Miami River, at the present town of Greenville, Ohio. The post was ultimately abandoned early in 1797.

FORT GRIFFIN [Texas, 1867–1881]. A post to replace Fort Belknap in protecting the settlements against hostile Comanche and Kiowa Indians was established on July 29, 1867, on the right bank of the Clear Fork of the Brazos River. It was first called Camp Wilson, but on February 6, 1868, it was designated Fort Griffin. The post was abandoned on May 31, 1881. **[105, 112, 245, 246]**

FORT HALE [South Dakota, 1870–1884]. A post was located on June 8, 1870, on the right bank of the Missouri River in the reservation of the Brulé Sioux. On July 21, 1870, it was moved fifteen miles north to the Agency. The post was known as Post at Lower Brulé Agency until December 30, 1878, when the name was changed to Fort Hale. The post was abandoned on July 8, 1884. Its site is now inundated by Fort Randall Reservoir.

FORT HALL [Idaho, 1870–1883]. The military post of Fort Hall was established on May 27, 1870, about a dozen miles east of the Snake River and twenty-five miles northeast of old Fort Hall, the trading post, to maintain proper control over the Shoshoni and Bannock Indians. The post was abandoned on May 1, 1883.

FORT HALLECK [Nevada, 1867–1886]. A post, called Camp Halleck, was established on July 26, 1867, in northeastern Nevada, about twelve miles south of the Humboldt River. The name of the post was changed to Fort Halleck on April 5, 1879, and the post was abandoned on December 1, 1886.

FORT HALLECK [Wyoming, 1862–1866]. Fort Halleck was established on the north base of Elk Mountain on July 20, 1862, to protect the overland trail, and troops from the fort were scattered along the trail at various points. The post was abandoned on July 4, 1866.

FORT HAMILTON [New York, 1831—]. This post, one of the defenses of New York, was located on the southwestern corner of Long Island, on the east side of the entrance to New York Harbor. Construction was begun on April 26, 1825, but the post was not garrisoned until November 1, 1831.

FORT HAMILTON [Ohio, 1791–1797]. As part of the advance against the Indians in the Northwest Territory, Fort Hamilton was established in September, 1791, on the east bank of the Miami River, thirty-five miles north of Cincinnati, at the present city of Hamilton, Ohio. The post was abandoned late in 1796 or early in 1797. **[213]**

FORT HAMPTON [Alabama, 1810–1817]. Fort Hampton was erected in 1810, north of the great bend of the Tennessee River, near the present town of Athens, Alabama, to protect settlers coming into the area from eastern Tennessee. The post was not used regularly after the War of 1812, but there was a garrison there in 1817.

HANCOCK BARRACKS [Maine, 1828–1845]. Hancock Barracks was established on May 5, 1828, at the present city of Houlton, Maine, on the Canadian frontier. The post was abandoned on September 9, 1845.

CAMP HANCOCK [North Dakota, 1872–1877]. Camp Hancock was established on August 9, 1872, on the east bank of the Missouri River, at Bismarck, where the Northern Pacific Railroad crosses the river. The post was abandoned in 1877.

FORT HANCOCK [Texas, 1881–1895]. A subpost of Fort Davis was established on

April 15, 1881, on a site six miles northwest of abandoned Fort Quitman. On July 9, 1882, the camp, then called Camp Rice, was moved to a new site on the Southern Pacific Railroad. On August 19, 1882, the post was moved once more to higher ground. It became independent of Fort Davis on July 1, 1884, and on May 14, 1886, the name was changed to Fort Hancock. The post was abandoned on October 5, 1895.

FORT HARKER [Kansas, 1864–1873]. A post, called Fort Ellsworth, was established in August, 1864, on the north bank of the Smoky Hill River near the crossing of the old Santa Fe stage road. The name of the post was changed on November 17, 1866, to Fort Harker. In January, 1867, the post was moved one mile east, to the site of present-day Kanopolis, Kansas. The post was discontinued on April 2, 1873.

FORT HARMAR [Ohio, 1785–1790]. As American troops moved into the Northwest after the Revolution, Fort Harmar was established in September, 1785, on the north side of the Ohio River near the mouth of the Muskingum River, at present-day Marietta, Ohio. The post was occupied by United States troops until September, 1790, when they were ordered to Fort Washington at Cincinnati.

FORT HARNEY [Oregon, 1867–1880]. A post was established on August 16, 1867, near the present town of Harney, Oregon. It was first called Camp Steele, but its name was changed to Camp Harney on September 14, 1867, and to Fort Harney on April 5, 1879. The post was abandoned on June 14, 1880.

FORT HARRISON [Indiana, 1811–1818]. Fort Harrison was established on the east bank of the Wabash River, at present-day

Terre Haute, Indiana, in the fall of 1811, as protection against the attacks of Tecumseh and the Prophet. The post was abandoned in 1818.   **[147]**

FORT HARTSUFF [Nebraska, 1874–1881]. A post was established on September 5, 1874, on the North Loup River in central Nebraska to protect settlers from roving bands of Sioux and to protect the Pawnee Indians on their reservation. The establishment was first called simply Post on the North Fork of the Loup River, but on December 9, 1874, the name was changed to Fort Hartsuff. The post was abandoned on May 1, 1881.   **[222]**

CAMP HATCH [Texas]. See Fort Concho.

FORT HAWKINS [Georgia, 1806–1817]. Fort Hawkins was established in 1806 near the Ocmulgee River at the site of the present city of Macon, Georgia. During the War of 1812 it was an assembly point for troops sent to the aid of General Andrew Jackson. The post was abandoned in 1817.

FORT HAYS [Kansas, 1865–1889]. A post was established on October 18, 1865, to protect construction crews of the Kansas Pacific Railroad, on Big Creek, a branch of the Smoky Hill River. It was first called Fort Fletcher, but on November 17, 1866, the post was designated Fort Hays. On June 8, 1867, the original site was abandoned because of flooding, and the post was moved fifteen miles west on the Big Creek near the crossing of the Union Pacific Railroad, at the site of the present city of Fort Hays, Kansas. The post was abandoned on November 8, 1889.   **[90]**

HIWASSEE GARRISON [Tennessee, 1806–1814]. For the protection of the Cherokee country, Hiwassee Garrison was established in 1806 at the junction of the Hiwassee and Tennessee rivers, replacing the posts at Southwest Point and Tellico. The fort was abandoned about 1814.

FORT HOSKINS [Oregon, 1856–1865]. Fort Hoskins was established on July 26, 1856, on the Willamette River north of Corvallis, Oregon. The post was moved to the Siletz River about forty miles northwest of Corvallis in September, 1856, where it guarded the eastern entrance to the Siletz Indian Reservation. The troops withdrew on April 10, 1865. **[178]**

CAMP HOWARD [Idaho, 1877–1881]. Camp Howard was established on August 12, 1877, two miles west of Mount Idaho, by troops operating against the Nez Percé Indians. The post was abandoned on July 11, 1881.

FORT HOWARD [Wisconsin, 1816–1852]. Fort Howard was established in 1816 on the west side of the Fox River at Green Bay, Wisconsin, as part of the movement of American forces into the Northwest after the War of 1812. The garrison was withdrawn in 1841, but the post was regarrisoned again after the Mexican War. The post was finally abandoned on June 8, 1852. **[191]**

FORT HUACHUCA [Arizona, 1877—]. Fort Huachuca (also called Camp Huachuca) was established at the mouth of the central canyon of the Huachuca Mountains on March 3, 1877.

CAMP HUALPAI [Arizona, 1869–1873]. A camp was established on Mohave Creek, one and one-half miles southeast of Aztec Pass and about forty miles northwest of Prescott on May 9, 1869. The post, first called Camp Devin, was designated Camp Toll Gate on May 25, 1869, and Camp Hualpai on August 1, 1870. The post was abandoned on August 27, 1873.

CAMP HUDSON [Texas, 1857–1868]. Camp Hudson was established on June 7, 1857, on Devils River, about eighty miles from Fort Clark. The post was abandoned on March 17, 1861, was reoccupied after the Civil War, and finally abandoned in April, 1868.

FORT HUMBOLDT [California, 1853–1867]. Fort Humboldt was established on January 30, 1853, at the mouth of the Humboldt River. The post was abandoned in January, 1867.

79

I-J-K

CAMP INDEPENDENCE [California, 1862–1877]. This post was established on July 4, 1862, on Oak Creek in the Owens River Valley, about three miles north of the town of Independence, California, to protect miners from Indian depredations. It was temporarily abandoned in 1864, then reoccupied in March, 1865, because of renewed Indian hostility. It was finally abandoned in July, 1877.   **[154]**

FORT INDEPENDENCE [Massachusetts, 1798–1879]. This harbor defense, located on Castle Island in Boston Harbor, was first occupied by United States troops in 1798 or 1799. It was not occupied between 1833 and 1850 and was finally abandoned on November 25, 1879.

INFANTRY CAMP [Arizona]. See Camp Pinal.

FORT INGE [Texas, 1849–1869]. Fort Inge was established on March 13, 1849, on the Leona River, near the present city of Uvalde, Texas. It was located where the principal road to El Paso branched off to Eagle Pass, but it was not garrisoned continuously. It

was abandoned by United States troops on March 19, 1861, reoccupied after the Civil War, then permanently abandoned on February 28, 1869.

FORT JACKSON [Alabama, 1814]. Fort Jackson was established in April, 1814, as a station in the Creek War. It was located near the junction of the Coosa and Tallapoosa rivers. The post was not continued after the war.

FORT JACKSON [Louisiana, 1822–1871]. Fort Jackson and Fort St. Philip were on the Mississippi about seventy-five miles below New Orleans, and the two forts were jointly administered. Fort Jackson was begun on the west bank of the river directly opposite Fort St. Philip in 1822. The forts were seized by Louisiana troops in January, 1861, but surrendered to Union forces April 28, 1862. The two forts were jointly garrisoned until July 7, 1871, when they were abandoned.

JACKSON BARRACKS [Louisiana]. See Post of New Orleans.

FORT JAMES [Georgia, 1797–1802]. Fort James was established on the south bank of

80

the Altamaha River in 1797. It was abandoned about 1802.

FORT JAMES [South Dakota, 1865–1866]. Fort James was established on the James River southeast of present-day Mitchell, South Dakota, in September, 1865. It was abandoned on October 8, 1866.

CAMP JAQUA [California, 1863–1866]. Camp Jaqua was established on August 5, 1863, on the road between Fort Humboldt and Fort Gaston. It was abandoned on August 9, 1866.

FORT JAY [New York, 1794–1806]. Fort Jay was located on Governors Island in New York Harbor. The post was built in the years 1794–1800, in anticipation of a war with France. It was demolished in 1806 and Fort Columbus was built on the site.

FORT JEFFERSON [Florida, 1861–1878]. Construction of a fortification on Garden Key was begun in 1846 and on November 4, 1850, the establishment was named Fort Jefferson. The post was first garrisoned on January 18, 1861, and was intended to control the door to the Gulf of Mexico. Its major function, however, was that of a federal prison. It was abandoned on January 11, 1874, but it was temporarily reoccupied from July 12 to November 9, 1878. [196, 274]

JEFFERSON BARRACKS [Missouri, 1826–]. On July 10, 1826, a site for a military post was occupied on the west bank of the Mississippi River below St. Louis. The post was first called Camp Adams, but on October 23, 1826, it was designated Jefferson Barracks. It was the starting point for numerous military and exploratory expeditions. On April 24, 1871, Jefferson Barracks

was turned over to the Ordnance Department and served as a recruiting station and for cavalry training. Orders of October 1, 1894, directed that the post again be garrisoned as a regular military post.   [283]

FORT JEFFERSON [Ohio, 1791–1796]. As the Americans advanced against the Indians in Ohio, Fort Jefferson was built in October, 1791, forty miles north of Fort Hamilton, at the present town of Fort Jefferson, Ohio. The post was abandoned in the fall of 1796.

FORT JESUP [Louisiana, 1822–1846]. Fort Jesup (called Cantonment Jesup in the early years) was established in May, 1822, on the ridge midway between the Red and Sabine rivers, about twenty-five miles southwest of Natchitoches. It was abandoned in February, 1846.   [51]

CAMP JOHN A. RUCKER [Arizona, 1878–1880]. A post was established in April, 1878, by troops in pursuit of Indians near the Mexican boundary. It was moved about six miles from its original site in May, 1878, and located on the White River, Chiricahua Mountains. The post was first called Camp Supply but was later designated Camp John A. Rucker. The post was discontinued on November 4, 1880.

FORT JOHN BUFORD [Wyoming]. See Fort Sanders.

FORT JOHNSON [South Carolina]. See Charleston Harbor.

FORT JOHNSTON [North Carolina, 1794–1881]. Fort Johnston was located on the west bank of the Cape Fear River, about four miles from its mouth. The site was occupied by United States troops in 1794 and construction begun. The post was repeatedly abandoned and then regarrisoned, and from April 17, 1861, to January 17, 1865, was in the hands of the Confederacy. The post was finally abandoned in February, 1881.

CAMP JOHNSTON [Texas, 1852]. Camp Johnston was a temporary post located on the south side of the north branch of the Concho River on March 15, 1852. It was abandoned in November, 1852, and its troops transferred to Fort Chadbourne.

FORT JONES [California, 1852–1858]. Fort Jones was established on October 16, 1852, on the Scott River about fifteen miles southwest of the present city of Yreka, California. It was evacuated on June 23, 1858.

POST AT KASKASKIA [Illinois, 1802–1807]. A garrison was established at Kaskaskia, Illinois, in 1802, and the post was part of the military frontier in the Northwest until 1807.

FORT KEARNY [Nebraska, 1846–1848]. On May 21, 1846, a post was established on the west bank of the Missouri River, at the site of present-day Nebraska City, Nebraska. The post was first called Camp Kearny, then Fort Kearny. It was not continuously occupied and in May, 1848, was completely abandoned, the troops establishing a new post on the Platte River.   **[267, 288]**

FORT KEARNY [Nebraska, 1848–1871]. A new post was established in May, 1848, on the south bank of the Platte River near present Kearney, Nebraska, to protect emigrants on the Oregon Trail. The post was first called Fort Childs, but on January 31, 1849, it was officially designated Fort Kearny. The troops were withdrawn from the fort on May 17, 1871.   **[205, 254, 282, 288]**

FORT KEARNY [Wyoming]. See Fort Phil Kearny.

CAMP KELLEY [Texas]. See Fort Concho.

FORT KENT [Maine, 1841–1845]. Fort Kent was established on September 17, 1841, at the junction of Fish River and St. John River in northern Maine. The post was abandoned on September 11, 1845.

FORT KEOGH [Montana, 1876–]. A site was occupied on August 28, 1876, at the mouth of the Tongue River at present-day Miles City, Montana, which was officially established as a military post on September 11, 1876. It was part of the movement of troops into the area after the Custer massacre. The post was known as Cantonment on Tongue River, as New Post on the Yellowstone, and as Tongue River Barracks. On November 8, 1877, it was named Fort Keogh.

KEY WEST BARRACKS [Florida, 1831–]. This post was established on January 2, 1831, on Key West on the north shore of the island. It served also as a garrison for Fort Taylor, an artillery fortification which was built on the key, beginning about 1845. The post was repeatedly abandoned and reoccupied.   **[287]**

FORT KING [Florida, 1827–1843]. Fort King was established in March, 1827, near the present city of Ocala, Florida, about forty miles east of Cedar Keys. It was abandoned on March 25, 1843.   **[123]**

FORT KLAMATH [Oregon, 1863–1889]. To protect settlers in the Klamath Lakes region from hostile Indians, Fort Klamath was established on September 5, 1863, near the northern end of Klamath Lake Valley, about forty miles north of the California line. The garrison abandoned the post on August 9, 1889.

FORT KNOX [Indiana, 1787–1816]. Fort Knox was established at Vincennes, Indiana, in August, 1787. A new garrison was later built nearby and troops were maintained at Vincennes until about 1816. [239]

POST AT KNOXVILLE [Tennessee, 1793–1807]. United States troops were stationed at Knoxville in 1793, and the city was a military center during the frontier period in Tennessee. The troops were withdrawn about 1807.

L

FORT LAFAYETTE [New York, 1822–1868]. This fortification, located at the left of the entrance to New York Harbor opposite Fort Hamilton, was begun in 1812 but not garrisoned until 1822. It was first known as Fort Diamond, but it was renamed Fort Lafayette on March 26, 1823. The fort was replaced in 1868.

FORT LANCASTER [Texas, 1855–1861]. Fort Lancaster (at first called Camp Lancaster) was established on Live Oak Creek, near its junction with the Pecos River, on August 20, 1855. It was abandoned on March 19, 1861. [138]

FORT LANE [Oregon, 1853–1856]. Fort Lane was established on September 28, 1853, about eight miles north of present Jacksonville, Oregon. The post was abandoned on September 17, 1856.

CAMP LA PAZ [Arizona, 1874–1875]. Camp La Paz was established on the Colorado Indian Reservation on April 20, 1874, and abandoned on May 23, 1875.

FORT LAPWAI [Idaho, 1862–1885]. Fort Lapwai was established on August 6, 1862, three miles south of the Clearwater River east of present-day Lewiston, Idaho, to keep order during the rush of gold seekers into the Nez Percé country. It was begun by volunteer troops, who were mustered out in 1865, but who were replaced by regulars on November 23, 1866. Fort Lapwai was made a subpost of Fort Walla Walla on July 25, 1884, and was finally abandoned on October 1, 1885.

FORT LARAMIE [Wyoming, 1849–1890]. Fort Laramie, a fur trading post, was located on the left bank of the Laramie River about half a mile from its confluence with the North Platte River. It was occupied as a United States military post on June 16, 1849, and on June 26 the trading company post was purchased by the government. The fort protected the Oregon Trail and served as the headquarters for campaigns against the Indians. The troops left the post on March 2, 1890, leaving only a small detachment to care for the government property.

[167, 174, 206, 207]

FORT LARNED [Kansas, 1859–1878]. A post was established on October 22, 1859, on the right bank of Pawnee Fork about eight miles from its confluence with the Arkansas River, near the present town of Larned, Kansas, to protect the Santa Fe Trail. It was first known as Camp on Pawnee Fork, and locally at one time as Camp Alert. On May 29, 1860, the station was officially designated Fort Larned. The troops were moved to Fort Dodge on October 28, 1878.   **[275]**

POST AT LAS VEGAS [New Mexico, 1848–1851]. A military post was established at Las Vegas, about fifty miles east of Santa Fe, New Mexico, in February, 1848. The post was abandoned on July 26, 1851.

FORT LEAVENWORTH [Kansas, 1827—]. A post was established on May 8, 1827, on the west bank of the Missouri River near present-day Leavenworth, Kansas. The post was designated Cantonment Leavenworth on November 8, 1827, and on February 8, 1832, was renamed Fort Leavenworth. Continuously garrisoned, it served as a starting point for military expeditions to the west during the frontier period.   **[180, 241, 242]**

CAMP ON LEON RIVER [Texas]. See Fort Gates.

FORT LEWIS [Colorado, 1878–1891]. On October 15, 1878, a post was established at Pagosa Springs on the San Juan River to guard the Ute Indian Reservation. It was named Camp Lewis on October 26, 1878, and in December, 1878, Fort Lewis. In 1880 the post was ordered to a new site and on August 30, 1880, a new Fort Lewis was established on the La Plata River, about twelve miles west of Durango, Colorado. The original post was then called Cantonment Pagosa Springs until it was soon abandoned. On October 15, 1891, the new Fort Lewis was also abandoned.   **[86]**

CAMP LEWIS [Montana, 1874]. Camp Lewis was established on May 10, 1874, on

a fork of the Judith River about two miles south of the present city of Lewistown, Montana. The post was abandoned on November 1, 1874.

CAMP LINCOLN [Arizona]. See Fort Verde.

CAMP LINCOLN [California, 1862–1869]. Established on June 13, 1862, near Crescent City, California, Camp Lincoln was abandoned on June 11, 1869.   **[67]**

FORT LINCOLN [North Dakota]. See Fort Abraham Lincoln.

FORT LINCOLN [Texas, 1849–1852]. This post was established on Seco Creek, a branch of the Nueces River, about fifty miles west of San Antonio, on July 7, 1849. It was abandoned on July 20, 1852.

LITTLE ROCK BARRACKS [Arkansas, 1873–1890]. The site of Little Rock Barracks, in the southeast part of the city, was purchased by the United States in 1836 and an arsenal constructed. On July 25, 1873, the facility became Little Rock Barracks. It was abandoned about September 25, 1890.

POST AT LOFTUS HEIGHTS [Mississippi]. See Fort Adams [Mississippi].

FORT LOGAN [Colorado, 1887—]. An installation, known simply as Post near Denver, was established in October, 1887, and designated Fort Logan on April 5, 1889. It was one of several troop centers which the government created once the decline of the Indian menace made it unnecessary to deploy soldiers at a large number of strategic locations.   **[231, 232]**

FORT LOGAN [Montana, 1869–1880]. In November, 1869, a post called Camp Baker was established in the Smith River Valley, thirteen miles northeast of Diamond City, Montana, to protect Diamond City and other mining camps in the vicinity from Indian depredations. The post was later moved to a new site about five miles to the north. On December 30, 1878, the name was changed to Fort Logan, and in October, 1880, the post was abandoned.

CAMP LOGAN [Oregon, 1865–1868]. Camp Logan was established on September 16, 1865, on a tributary of the Middle Fork of the John Day River, about thirteen miles east of Canyon City, Oregon, to protect the settlers from Indian attacks. The troops were evacuated from the post on November 28, 1868, although the post was later reoccupied temporarily by a small detachment to guard the property.

FORT LOOKOUT [South Dakota, 1856–1857]. A post was established on July 31, 1856, near the trading post of Fort Lookout on the west bank of the Missouri River about sixty miles below Fort Pierre. The post was evacuated on June 17, 1857.

POST AT LORAMIE'S [Ohio, 1794–1798]. A trading post known as Loramie's Store was occupied by the English as early as 1750 or 1751. It was located in western Ohio on Loramie Creek, a branch of the Miami River. In 1794 General Anthony Wayne built a post there, which was sometimes called Fort Loramie. The post was abandoned early in 1798.

CANTONMENT LORING [Idaho, 1849–1850]. Cantonment Loring, a post on the Snake River, about three miles above the trading post of Fort Hall, was established in July, 1849, in order to protect the Oregon

Trail. The post was abandoned on May 6, 1850.

POST AT LOS LUNAS [New Mexico, 1852–1862]. A military post was established at Los Lunas, about twenty miles south of Albuquerque, New Mexico, on January 3, 1852. The post was abandoned in October, 1862.

FORT LOWELL [Arizona, 1862–1891]. A post was established on May 21, 1862, at the city of Tucson, Arizona. On August 29, 1866, it was named Camp Lowell, and on March 28, 1873, it was directed that the post be moved to a new site seven miles southeast of Tucson. The post was named Fort Lowell on April 5, 1879, and was abandoned in March, 1891.

FORT LOWELL [New Mexico, 1866–1869]. A post, called Camp Plummer, was established on November 6, 1866, on the Rio Chama at the Spanish Trail crossing in northern New Mexico. The name was changed to Fort Lowell on July 13, 1868, and on July 27, 1869, the post was abandoned.

POST AT LOWER BRULE AGENCY [South Dakota]. See Fort Hale.

FORT LYON [Colorado, 1860–1889]. On August 29, 1860, a military post was built in the vicinity of Bent's Fort on the Arkansas River, near present-day Lamar, Colorado. It was first called Fort Wise; then on June 25, 1862, it was designated Fort Lyon. In June, 1867, the original site of the post was abandoned and a new Fort Lyon established about twenty miles upstream on the left bank of the Arkansas, two and one-half miles below the mouth of the Purgatoire River.

The post was ordered abandoned on August 31, 1889.

CAMP LYON [Idaho, 1865–1869]. Camp Lyon was established on June 27, 1865, on the north fork of Jordan Creek, the most northern tributary of the Owyhee River. The post was abandoned on April 27, 1869.

FORT LYON [New Mexico, 1860–1861]. A post, first called Fort Fauntleroy, was established on August 31, 1860, on the road from Albuquerque to Fort Defiance. The name was changed to Fort Lyon in September, 1861, and the post was abandoned on December 10, 1861. Fort Wingate was moved from its original location and reestablished on the site of Fort Lyon in 1868.

M

FORT McDERMIT [Nevada, 1865–1889]. A post established on August 14, 1865, on the east bank of Quinn River, near the northern boundary of Nevada, was first called Camp McDermit, then, on April 5, 1879, Fort McDermit. It was abandoned on June 22, 1889.

FORT McDOWELL [Arizona, 1865–1891]. Camp McDowell was established on September 7, 1865, on the west bank of the Verde River, about eight miles from its confluence with the Salt River. On April 5, 1879, its name was changed to Fort McDowell, and on January 17, 1891, it was finally abandoned.

FORT McDOWELL [California]. See Post of Angel Island.

CAMP McGARRY [Nevada, 1865–1868]. Camp McGarry was established in October, 1865, at Summit Springs near Summit Lake, Nevada. It was abandoned on December 18, 1868.

FORT McHENRY [Maryland, 1794–]. The construction of Fort McHenry at Baltimore, Maryland, began in 1794. Although an important coastal defense, it was not continuously garrisoned. **[93, 200, 281]**

FORT McHENRY [Mississippi, 1798]. Fort McHenry was established at Vicksburg, Mississippi, in the spring of 1798, after the withdrawal of Spanish troops from the area. The post does not seem to have been regularly garrisoned.

FORT McINTOSH [Pennsylvania, 1778–1791]. Built in the autumn of 1778 on the north side of the Ohio River, about thirty miles below Pittsburgh, Fort McIntosh was one of the few American forts on the frontier at the end of the Revolutionary War. The post was abandoned in the winter of 1790–1791. **[78, 157, 237]**

FORT McINTOSH [Texas, 1849–]. A post was established on March 3, 1849, on the Rio Grande just above Laredo, Texas. It was first called Camp Crawford but on December 28, 1849, the name was changed to Fort McIntosh. The post was evacuated on March 12, 1861, and reoccupied on October 23, 1865.

FORT McKAVETT [Texas, 1852–1883]. Fort McKavett (originally called Camp Mc-

Kavett) was established on March 14, 1852, on the south bank of the San Saba River, a branch of the Colorado, as part of the line of defense against Indian depredations. The post was abandoned pursuant to orders of February 5, 1859, but it was reoccupied about April 1, 1868. The post was ultimately abandoned on June 29, 1883.   **[115]**

CANTONMENT McKEAN [Nebraska]. See Fort McPherson [Nebraska].

FORT McKEEN [North Dakota]. See Fort Abraham Lincoln.

FORT McKINNEY [Wyoming, 1876–1894]. A post, called Cantonment Reno, was established on October 12, 1876, on the north bank of the Powder River about three miles above abandoned Fort Reno. Its name was changed on August 30, 1877, to Fort McKinney, and on July 18, 1878, the site was changed to a spot on the north bank of the Clear Fork, near the present city of Buffalo, Wyoming. The post was abandoned on November 7, 1894.

FORT McLANE [New Mexico, 1860–1861]. A post was established on September 16, 1860, about fifteen miles south of the Santa Rita copper mines and a dozen miles west of the point where the overland mail route crossed the Mimbres River. The post was first called Camp Wheeler. Its name was changed on December 1, 1860, to Fort Floyd and on January 18, 1861, to Fort McLane. The post was abandoned on July 3, 1861.

CAMP McPHERSON [Arizona]. See Camp Date Creek.

FORT McPHERSON [Georgia, 1865—]. Atlanta, Georgia, was occupied by Union forces

on May 4, 1865, and the facilities built there were designated McPherson Barracks on December 30, 1867. The post was abandoned in 1882 and reoccupied in May, 1889, at which time its name was changed to Fort McPherson.

FORT McPHERSON [Nebraska, 1863–1880]. A post was established on September 18, 1863, on the south side of the Platte River near present-day North Platte, Nebraska. The post was named Cantonment McKean on September 27, 1863, then successively renamed Post at Cottonwood Springs, Fort Cottonwood, and finally on February 26, 1866, Fort McPherson. The post was abandoned in April, 1880.

FORT McRAE [New Mexico, 1863–1876]. Fort McRae was established on April 3, 1863, at Ojo del Muerto about three miles east of the Rio Grande for the protection of the Jornado del Muerto from the Apaches. The post was abandoned on October 30, 1876.

FORT MACKINAC [Michigan, 1796–1894]. Fort Mackinac, originally a French but later a British post, stood on a bluff on the southeast part of Mackinac Island in the straits between Lakes Michigan and Huron. It was occupied by United States troops in October, 1796. The post was captured by the British in 1812 and reoccupied by American troops in 1815. The post was irregularly occupied until it was finally abandoned pursuant to orders of September 15, 1894.   **[83]**

FORT MACOMB [Louisiana, 1827–1867]. A post was established about 1827 on the west side of Chef Menteur Pass, about twenty-five miles from New Orleans. It was first called Fort Wood, but the name was changed to Fort Macomb on June 23, 1851.

In 1861 and 1862 the fort was held briefly by the Confederacy. Troops were finally withdrawn on January 27, 1867. [215]

FORT MACON [North Carolina, 1834–1876]. Fort Macon was constructed between 1826 and 1834 on the point of Bogue Island, near Beaufort, North Carolina. It was first occupied by troops on December 4, 1834. The fort was not garrisoned in 1836–1842 and 1849–1862. From 1862 to 1876 it was a military prison. The garrison was finally withdrawn on September 25, 1876, and orders of April 21, 1877, directed the abandonment of the fort. [89]

FORT MADISON [Iowa, 1808–1813]. Fort Madison was established on September 26, 1808, on the right bank of the Mississippi River twenty-five miles above the mouth of the Des Moines River, at the site of the present city of Fort Madison, Iowa. Its purpose was to control the Sacs and Foxes and other Indians of the upper Mississippi, and to oppose British traders. The fort was besieged by Indians during the War of 1812 and, not being suitable for defense, was abandoned on September 3, 1813. [182, 279]

MADISON BARRACKS [New York, 1815—]. Madison Barracks (first known as Cantonment at Sackets Harbor) was located on the south shore of Black River Bay, about ten miles from Lake Ontario, at the site of the present town of Sackets Harbor, New York. It was occupied in 1815 or 1816 and was only irregularly garrisoned until after the Civil War.

FORT MAGINNIS [Montana, 1880–1890]. Fort Maginnis was established on August 22, 1880, about twenty miles northeast of Lewistown, Montana. It was abandoned on July 10, 1890.

FORT MANN [Kansas, 1845–1850]. Fort Mann was established about 1845 near the Cimarron crossing of the Arkansas River, near present-day Dodge City, Kansas. The post was maintained until about 1850, when Fort Atkinson was established.

FORT MARCY [New Mexico, 1846–1894]. Santa Fe, New Mexico, was occupied by United States troops on August 18, 1846, and construction of a fort, named Fort Marcy, was begun in September. The post was abandoned in 1867 and re-established as a post in 1875. Orders of September 15, 1894, directed the post to be abandoned.

FORT MARION [Florida]. See Post of St. Augustine.

CANTONMENT MARTIN [Kansas, 1818–1820]. Cantonment Martin was established in 1818 as a base of supplies for Stephen H. Long's expedition. It was located on Cow Island in the Missouri River north of present-day Leavenworth, Kansas, and was occupied until the return of Long's expedition in October, 1820.

FORT MARTIN SCOTT [Texas, 1848–1866]. Fort Martin Scott was established on December 5, 1848, about two miles south of Fredericksburg, Texas. It was abandoned in December, 1853, as the line of frontier forts reached farther west. The post was held by the Confederates from 1861 to 1865 and reoccupied by United States troops on October 18, 1866. It was discontinued on December 28, 1866. [221]

FORT MASON [California, 1863—]. A post was established on October 13, 1863, on the south side of San Francisco Bay. It was first called Fort Point San José, but was designated Fort Mason on November 25, 1882.

FORT MASON [Texas, 1851–1869]. Fort Mason was established on July 6, 1851, near the Llano River, a tributary of the Colorado. It was irregularly occupied until the Civil War and on March 29, 1861, was abandoned to the Confederacy. It was reoccupied in 1866 and then finally abandoned on March 23, 1869.

FORT MASSAC [Illinois, 1794–1814]. Fort Massac, an old French fort on the north bank of the Ohio River about ten miles below present-day Paducah, Kentucky, was repaired and reoccupied by American troops in 1794 for Indian control in the Ohio Valley and because of fear of French disturbances in the Kaskaskia region. The post was abandoned in 1814.   **[100, 101, 252, 253]**

FORT MASSACHUSETTS [Colorado, 1852–1858]. Fort Massachusetts was established on June 22, 1852, on Ute Creek at an opening into the San Luis Valley as defense against the Utes and Apaches. The post was garrisoned until June 24, 1858, when the troops were transferred to a new post, Fort Garland, a few miles to the south.   **[116]**

FORT MEADE [Florida, 1849–1857]. Fort Meade was established on December 19, 1849, on Peace River, about forty-five miles east of Tampa Bay. It was abandoned on September 20, 1857.

FORT MEADE [South Dakota, 1878–]. A post was established on August 28, 1878, on the east side of Bear Butte Creek in the Black Hills, about fifteen miles east of Deadwood, South Dakota. It was originally called Camp Ruhlen, but on December 30, 1878, the name was changed to Fort Meade.

CAMP MEDICINE BUTTE [Wyoming, 1885–1887]. Camp Medicine Butte was es-tablished at Evanston, Wyoming, on September 5, 1885, to protect the United States mails from anti-Chinese rioters who were destroying the property of the Union Pacific Railroad. The post was discontinued on April 4, 1887.

FORT MERRILL [Texas, 1850–1855]. Fort Merrill was established on February 26, 1850, on the right bank of the Nueces River about fifty miles northwest of Corpus Christi. It was abandoned on December 1, 1855.

CAMP MERRITT [Montana, 1890–]. Camp Merritt was established in April, 1890, at the Tongue River Indian Agency. In 1898 it became a subpost of Fort Keogh.

FORT MIAMI [Ohio, 1796–1797]. Fort Miami (or Miamis) was built by the British on the Maumee River in the spring of 1794. American troops occupied the post on July 11, 1796, and abandoned it in 1797.   **[87]**

FORT MIFFLIN [Pennsylvania, 1798–1866]. Fort Mifflin was built on Mud Island in the Delaware River a short distance below Philadelphia on the site of a Revolutionary War fort. Construction on the new fort was begun in 1798. The post was irregularly garrisoned and was abandoned by troops in April, 1866.   **[97]**

FORT MILLER [California, 1851–1864]. Because of Indian uprisings in the foothills of the Sierras, Fort Miller (first called Camp Barbour) was established in the mining district of the San Joaquin River on May 26, 1851. The post was abandoned in 1856 or 1857, then regarrisoned by California Volunteers in 1863. It was finally abandoned late in 1864.   **[155]**

FORT MISSOULA [Montana, 1877–]. A

post was established on June 25, 1877, on the east bank of the Bitterroot River, four miles from Missoula, Montana, for Indian control in the region. It was named Fort Missoula on November 8, 1877.   **[92, 247]**

CANTONMENT MISSOURI [Nebraska]. See Fort Atkinson [Nebraska].

FORT MITCHELL [Alabama, 1813–1837]. Fort Mitchell was built on the west bank of the Chattahoochee River, at the site of the present town of Fort Mitchell, Alabama. The post was originally built by Georgia militia and was first occupied by federal troops in 1813. It was abandoned after the War of 1812 but was reoccupied in 1828 and maintained until November 14, 1837.

FORT MITCHELL [Nebraska, 1864–1867]. Fort Mitchell, an outpost of Fort Laramie, was established in 1864 on the North Platte River, just above Scotts Bluff. It was abandoned in 1867.   **[208, 209]**

FORT MOGOLLON [Arizona]. See Fort Apache.

FORT MOHAVE [Arizona, 1859–1890]. To control the Mohave and Paiute Indians in the vicinity of the thirty-fifth parallel, a camp was established in April, 1859, on the left bank of the Colorado River near the head of Mohave Valley. It was originally called Camp Colorado but was renamed Fort Mohave by the garrison commander. It was also known as Camp Mohave until officially designated Fort Mohave on April 5, 1879. The post was abandoned between May, 1861, and April, 1863, and was finally abandoned pursuant to orders of May 23, 1890.

FORT MONROE [Virginia, 1823–]. A defense work called Fortress Monroe was built at Point Comfort, at the west side of the

entrance to Chesapeake Bay. Construction was begun in March, 1819, and the post was first garrisoned in July, 1823. The post was renamed Fort Monroe by orders of February 8, 1832. It was almost continuously garrisoned and was the site of the Coast Artillery School.   **[84, 85]**

POST OF MONTEREY [California, 1847–1865]. The Presidio of Monterey became a United States military post on January 28, 1847. It was variously designated—Monterey Redoubt and Post of Monterey—and was abandoned on August 19, 1852. The post was briefly re-established as Monterey Barracks by California Volunteers from February 17 to October 18, 1865. The post was reactivated in 1902.

FORT MONTGOMERY [Alabama, 1814–1818]. Fort Montgomery was established in the summer of 1814, ten or twelve miles above the junction of the Alabama and Tombigbee rivers, about three miles east of the Alabama. The post was abandoned about 1818.

CANTONMENT MONTPELIER [Alabama, 1817–1820]. Cantonment (or Camp) Montpelier was located about seven miles northeast of Fort Montgomery, Alabama, and about ten miles from the Alabama River. There were troops at the camp from about 1817 to 1820.

FORT MONUMENT [Kansas, 1865–1868]. Troops were stationed at Monument Station of the Butterfield Overland Dispatch in 1865 to protect the stage road. The post was abandoned in 1868.

FORT MORGAN [Alabama, 1834–1868]. This fort was built at Mobile Point at the entrance to Mobile Bay on the site of a previous fort called Fort Bowyer. The post was named Fort Morgan on April 18, 1833, and was first garrisoned on March 7, 1834. It was irregularly garrisoned and was occupied by Confederate forces during the Civil War. It was abandoned pursuant to orders of January 28, 1868.

FORT MORGAN [Colorado, 1865–1868]. A post was established on July 1, 1865, on the south bank of the South Platte River in northwestern Colorado. It was first called Camp Wardwell, but on June 23, 1866, it was designated Fort Morgan. The post protected the stage route between the Missouri River and Denver, until it was abandoned on May 18, 1868.

FORT MOULTRIE [South Carolina, 1798–1860]. A Revolutionary War fort was built on Sullivans Island in the main entrance to Charleston Harbor. It was first called Fort Sullivan and then renamed Fort Moultrie. A second fort was built on the site in 1798. The troops were generally reported as "Troops in Charleston Harbor," but from 1842 to 1860 Fort Moultrie was a separate post.   **[243]**

MOUNT VERNON BARRACKS [Alabama, 1873–1894]. Mount Vernon Barracks on the west side of the Mobile River at the town of Mount Vernon, Alabama, was established on orders of July 25, 1873, which changed the designation from Mount Vernon Arsenal, established on January 1, 1829. The post was abandoned in December, 1894.

CAMP ON MUCKLESHUTE PRAIRIE [Washington, 1856–1857]. A camp was established on Muckleshute Prairie on the White River on March 20, 1856. The troops were withdrawn in July, 1857.

FORT MYER [Virginia, 1863–]. This post on the south bank of the Potomac was one of the principal defenses of Washington, and earthworks were constructed in 1863. The post was first called Fort Whipple, but the name was changed to Fort Myer on February 4, 1881.

FORT MYERS [Florida, 1850–1858]. Fort Myers was established on the left bank of the Caloosahatchee River about twenty miles from the Gulf of Mexico on February 20, 1850, and abandoned May 31, 1858.   **[162]**

N-O-P

POST AT NATCHEZ [Mississippi, 1798–1808]. Natchez, Mississippi, was occupied by troops in about 1798 and was used briefly as headquarters by General James Wilkinson. He designated the post Fort Sargent, but the name does not seem to have been used regularly. The installation was used until about 1808.

POST AT NATCHITOCHES [Louisiana, 1804–1822]. Natchitoches, Louisiana, on the Red River, was occupied by United States troops in 1804, and was an important military post in the Southwest, exerting American authority after that area had been acquired from France. The post was sometimes called Fort Claiborne, and in 1820 a new facility, Fort Selden, was established at Natchitoches. The troops were withdrawn from the area when Fort Jesup was established in 1822.

FORT NELSON [Virginia, 1794–1824]. Fort Nelson was located on the west side of Norfolk Harbor, opposite Fort Norfolk. Construction was begun on the fort in 1794. The post was abandoned in April, 1824.

CANTONMENT NEW HOPE [Minnesota]. See Fort Snelling.

POST AT NEW MADRID [Missouri, 1804–1808]. A post was established in 1804 at New Madrid, the Spanish settlement on the Mississippi below the mouth of the Ohio, as part of American military occupation of the Louisiana Purchase. The garrison was maintained until about 1808.

POST OF NEW ORLEANS [Louisiana, 1803—]. The first United States troops arrived in New Orleans on December 20, 1803, and the city was garrisoned intermittently, with the intention of guarding against slave insurrections. In 1834 new barracks were erected on the left bank of the Mississippi below the city, which were originally called New Orleans Barracks. After the Civil War the post was known as Jackson Barracks.

NEWPORT BARRACKS [Kentucky, 1803–1894]. Military barracks were first established at Newport, Kentucky, about 1803, and an arsenal was also established. The post was later used as a recruiting depot. It was finally abandoned on November 10, 1894.

NEW SAN DIEGO BARRACKS [California]. See San Diego Barracks.

NEW YORK HARBOR [New York]. New

York City, as a critical point on the Atlantic coast, was protected by a number of forts and batteries. Among the more important of these were Fort Jay, constructed on Governors Island in 1794–1800 and replaced by Fort Columbus in 1806; Fort Lafayette, begun in 1812, and Fort Hamilton, begun in 1825, guarding the entrance to the harbor; Fort Wood, begun on Bedloe's Island in 1822; and Fort Schuyler, begun on Throgs Neck in 1833.

FORT NIAGARA [New York, 1796—]. Fort Niagara, located on a point of land at the junction of the Niagara River and Lake Ontario, was surrendered to the United States by the British on August 11, 1796. The post was again in British possession from December, 1813, to March, 1815, but thereafter was continuously garrisoned except for brief intervals. **[148, 201]**

FORT NIOBRARA [Nebraska, 1880—]. Fort Niobrara was established on April 22, 1880, on the south bank of the Niobrara River just below the town of Valentine, Nebraska.

POST AT NOME LACKEE [California, 1855–1858]. A military post was established on January 4, 1855, on the Nome Lackee Indian Reservation. It was abandoned on April 21, 1858.

FORT NORFOLK [Virginia, 1794–1824]. Fort Norfolk, located on the east side of Norfolk Harbor, was established about 1794. The post was turned over to the Navy in March, 1824.

CANTONMENT ON THE NORTH FORK OF THE CANADIAN RIVER [Oklahoma, 1879–1882]. A post was established on March 6, 1879, on the North Fork of the Canadian River about sixty miles up the river from Fort Reno, to check the movements of the Cheyenne and other Indians. The post was never given a formal designation. The troops were withdrawn in June, 1882.

POST ON THE NORTH FORK OF THE LOUP RIVER [Nebraska]. See Fort Hartsuff.

CANTONMENT ON THE NORTH FORK OF THE RED RIVER [Texas]. See Fort Elliott.

NORTH PLATTE STATION [Nebraska, 1867–1877]. This post, called also Camp Sergeant, was established on January 30, 1867, for protection of the Union Pacific Railroad and as a base of supplies for troops scouting the area. It was located between the North Platte and South Platte rivers at their junction. The station was considered a subpost of Fort McPherson. Although abandoned on November 4, 1877, it was garrisoned by small, temporary detachments after that date.

OGLETHORPE BARRACKS [Georgia, 1821–1851]. This post, located at Savannah, Georgia, was established in 1821. It was abandoned in January, 1851, after being irregularly garrisoned. The post was taken by Georgia troops in January, 1861, and was reoccupied by United States troops on December 21, 1864. It served as a garrison for troops until the end of the Reconstruction period.

POST AT OJO CALIENTE [New Mexico, 1874–1882]. A camp was established on the western slope of the San Mateo Range in southwestern New Mexico on September 2,

1874. It was an outpost of Fort Craig, about fifty miles to the east. The post was abandoned on October 5, 1882.

FORT OMAHA [Nebraska, 1868—]. A post was established at Omaha on August 19, 1863, and used for the training of volunteer troops during the Civil War, and in 1866 Omaha became the headquarters of the Department of the Platte. In 1868 a new post north of the city was occupied by troops on November 20. At first called Sherman Barracks, the post was designated Omaha Barracks on November 24, 1868. The name was changed to Fort Omaha on December 30, 1878. In 1891 a new post was established ten miles south of the city and called Fort Crook.

FORT ONTARIO [New York, 1796—]. Fort Ontario, on the right bank of the Oswego River at its junction with Lake Ontario, was surrendered to the United States by the British on July 15, 1796. Occupied until 1803 by a small detachment, it was then abandoned. The fort was defended against the attack of the British during the War of 1812 and then was allowed to fall into ruin. On November 23, 1839, the site was again garrisoned by United States troops and a new fort constructed. **[91]**

POST AT OPELOUSAS [Louisiana, 1804–1808]. The town of Opelousas, Louisiana, was one of the sites garrisoned by United States troops early in 1804 as part of American occupation of the Louisiana Purchase. The post was maintained until about 1808.

CAMP ORD [Arizona]. See Fort Apache.

FORT ORFORD [Oregon, 1851–1856]. Fort Orford was established in September, 1851, ten miles south of Cape Blanco àt Port Orford, Oregon. It was abandoned during July and August, 1856.

FORT OSAGE [Missouri, 1808–1819]. Fort Osage (sometimes called Fort Clark) was established in September, 1808, on the right bank of the Missouri River near the site of the present town of Sibley, Missouri, for the protection of the government trading house. The post was evacuated in 1813 during the War of 1812 but regarrisoned in 1815 or 1816. The troops withdrew permanently at the time of the Yellowstone Expedition of 1819. **[81, 161]**

POST AT OUACHITA [Louisiana, 1804–1808]. A military garrison was maintained at Ouachita, Louisiana, from 1804 to 1808 as part of American occupation of the Louisiana Purchase.

CANTONMENT PAGOSA SPRINGS [Colorado]. See Fort Lewis [Colorado].

POST AT PASS CHRISTIAN [Mississippi, 1812–1818]. Troops were stationed at Pass Christian at the entrance of Lake Borgne in 1812, and the site was used for troops after the War of 1812 until 1817 or 1818.

CAMP ON PAWNEE FORK [Kansas]. See Fort Larned.

FORT PEMBINA [North Dakota, 1870–1895]. A post was established on July 9, 1870, on the left bank of the Red River of the North near the Canadian border, about a mile and a half south of the present town of Pembina, North Dakota. It was first named Fort George H. Thomas, but it was renamed Fort Pembina on September 6, 1870. The post was abandoned on September 26, 1895.

CAMP PENA COLORADO [Texas, 1880–1893]. Camp Pena Colorado was established in March, 1880, about fifty miles southeast of Fort Davis. It was abandoned on February 11, 1893.

POST OF PETITE COQUILLE [Louisiana]. See Fort Pike.

FORT PHANTOM HILL [Texas]. See Post on Brazos River.

FORT PHIL KEARNY [Wyoming, 1866–1868]. Fort Phil Kearny, the principal post on the Bozeman Trail, was established on July 13, 1866, on the Piney Fork of the Powder River in the foothills of the Big Horn Mountains. The site was known as New Fort Reno until orders of June 28, 1866, designating it Fort Phil Kearny were received. The post was abandoned on July 31, 1868. **[98, 260]**

FORT PICKENS [Florida, 1834–1867]. Fort Pickens was located on the western tip of Santa Rosa Island, commanding the eastern entrance of Pensacola Harbor. Construction was begun in 1828, and the post was first garrisoned in October, 1834. The post was not regularly garrisoned and the last report of troops at the fort was in 1867.

FORT PICKERING [Tennessee, 1797–1810]. On July 20, 1797, American troops occupied Chickasaw Bluffs, at the present city of Memphis, Tennessee. The post established there was first named Fort Adams, but its name was changed to Fort Pickering. It was abandoned about 1810.

CAMP PICKETT [Washington]. See Camp San Juan Island.

FORT PIERCE [Florida, 1838–1842]. Fort Pierce was established in January, 1838, at the Indian River Inlet on the shore of St. Lucie Sound. It was abandoned on May 16, 1842.

FORT PIERRE [South Dakota, 1855–1857]. Fort Pierre, originally a fur trading post, was established as a military post on July 7, 1855. It was located on the west bank of the Missouri River, opposite the present city of Pierre, South Dakota. The post was abandoned on May 16, 1857. **[128, 290]**

FORT PIKE [Louisiana, 1816–1871]. A post was established on Petite Coquille Island at the entrance of Lake Pontchartrain in May, 1816. The post was originally designated Petite Coquille, but on November 8, 1827, the name was changed to Fort Pike. The post was abandoned on August 11, 1849, and on January 14, 1861, the site was seized by Louisiana troops. It was reoccupied by United States troops on August 18, 1862. The troops were withdrawn on May 22, 1871.

FORT PIKE [New York, 1812–1818]. Fort Pike was built in 1812 at Sackets Harbor, New York. The post was continued as a military garrison after the War of 1812 and was finally abandoned about 1818.

CAMP PILOT BUTTE [Wyoming, 1885—]. A post was established at Rock Springs, Wyoming, pursuant to orders of September 5, 1885, to restore order after an anti-Chinese riot. The post was named Camp Pilot Butte on October 20, 1885.

CAMP PINAL [Arizona, 1870–1871]. A post, called Infantry Camp, was established in the Pinal Mountains on November 28, 1870. The name was changed to Camp Pinal on April 4, 1871, and on July 24, 1871, the post was abandoned by the government.

CASTLE PINCKNEY [South Carolina]. See Charleston Harbor.

FORT PITT [Pennsylvania]. See Forts at Pittsburgh.

FORTS AT PITTSBURGH [Pennsylvania, 1777–1811]. The British post Fort Pitt, at present-day Pittsburgh, Pennsylvania, was taken by Virginia militia in 1775 and turned over to the United States forces in 1777. There was a military post there until about 1811 and an arsenal until many years later. The American installation at Pittsburgh was first known as Fort Pitt. Then, beginning about 1794, it was known as Fort Fayette, which was at a new site. Dependencies of the Pittsburgh post were maintained at Fort Franklin, Presque Isle, Big Beaver, and Le Boeuf.   **[127]**

PLATTE BRIDGE STATION [Wyoming, 1855–1859]. A detachment of troops established a post at the Platte Bridge, about one hundred and twenty-five miles west of Fort Laramie, on November 2, 1855, in order to protect the bridge. In the early post returns the facility was also referred to as Fort Clay and as Camp Davis. On November 3, 1856, the station was abandoned, but it was re-occupied on July 29, 1858. The camp was finally abandoned on May 1, 1859. The later post of Fort Casper was built in the same locality.   **[168]**

PLATTSBURGH BARRACKS [New York, 1812–]. Troops were stationed on the west shore of Lake Champlain in the vicinity of the present city of Plattsburgh, New York, beginning in 1812. The post was abandoned and regarrisoned several times and after the Civil War it was continuously garrisoned.

CAMP PLUMMER [New Mexico]. See Fort Lowell [New Mexico].

FORT POINT [California]. See Fort Winfield Scott [California].

POST AT POINTE COUPEE [Louisiana, 1805–1808]. A garrison of United States troops was maintained at Pointe Coupee on the lower Mississippi from 1805 to 1808 as part of the movement of American troops into the Louisiana Purchase.

FORT POINT SAN JOSE [California]. See Fort Mason [California].

FORT POLK [Texas, 1846–1850]. Fort Polk was established on March 26, 1846, at Point Isabel, nine miles from the mouth of the Rio Grande. It was abandoned on February 9, 1850.

POST POND CREEK [Kansas]. See Fort Wallace.

CAMP POPLAR RIVER [Montana, 1880–1893]. Camp Poplar River, on the south bank of the Poplar River two miles north of the Missouri River, was established on October 12, 1880. The post was abandoned on October 2, 1893.

CAMP PORTER [Montana, 1880–1881]. Camp Porter was established on November 12, 1880, on the Yellowstone River near the mouth of Glendive Creek, to protect the construction crews of the Northern Pacific Railroad. The post was abandoned on November 29, 1881.

FORT PORTER]New York, 1863–]. Fort Porter, named in orders of January 13, 1849, was first occupied in 1863 as a camp for collecting and organizing volunteers. It was garrisoned by regular troops beginning in 1866. The post was located within the city of Buffalo, New York, on the right bank of the Niagara River about half a mile from the outlet of Lake Erie.

FORT IN POWELL VALLEY [Tennessee, 1797]. To prevent encroachment on the Cherokee lands a fort was built in the Powell River Valley in eastern Tennessee in 1797.

FORT PREBLE [Maine, 1808—]. Fort Preble, located on Cape Elizabeth on the south side of the harbor at Portland, Maine, was established in 1808. With some short interruptions it was garrisoned continuously.

FORT PULASKI [Georgia, 1862–1873]. The construction of this fort was begun in 1829 on Cockspur Island, commanding both channels of the Savannah River. The work was named Fort Pulaski on April 18, 1833, but it was not occupied until the Civil War, first by Georgia troops on January 3, 1861, and then by United States forces on April 11, 1862. The post was closed on October 25, 1873. **[199, 296]**

Q-R

FORT QUITMAN [Texas, 1858–1877]. Fort Quitman was established on September 28, 1858, on the east bank of the Rio Grande, about seventy miles below El Paso. The post was abandoned on April 5, 1861, and re-established on January 1, 1868. It was finally abandoned on January 5, 1877.

CAMP RADZIMINSKI [Oklahoma, 1858–1859]. Camp Radziminski was established in September, 1858, on Otter Creek, at the base of the Wichita Mountains. It was abandoned on December 6, 1859.

POST AT RANCHO DE JURUPA [California, 1852–1854]. A post at Rancho de Jurupa, in the valley of the Santa Ana River, about fifteen miles northeast of Rancho del Chino, was established on September 17, 1852, and abandoned on April 11, 1854.

POST AT RANCHO DEL CHINO [California, 1850–1852]. A post was established on September 14, 1850, at Rancho del Chino, near the Santa Ana River, about thirty miles southeast of Los Angeles. On September 17, 1852, the post was abandoned

and the troops transferred to Rancho de Jurupa.

FORT RANDALL [South Dakota, 1856–1892]. Fort Randall was established on June 26, 1856, on the right bank of the Missouri River as a base of supplies for posts on the upper Missouri and for protection of settlers against hostile Indians. The troops were withdrawn on December 6, 1892. **[210, 257]**

CAMP RANKIN [Colorado]. See Fort Sedgwick.

FORT RANSOM [North Dakota, 1867–1872]. Fort Ransom was built on the Sheyenne River about sixty miles west of the Minnesota line to keep the hostile Sioux in check. It was established on June 18, 1867, and abandoned on May 26, 1872.

FORT RAWLINS [Utah, 1870–1871]. Fort Rawlins was established on July 30, 1870, about two miles from the city of Provo, Utah. It was abandoned on July 9, 1871.

POST AT RAYADO [New Mexico, 1850–

1854]. A post was established at Rayado, New Mexico, on May 31, 1850. The troops were withdrawn on August 7, 1851, but the post was reoccupied between July 16 and September 18, 1854.

FORT READING [California, 1852–1867]. Fort Reading was established on May 26, 1852, on Cow Creek, two and one-half miles from its confluence with the Sacramento River. The troops were withdrawn in 1857, but the post was reoccupied on December 5, 1866. The post was finally abandoned in June, 1867.

FORT RECOVERY [Ohio, 1793–1796]. Fort Recovery was established in December, 1793, on a branch of the Miami River about a hundred miles north of Cincinnati, at the present town of Fort Recovery, Ohio. The post was abandoned in 1796.   **[152]**

POST AT RED CLOUD AGENCY [Nebraska]. See Fort Robinson.

CAMP RED WILLOW [Nebraska, 1872]. Camp Red Willow was established on May 18, 1872, near the mouth of Red Willow Creek, a tributary of the Republican River, east of present-day McCook, Nebraska. The post was abandoned on November 4, 1872.

CAMP RENO [Arizona, 1868–1870]. Camp Reno, in the Tonto Valley, was garrisoned on October 31, 1868, although construction had begun a year earlier. The post was used as a point of departure for expeditions against the Apaches. It was abandoned in March, 1870.

FORT RENO [Oklahoma, 1874–]. A post was established on the North Fork of the Canadian River, about two miles from the

Cheyenne and Arapaho Indian Agency, in August, 1874. It was first known simply as Camp near Cheyenne Agency, but on February 21, 1876, it was officially designated Fort Reno. The fort was important in the campaign of 1874–1875 against the Kiowa, Comanche, and Cheyenne Indians and in the campaign of 1878–1879 against the northern Cheyennes.

FORT RENO [Wyoming, 1865–1868]. A post was established on August 28, 1865, on the Powder River, one hundred and eighty miles northwest of Fort Laramie as part of the line of defense for the Bozeman Trail. It was originally called Fort Connor, but its name was changed to Fort Reno on November 11, 1865. The post was abandoned on August 18, 1868, when the United States was forced to withdraw its garrisons in the area.

CANTONMENT RENO [Wyoming]. See Fort McKinney.

NEW FORT RENO [Wyoming]. See Fort Phil Kearny.

CAMP REYNOLDS [California]. See Post of Angel Island.

FORT REYNOLDS [Colorado, 1867–1872]. Fort Reynolds was established on July 3, 1867, on the right bank of the Arkansas River about twenty miles east of Pueblo, Colorado. The post was abandoned on July 15, 1872.

CAMP REYNOLDS [Montana]. See Fort Shaw.

FORT RICE [North Dakota, 1864–1878]. Fort Rice was established by General Alfred

Sully on July 7, 1864, as a supply base for his operations against the Sioux. It was located on the right bank of the Missouri River, about ten miles north of the mouth of the Cannonball River. The fort was abandoned on November 25, 1878. **[211]**

CAMP RICE [Texas]. See Fort Hancock.

FORT RICHARDSON [Texas, 1867–1878]. A post was established on November 26, 1867, on a tributary of the Trinity River near the present town of Jacksboro, Texas, as defense against the Indians and to protect the cattle trade. The post was abandoned on May 23, 1878. **[106, 122]**

FORT RICHMOND [New York]. See Fort Wadsworth [New York].

FORT RIDGELY [Minnesota, 1853–1867]. Established on April 29, 1853, on the north side of the Minnesota River, Fort Ridgely guarded the Sioux reservation along the river. The post was abandoned on May 22, 1867.

FORT RILEY [Kansas, 1853–]. Camp Center was established on May 17, 1853, on the north bank of the Kansas River at the junction of the Smoky Hill and Republican forks near present-day Junction City, Kansas. The name was changed to Fort Riley on June 27, 1853. **[235]**

FORT RILEY [Texas]. See Fort Clark [Texas].

FORT RINGGOLD [Texas, 1848–]. A post was established on October 26, 1848, on the Rio Grande, just below Rio Grande City, Texas. It was first called Camp Ringgold, then on July 16, 1849, its name was changed to Ringgold Barracks, and finally on Decem-

ber 30, 1878, to Fort Ringgold. The post was abandoned on March 7, 1861, but was occupied once more by United States troops on June 24, 1865.

POST ON THE RIO LLANO [Texas]. See Fort Terrett.

FORT RIPLEY [Minnesota, 1849–1877]. A post was established on April 13, 1849, on the west bank of the Mississippi River just below the mouth of the Crow Wing River, to control the Winnebago Reservation. It was first called Fort Gaines, but the name was changed to Fort Ripley on November 4, 1850. The post was abandoned on July 11, 1877. **[236]**

FORT ROBINSON [Nebraska, 1874–]. Fort Robinson (first called Camp Robinson) was established on March 8, 1874. It was built on the left bank of the White River in northwestern Nebraska at the Red Cloud Agency near present-day Crawford, Nebraska, to maintain order among the Sioux warriors settled there. It was an important base of operations against the Indians. **[158]**

CAMP ROCK SPRING [California, 1867–1868]. A camp was established on March 28, 1867, at Rock Spring, on the road from Camp Cady to Fort Mohave. The post was abandoned in January, 1868.

POST AT ROCK SPRINGS [Wyoming]. See Camp Pilot Butte.

FORT ROSECRANS [California]. See San Diego Barracks.

CAMP RUBY [Nevada, 1862–1869]. Camp Ruby was established on September 14, 1862, on the western side of Ruby Valley. The post was abandoned on September 20, 1869.

CAMP RUCKER [Arizona]. See Camp John A. Rucker.

CAMP RUHLEN [South Dakota]. See Fort Meade [South Dakota].

FORT RUSSELL [Wyoming]. See Fort D. A. Russell.

S

FORT SABINE [Louisiana, 1836–1838]. Fort Sabine was established on April 17, 1836, on the west side of Sabine Pass, three miles from the Gulf of Mexico. The post was abandoned in September, 1838.

POST AT SAC AND FOX AGENCY [Iowa]. See Fort Sanford.

CANTONMENT AT SACKETS HARBOR [New York]. See Madison Barracks.

FORT SAGINAW [Michigan, 1822–1824]. On July 25, 1822, a detachment of troops from Fort Howard established a post on the west bank of the Saginaw River, twenty-five miles from its mouth, at the present city of Saginaw, Michigan, to overawe the neighboring Chippewa Indians. The post returns are all headed Post of Saguina. The troops withdrew in September, 1823, leaving a small detachment until July, 1824. [133, 134]

FORT ST. ANTHONY [Minnesota]. See Fort Snelling.

POST OF ST. AUGUSTINE [Florida, 1821–]. The military post at St. Augustine, Florida, was occupied after Florida was acquired by the United States in 1821. The

post was designated Fort Marion on January 7, 1825, and the place was irregularly garrisoned until abandoned on February 26, 1852. It was seized by state troops in 1861, but it was established again as a United States post on March 21, 1862. The post was sometimes reported as Fort Marion, sometimes as St. Augustine, and finally as St. Francis Barracks.   [297]

FORT ST. CLAIR [Ohio, 1791–1796]. Fort St. Clair was begun in December, 1791, midway between Fort Jefferson and Fort Hamilton, about a mile north of the present town of Eaton, Ohio. The fort, designed as one of the posts in the advance against the Indians, was maintained until 1796.   [149, 240]

ST. FRANCIS BARRACKS [Florida]. See Post of St. Augustine.

FORT ST. MARYS [Ohio, 1794–1796]. Fort St. Marys was built in 1794 on the west bank of the St. Marys River, at the site of the present city of St. Marys, Ohio. It was erected as a supply depot and was maintained as a post until 1796.

FORT ST. PHILIP [Louisiana, 1803–1871]. Fort St. Philip, originally a Spanish fort located on the east bank of the Mississippi River about seventy-five miles below New Orleans, was occupied by American forces late in 1803, with the transfer of Louisiana to the United States. After the building of Fort Jackson directly across the river in 1822, the two forts were jointly administered. From January, 1861, to April, 1862, the fort was controlled by state forces. After a history of periodic abandonment and reoccupation, the fort was abandoned on July 7, 1871.

FORT ST. STEPHENS [Alabama, 1799–1808]. Fort St. Stephens, a Spanish post on the Tombigbee River north of Mobile, Alabama, was transferred to the United States on May 5, 1799, when it was ascertained that the fort was in United States territory. Instead of occupying this post, the United States built Fort Stoddert to the south. However, Fort St. Stephens seems to have been garrisoned from 1805 to 1808.

CAMP SALUBRITY [Louisiana, 1844–1845]. Camp Salubrity, about three miles from Natchitoches, Louisiana, was established on May 24, 1844, and abandoned on July 3, 1845. **[51]**

FORT SAM HOUSTON [Texas, 1845–]. A post was established at San Antonio, Texas, on October 28, 1845. It was intermittently occupied before the Civil War and in April, 1861, was abandoned to Texas troops. The post at San Antonio was re-established on September 22, 1865, and a new site occupied on December 22, 1879. On September 11, 1890, the post was renamed Fort Sam Houston. **[170, 194]**

POST OF SAN ANTONIO [Texas]. See Fort Sam Houston.

POST OF SAN CARLOS [Arizona, 1882–1894]. Military troops were stationed at San Carlos, Arizona, as part of the policy of restricting Indians to reservations. The post was at first considered a subpost of Fort Apache, but it had status as a separate post from 1882 to September, 1894, when it became a subpost of Fort Grant. It was finally abandoned altogether in 1900.

FORT SANDERS [Wyoming, 1866–1882]. A post was established near the present city of Laramie, Wyoming, on July 4, 1866, to protect the stage route. On July 23, 1866, it was named Fort John Buford, and on September 5, 1866, it was renamed Fort Sanders. The post was abandoned on May 18, 1882.

SAN DIEGO BARRACKS [California, 1849–]. A post at San Diego, California, established on April 20, 1849, was known for a while as Mission of San Diego and from 1858 to 1876 as New San Diego Barracks. After 1876 it was called San Diego Barracks. In 1903 it became Fort Rosecrans.

POST OF SAN ELIZARIO [Texas, 1849–1851]. A post was established on the Rio Grande at San Elizario, about twenty miles below El Paso, on September 15, 1849. It was evacuated in September, 1851.

POST OF SAN FELIPE [Texas]. See Camp Del Rio.

FORT SANFORD [Iowa, 1842–1843]. Fort Sanford was a temporary post established on the left bank of the Des Moines River near the Sac and Fox Agency on October 12, 1842, to prevent white intruders from entering Indian lands. The post was abandoned in May, 1843, when the troops moved to the site of the new Fort Des Moines. **[150]**

PRESIDIO OF SAN FRANCISCO [California, 1847–]. The Presidio of San Francisco, a post dating back to the eighteenth century, was occupied by United States troops in April, 1847, and has been continuously occupied.

CAMP SAN JUAN ISLAND [Washington, 1859–1874]. On July 27, 1859, a company of United States troops established a post on San Juan Island, then in dispute between the United States and Great Britain. The post was named Camp Pickett on August 10, 1859. In June, 1863, the name was changed to Post of San Juan Island, and in March, 1867, to Camp Steele. Finally, on November 23, 1868, the post was designated Camp San Juan Island. The post was abandoned on July 1, 1874.

POST OF SAN LUIS REY [California, 1847–1852]. A camp was established on February 3, 1847, on the San Luis River, two miles from the sea and about thirty-five miles northwest of San Diego. It was abandoned on June 23, 1849, but a new post nearby was established on April 18, 1850. The troops were withdrawn from this second post in June, 1852.

CAMP ON SAN PEDRO RIVER [Arizona]. See Fort Grant [Arizona].

POST OF SANTA FE [New Mexico]. See Fort Marcy.

FORT SARGENT [Mississippi]. See Post at Natchez.

POST AT SAULT STE. MARIE [Michigan]. See Fort Brady.

FORT SCHUYLER [New York, 1861–]. Construction of Fort Schuyler at Throgs

Neck, New York Harbor, was begun in 1833. The post was first garrisoned on January 17, 1861. Between 1870 and 1877 the post was not occupied.

FORT SCOTT [California]. See Fort Winfield Scott.

FORT SCOTT [Georgia, 1816–1821]. Fort Scott, located on the Flint River near its junction with the Chattahoochee, was established in 1816 and abandoned in 1821.

FORT SCOTT [Kansas, 1842–1873]. Fort Scott was established on May 30, 1842, in eastern Kansas, four miles west of the Missouri line, at the site of the present town of Fort Scott, Kansas. It served as an intermediate post on the military road from Fort Leavenworth to Fort Gibson. The post was abandoned on April 22, 1853, but was reoccupied by troops in March, 1862. It was abandoned again in October, 1865, but from December, 1869, to April, 1873, the post served as headquarters for troops operating in southeastern Kansas.   [32]

CAMP SCOTT [Nevada]. See Camp Winfield Scott.

FORT SCOTT [Texas]. See Fort Martin Scott.

CAMP SCOTT [Wyoming, 1857–1858]. Camp Scott was established on November 17, 1857, in the valley of Black's Fork of the Green River, two miles from Fort Bridger, as the wintering place for the Army of Utah. The post was abandoned on June 14, 1858.

FORT SEDGWICK [Colorado, 1864–1871]. A post, called Camp Rankin, was established on the south bank of the South Platte River opposite the mouth of Lodgepole Creek, on

May 19, 1864. On September 27, 1865, the name was changed to Fort Sedgwick, and on May 31, 1871, the troops were withdrawn.

FORT SELDEN [Louisiana, 1820–1822]. Fort Selden was established at Natchitoches, Louisiana, in November, 1820. With the establishment of Fort Jesup in 1822 the troops were transferred to the new post.   **[51]**

FORT SELDEN [New Mexico, 1865–1890]. Fort Selden was established on May 8, 1865, about a mile and a half from the east bank of the Rio Grande at the lower end of the Jornado del Muerto. The troops were withdrawn on March 11, 1877, but the post was reoccupied on December 25, 1880. On August 23, 1890, Fort Selden became a subpost of Fort Bayard.

CAMP SERGEANT [Nebraska]. See North Platte Station.

FORT SEVERN [Maryland, 1814–1845]. Fort Severn, located at Annapolis on the Severn River at its entrance into Chesapeake Bay, was established in 1814. It was turned over to the Navy Department for a naval academy on September 3, 1845.   **[130]**

FORT SEWARD [North Dakota, 1872–1877]. A post, first called Fort Cross, was established on June 3, 1872, at the Northern Pacific Railroad crossing of the James River at the present city of Jamestown, North Dakota. On November 9, 1872, the name was changed to Fort Seward. The post was abandoned on September 30, 1877.

FORT SHAW [Montana, 1867–1891]. This post was established on June 20, 1867, on the right bank of the Sun River, about fifteen miles from its confluence with the Missouri, to keep open the route from Helena

to Fort Benton. It was originally called Camp Reynolds but was renamed Fort Shaw on July 4, 1867. The post was abandoned on July 21, 1891.

FORT SHELBY [Michigan]. See Post at Detroit.

FORT SHERIDAN [Illinois, 1887—]. Fort Sheridan was established near Highland Park, Illinois, on November 8, 1887, and officially named on February 27, 1888.

CAMP SHERIDAN [Nebraska, 1874–1881]. A post was located at the Spotted Tail Agency on March 12, 1874. When the Agency was moved in September, 1874, the post was established on September 9, 1874, on the right bank of the west fork of Beaver Creek, twelve miles above its confluence with the White River. The post was abandoned in May, 1881.

CAMP SHERIDAN [Wyoming]. See Fort Yellowstone.

FORT SHERMAN [Idaho, 1878—]. A post called Fort Coeur d'Alene was established on April 16, 1878, on the north shore of the lake of that name in the angle formed by the Spokane River. Its name was changed to Fort Sherman on April 6, 1887.

FORT SIDNEY [Nebraska, 1867–1894]. This post was established as Sidney Barracks on December 13, 1867, on the line of the Union Pacific Railroad at Sidney, Nebraska. Its name was changed to Fort Sidney on December 30, 1878. The troops were withdrawn on June 1, 1894.

FORT SILL [Oklahoma, 1869—]. A post, named Camp Wichita, was established on March 4, 1869, near the foot of the Wichita

Mountains at the junction of Cache and Medicine Bluff creeks. The name of the post was changed to Fort Sill on July 2, 1869. The post was an important headquarters in the wars against the southern Plains Indians.

[95, 165, 227, 268]

FORT SIMCOE [Washington, 1856–1859]. Fort Simcoe was established in Simcoe Valley on August 8, 1856, after the Yakima Indian War of 1855–1856, in order to discourage white settlement in the area. The post was abandoned on May 22, 1859.

[125, 126, 166]

FORT SISSETON [South Dakota, 1864–1889]. This post was established as Fort Wadsworth on July 26, 1864, at the head of the Coteau des Prairies in what is now the northeastern section of South Dakota, to control the Indians in the region and to protect the wagon routes to the gold fields of Idaho and Montana. On August 29, 1876, its name was changed to Fort Sisseton. The post was abandoned June 1, 1889. **[131, 179]**

FORT SMITH [Arkansas, 1817–1871]. Fort Smith was established late in the year 1817 on the south side of the Arkansas River at the mouth of the Poteau River. The post was abandoned and then reoccupied, and on April 23, 1861, the troops were withdrawn and the post seized by Arkansas troops. The fort was reoccupied by United States troops on September 1, 1863, and was finally abandoned in August, 1871.

FORT SMITH [Montana]. See Fort C. F. Smith.

CAMP SMITH [Oregon]. See Camp C. F. Smith.

CAMP ON SNAKE RIVER [Wyoming, 1879–1883]. This post was established on the Snake River on November 7, 1879, and was abandoned on July 16, 1883.

FORT SNELLING [Minnesota, 1819–]. A post was established at the confluence of the Minnesota River (then called the St. Peter's River) with the Mississippi River on August 24, 1819. It was first called Cantonment New Hope and later Fort St. Anthony. The post was named Fort Snelling on January 7, 1825, and was the key post on the upper Mississippi.   **[159, 172, 173, 176, 177, 185, 186]**

POST AT SOCORRO [New Mexico, 1849–1851]. A post was established in November, 1849, at Socorro, on the west bank of the Rio Grande. It was abandoned in August, 1851.

CAMP AT SONOMA [California, 1847–1851]. A camp was established at the town of Sonoma, California, on April 4, 1847. It was repeatedly abandoned and then reoccupied, and it was finally abandoned on October 16, 1851.

POST AT SOUTHWEST POINT [Tennessee, 1794–1806]. A post was established at Southwest Point, at the junction of the Clinch and Tennessee rivers at present-day Kingston, Tennessee, in 1794. The garrison was withdrawn and moved to Hiwassee Garrison in 1806.

FORT SPOKANE [Washington, 1880–]. A post, called Camp Spokane, was established on the south side of the Spokane River about one mile from the Columbia River, on October 16, 1880, to control the Indians of the area. Its name was changed to Fort Spokane on February 11, 1882.

POST AT SPOTTED TAIL AGENCY [Nebraska]. See Camp Sheridan [Nebraska].

CAMP STAMBAUGH [Wyoming, 1870–1878]. Camp Stambaugh was established on June 20, 1870, in the region of the Sweetwater gold mines, as a subpost of Fort Bridger. It became an independent post on August 20, 1870, and was discontinued on May 16, 1878.

POST AT STANDING ROCK AGENCY [North Dakota]. See Fort Yates.

FORT STANFORD [Arizona]. See Fort Breckinridge.

FORT STANTON [New Mexico, 1855—]. Fort Stanton was established for control of the Apaches on May 4, 1855, on the Rio Bonita, about twenty miles east of the Sierra Blanca Range. It was abandoned on August 2, 1861, but reoccupied on April 8, 1863.

CAMP STEELE [Oregon]. See Fort Harney.

CAMP STEELE [Washington]. See Camp San Juan Island.

FORT STEELE [Wyoming]. See Fort Fred Steele.

FORT STEILACOOM [Washington, 1849–1868]. Fort Steilacoom was established at the southern extremity of Puget Sound on August 22, 1849. The post was abandoned on April 22, 1868.

FORT STEUBEN [Ohio, 1786–1796]. Fort Steuben was established on August 2, 1786, on the Ohio River, about fifty miles below Fort McIntosh, at present Steubenville, Ohio. The post was abandoned late in 1796.

FORT STEVENS [Oregon, 1865–1884]. Fort Stevens, on the left bank of the Colum-

bia River at its mouth about nine miles from Astoria, was occupied on April 25, 1865. The troops were withdrawn on December 1, 1884.

FORT STEVENSON [North Dakota, 1867–1883]. Fort Stevenson was established on June 22, 1867, on the left bank of the Missouri River on a site now inundated by Garrison Reservoir. The post was part of the chain of military posts guarding the routes of travel to Montana. It was abandoned on August 31, 1883.   [212]

FORT STOCKTON [Texas, 1858–1886]. Troops were on the site of this post in December, 1858, but the post was not formally established until March 23, 1859. The station, first called Camp Stockton, then renamed Fort Stockton on May 23, 1860, was established to protect the mail route from San Antonio to El Paso. The post was closed down in April, 1861, reoccupied on July 7, 1867, and finally abandoned on June 30, 1886.   [117]

FORT STODDERT [Alabama, 1799–1814]. After the evacuation of the area by the Spanish, Fort Stoddert was established in 1799 four miles below the junction of the Alabama and Tombigbee rivers. The post was not continued after the War of 1812.

FORT STROTHER [Alabama, 1813]. Fort Strother was established in 1813 on the Coosa River during the Creek War. It had only a temporary existence.

FORT SULLIVAN [Maine, 1808–1873]. Fort Sullivan was established on Moose Island in Passamaquoddy Bay, near Eastport, Maine. Construction was probably begun in 1808. The post was intermittently occupied until the troops were finally withdrawn in 1873.

FORT SULLY [South Dakota, 1863–1894]. Fort Sully, established in September, 1863, as a result of the Sioux uprising, was first located on the east bank of the Missouri River about three miles below Pierre, South Dakota. This location was abandoned on July 25, 1866, when the garrison moved to a new site about twenty-five miles above Pierre. The troops were withdrawn on October 20, 1894, although a few men remained until November 30 to wind up the affairs of the post.

POST AT SULPHUR FORK [Arkansas]. See Cantonment Taylor.

FORT SUMNER [New Mexico, 1862–1869]. Fort Sumner was established on November 30, 1862, on the left bank of the Pecos River at Bosque Redondo to guard Apache and Navaho prisoners. The post was abandoned by the government on August 30, 1869.

FORT SUMTER [South Carolina]. See Charleston Harbor.

CAMP SUPPLY [Arizona]. See Camp John A. Rucker.

FORT SUPPLY [Oklahoma, 1868–1894]. This post was established as Camp Supply on November 8, 1868, at the confluence of Wolf Creek and the North Fork of the Canadian River. The name was changed to Fort Supply on December 30, 1878. The main body of troops were withdrawn from the post on October 6, 1894, leaving a detachment to garrison it until February 25, 1895.

CANTONMENT ON THE SWEETWATER [Texas]. See Fort Elliott.

T-U-V

POST OF TAOS [New Mexico, 1847–1852]. A post was established at Taos, New Mexico, in October, 1847, and abandoned on June 14, 1852.

CANTONMENT TAYLOR [Arkansas, 1821–1824]. In June, 1821, troops were sent to protect the trading factory at the mouth of the Sulphur Fork of Red River, just above the Louisiana-Arkansas line. The troops in the following year constructed the post known as Cantonment Taylor. The position was occupied until May, 1824.

FORT TAYLOR [Florida]. See Key West Barracks.

FORT TAYLOR [Texas]. See Fort Brown.

FORT TEJON [California, 1854–1864]. Fort Tejon, established on August 10, 1854, near the Tejon Indian Reservation, was intended to quiet the reservation Indians and to command Tejon Pass. The post was not occupied between June, 1861, and August, 1863, and was finally abandoned on September 11, 1864. **[124, 294]**

FORT TELFAIR [Georgia, 1790–1795]. One of the early defenses on the Georgia frontier, Fort Telfair was established in 1790 on the Altamaha River. The post was abandoned about 1795.

TELLICO BLOCKHOUSE [Tennessee, 1794–1806]. Troops were stationed at Tellico Blockhouse on the Little Tennessee River, at the present town of Loudon, Tennessee, in 1794. In 1806 the garrison was withdrawn and transferred to Hiwassee Garrison.

FORT TERRETT [Texas, 1852–1854]. Fort Terrett was established on February 2, 1852, on the north fork of the Llano River, a tributary of the Colorado. First known as Post on the Rio Llano, it was designated Fort Terrett on October 16, 1852, and abandoned on February 26, 1854.

FORT TER-WAW [California, 1857–1862]. Fort Ter-Waw was established on October 13, 1857, at the Klamath Indian Reservation near Crescent City, California. The post was finally abandoned in June, 1862, the troops moving to the Smith River Valley to establish Camp Lincoln. **[67]**

CAMP THOMAS [Arizona]. See Fort Apache.

FORT THOMAS [Arizona, 1876–1890]. A post was established on August 12, 1876, about a mile south of the Gila River, a short distance above the site of old Fort Goodwin. First known simply as New Post on the Gila, it was designated Camp Thomas on September 18, 1876, then Fort Thomas in February, 1882. By orders of December 22, 1890, the installation lost its independent status and became a subpost of Fort Grant. However, troops garrisoned the post through April, 1892.

FORT THOMAS [Kentucky, 1890–]. Fort Thomas, near Newport, Kentucky, was first occupied on August 15, 1890.

FORT THOMAS [North Dakota]. See Fort Pembina.

FORT THOMPSON [South Dakota, 1864–1871]. Fort Thompson was established at the Crow Creek Agency on the Missouri River in September, 1864. The troops were withdrawn in June, 1867, but the post was reoccupied from 1870 to 1871.

FORT THORN [New Mexico, 1853–1859]. Fort Thorn was established on the west bank of the Rio Grande opposite the center of the Jornado del Muerto, on December 24, 1853, and was officially named on March 8, 1854. The post was abandoned in March, 1859.

FORT THORNBURGH [Utah, 1881–1883]. This fort was established on September 17, 1881, at the junction of the Duchesne and Green rivers in northeastern Utah. A new site on Ashley Creek, a tributary of the Green River, was occupied on April 10, 1882.

The post was abandoned on October 3, 1883.

CAMP THORNTON [Texas]. See Fort Graham.

CAMP THREE FORKS OWYHEE [Idaho, 1866–1871]. A post, called Camp Winthrop, was established on September 25, 1866, near the south fork of the Owyhee River, about fifteen miles from the junction of the three forks. The name of the post was changed to camp Three Forks Owyhee in April, 1867. The post was abandoned on October 23, 1871.

CAMP TOLL GATE [Arizona]. See Camp Hualpai.

TONGUE RIVER BARRACKS [Montana]. See Fort Keogh.

FORT TOTTEN [North Dakota, 1867–1890]. Fort Totten was established on July 17, 1867, on the southeast shore of Devils Lake, as part of the plan to place the Indians of the region on a reservation and as one of the posts to protect the overland route from Minnesota to Montana. The troops were withdrawn on November 18, 1890. **[129]**

FORT TOWNSEND [Washington, 1856–1895]. Fort Townsend, about two miles from the town of Port Townsend, Washington, was established on October 26, 1856, to protect the Puget Sound area. It was abandoned in 1859, when troops were sent to San Juan Island. On July 1, 1874, when Camp San Juan Island was abandoned, Fort Townsend was re-established. The troops were withdrawn on March 5, 1895. **[111]**

FORT TOWSON [Oklahoma, 1824–1854]. A post, called Cantonment Towson, was established six miles north of the Red River and the same distance east of the Kiamichi River in May, 1824, to protect the Choctaw Indians from the Plains Indians. It was temporarily abandoned in April, 1829, but was re-established in 1831. The name was changed to Fort Towson on February 8, 1832, and the post was finally abandoned on June 8, 1854.   **[219]**

FORT TRUMBULL [Connecticut, 1812—]. Fort Trumbull at New London, Connecticut, was first built during the Revolutionary War. This original work fell into decay, but a new fort was constructed during the War of 1812. The post was intermittently occupied.

FORT TULAROSA [New Mexico, 1872–1874]. Fort Tularosa was established on the left bank of the Tularosa River in western New Mexico near the present town of Aragon on April 30, 1872. The post was abandoned on November 26, 1874.

FORT UMPQUA [Oregon, 1856–1862]. Fort Umpqua was established on July 28, 1856, on the north side of the Umpqua River. The post was abandoned on July 16, 1862.

CANTONMENT ON THE UNCOMPAHGRE [Colorado]. See Fort Crawford [Colorado].

FORT UNION [New Mexico, 1851–1891]. Fort Union was established on July 26, 1851, north of the present town of Watrous, New Mexico, to check the northern tribes of Apache and Ute Indians and to protect the Santa Fe Trail. It served as an important supply center for lesser forts in the region. The post was abandoned on May 15, 1891.
[266, 276, 277, 293]

FORT UNION [North Dakota, 1864–1865]. Fort Union, originally a fur trading post located at the mouth of the Yellowstone River, was garrisoned as a military post from 1864 to 1865.

VANCOUVER BARRACKS [Washington, 1849—]. A post called Columbia Barracks was established on May 15, 1849, at the Hudson's Bay Company post of Fort Vancouver, on the north bank of the Columbia River, about eight miles north of Portland, Oregon. The military post was designated Fort Vancouver on July 13, 1853, and on April 5, 1879, the name was changed to Vancouver Barracks.   **[82, 278]**

FORT VERDE [Arizona, 1866–1891]. A post, known first as Camp Lincoln, was established on January 5, 1866, on the left bank of the Verde River, near the junction with Beaver Creek. The name of the post was changed to Camp Verde on November 23, 1868, and to Fort Verde on April 5, 1879. The post was abandoned on April 25, 1891.   **[233]**

CAMP VERDE [Texas, 1856–1869]. Camp Verde was established on July 8, 1856, on the northern bank of Verde Creek near Bandera Pass. It was abandoned on March 7, 1861, but reoccupied by United States troops on November 30, 1866. The troops were finally withdrawn on April 1, 1869.

W

FORT WADSWORTH [New York, 1861—]. A fort on Staten Island in New York Harbor was acquired by the federal government in 1847. Occupied by federal forces on August 9, 1861, it was first called Fort Richmond. The name of the post was changed to Fort Wadsworth on November 7, 1865.

FORT WADSWORTH [South Dakota]. See Fort Sisseton.

CAMP WALBACH [Wyoming, 1858–1859]. Camp Walbach was established on September 30, 1858, on Lodgepole Creek, Cheyenne Pass, east of present-day Laramie, Wyoming. It was abandoned on April 19, 1859.

FORT WALLACE [Kansas, 1865–1882]. A post, first called Post Pond Creek, was established in western Kansas on October 26, 1865. After two changes in site, the post was located at the junction of Pond Creek with the south fork of the Smoky Hill River. On April 18, 1866, the name was changed to Fort Wallace. The post was abandoned on May 31, 1882.   **[217]**

FORT WALLA WALLA [Washington, 1856—]. This fort was established on September 23, 1856, on the Walla Walla River near the present city of Walla Walla, Washington. The post was temporarily abandoned from June 7, 1867, to July 28, 1873.

CAMP WALLEN [Arizona, 1866–1869]. Camp Wallen was established on May 9, 1866, near the San Pedro River, about sixty-five miles southeast of Tucson. It was abandoned on October 31, 1869.

FORT WARBURTON [Maryland]. See Fort Washington [Maryland].

CAMP WARDWELL [Colorado]. See Fort Morgan [Colorado].

CAMP WARNER [Oregon, 1866–1874]. Camp Warner was established on August 10, 1866, and was originally located twenty miles east of Warner Lakes in southern Oregon. In September, 1867, it was relocated fifteen miles west of Warner Lakes and thirty-five miles from the California line. The post was abandoned on September 3, 1874.

FORT WARREN [Massachusetts, 1861—]. Fort Warren, at the mouth of Boston Har-

114

bor, was first occupied on October 30, 1861, although construction had begun about 1833.   [259]

FORT WASHAKIE [Wyoming, 1869—]. In compliance with the terms of a treaty with the Shoshoni and Bannock Indians for their protection against the Sioux, Arapaho, Cheyenne, and other hostile Indians, a post was established on the Popo Agie River at the site of present Lander, Wyoming, on June 28, 1869. The post was first named Camp Augur, but its name was changed to Camp Brown on March 28, 1870. In June, 1871, a new site was selected on the south bank of the south fork of the Little Wind River at its junction with the north fork. On December 30, 1878, the name of the post was changed to Fort Washakie.

WASHINGTON BARRACKS [District of Columbia, 1881—]. This post, begun as Washington Arsenal, was designated Washington Barracks on May 12, 1881.

FORT WASHINGTON [Maryland, 1815–1872]. Fort Washington, located on the east bank of the Potomac River about fourteen miles below Washington, was occupied after the War of 1812, replacing a pre-war work called Fort Warburton. Fort Washington was repeatedly abandoned and reoccupied until the troops were withdrawn on September 16, 1872.   [108]

CANTONMENT WASHINGTON [Mississippi, 1809–1811]. A cantonment was garrisoned at Washington, the first capital of Mississippi Territory, from 1809 to 1811, and was used at times as headquarters by General James Wilkinson.

FORT WASHINGTON [Ohio, 1789–1804]. As part of the drive against the Indians of the Northwest Territory, Fort Washington was established at Cincinnati in the autumn of 1789. For a decade or more the strongest and most important of the posts in the Northwest Territory, it was abandoned in 1804.   [190, 195, 198]

FORT WASHITA [Oklahoma, 1842–1861]. Fort Washita was established on April 23, 1842, on the left bank of the Washita River, about thirty miles from its confluence with the Red River, to protect the Chickasaw and Choctaw Indians from the wild tribes of the Southwest. The post was abandoned on May 1, 1861. It was occupied by the Confederacy during the Civil War but never reoccupied by federal troops.   [220]

CAMP WATSON [Oregon, 1864–1869]. Camp Watson was established on July 12, 1864, near the Middle Fork of the John Day River, to protect the road between The Dalles and Canyon City from the Snake Indians, who opposed the influx of miners. It was abandoned on May 24, 1869.   [193]

FORT WAYNE [Georgia, 1821–1823]. This fort was established near the present-day Brunswick, Georgia, in October, 1821. It was abandoned in June, 1823.

FORT WAYNE [Indiana, 1794–1819]. Fort Wayne was established on October 22, 1794, on the Maumee River at the site of the present city of Fort Wayne, Indiana. The troops departed on April 19, 1819. [163, 164]

FORT WAYNE [Michigan, 1861—]. Fort Wayne was built on the right bank of the Detroit River, on a site then about two and one-half miles from the city of Detroit. The post was first garrisoned by regular troops on December 15, 1861. [181, 184, 214, 234]

FORT WAYNE [Oklahoma, 1838–1842]. Fort Wayne was established on October 29, 1838, on the Illinois River, a tributary of the Arkansas. In the summer of 1840 the post was moved to a new site on the north bank of Spavinaw Creek, almost on the Arkansas line. The post was abandoned on May 26, 1842.

FORT WEBSTER [New Mexico, 1852–1853]. Fort Webster was established at the Santa Rita copper mines on January 23, 1852. The post was moved to a new site on the Mimbres River about twelve miles away on September 9, 1852, and was abandoned on December 20, 1853.

FORT WELLER [California, 1859]. Fort Weller was established on January 3, 1859, on the headwaters of the Russian River. It was abandoned in September or October of the same year and its garrison sent to Fort Bragg. **[68]**

FORT WEST [New Mexico, 1863–1864]. Fort West was established on February 24, 1863, near the headwaters of the Gila River. The post was abandoned on January 8, 1864.

CAMP WHEELER [New Mexico]. See Fort McLane.

POST AT WHETSTONE AGENCY [South Dakota, 1870–1872]. A post was established on the right bank of the Missouri River about thirty miles above Fort Randall at the Whetstone Indian Agency on May 10, 1870. It was abandoned on April 30, 1872.

WHIPPLE BARRACKS [Arizona, 1863–]. A post, first called Fort Whipple, was established on December 23, 1863, twenty-four miles northeast of Prescott, Arizona, and was intended to protect miners in the region. On May 18, 1864, the post was moved to a

site two miles from Prescott. The name was changed to Whipple Barracks on April 5, 1879.

FORT WHIPPLE [Virginia]. See Fort Myer.

CAMP ON WHITE RIVER [Colorado, 1879–1883]. A post was established on the White River on October 11, 1879, and abandoned on July 12, 1883.

CAMP WICHITA [Oklahoma]. See Fort Sill.

FORT WILKINS [Michigan, 1844–1870]. Fort Wilkins was established on May 28, 1844, at Copper Harbor, Keweenaw Point, on the upper peninsula of Michigan, to protect the copper mining region. It was evacuated on July 25, 1846, as troops were withdrawn for the Mexican War. The post was reoccupied in the fall of 1867 and finally discontinued on August 30, 1870.

[107, 135, 136]

FORT WILKINSON [Georgia, 1797–1806]. Fort Wilkinson was established in 1797 west of the Oconee River, near present Milledgeville, Georgia. It was the principal fort on that part of the frontier until displaced by Fort Hawkins in 1806.

CANTONMENT WILKINSONVILLE [Illinois, 1801–1802]. Cantonment Wilkinsonville was established in January, 1801, on the lower Ohio River, as part of a plan to move troops to the West out of fear of French action against the United States. The post was abandoned in 1802. **[99, 272]**

CAMP WILLOW GROVE [Arizona, 1867–1869]. Camp Willow Grove was established in August, 1867, about ninety-five miles northeast of Fort Mohave. It was abandoned on October 12, 1869.

CAMP WILSON [Texas]. See Fort Griffin.

FORT WINFIELD SCOTT [California, 1861–1886]. A military installation called Fort Point was one of the principal defenses of San Francisco Bay and was begun in 1853. The post was first occupied on February 15, 1861, and from 1865 to 1878 it was a subpost of the Presidio of San Francisco. The name of the post was changed to Fort Winfield Scott on November 25, 1882. The fort was discontinued as an independent post on September 15, 1886, again becoming a subpost of the Presidio of San Francisco.

CAMP WINFIELD SCOTT [Nevada, 1866–1871]. Camp Winfield Scott was established on December 12, 1866, at the foot of the Santa Rosa Mountains near the head of Paradise Valley. The post was abandoned on February 19, 1871.

FORT WINGATE [New Mexico, 1862—]. Fort Wingate was originally established on October 22, 1862, about twenty miles southwest of Mount Taylor. In July, 1868, the post was moved to a new site sixty-five miles away, near the headwaters of the Puerco River, at the location of abandoned Fort Lyon, east of present-day Gallup, New Mexico.

FORT WINNEBAGO [Wisconsin, 1828–1845]. Fort Winnebago was established on October 7, 1828, on the right bank of the Fox River at the portage between the Fox and Wisconsin rivers. The post was abandoned on September 10, 1845. **[273]**

CAMP WINTHROP [Idaho]. See Camp Three Forks Owyhee.

FORT WISE [Colorado]. See Fort Lyon [Colorado].

FORT WOLCOTT [Rhode Island, 1798–1836]. Fort Wolcott, located on Goat Island in the center of Newport Harbor, was begun in 1798. The troops were withdrawn on May 22, 1836.

FORT WOOD [Louisiana]. See Fort Macomb.

FORT WOOD [New York]. See New York Harbor.

CAMP WOOD [Texas, 1857–1861]. Camp Wood was established on the east bank of the Nueces River, about fifty miles northwest of Fort Inge, on May 20, 1857. The post was abandoned in March, 1861.

FORT WORTH [Texas, 1849–1853]. Fort Worth was established on June 6, 1849, on the West Fork of the Trinity River, at the site of the present city of Fort Worth, Texas. The post was abandoned on September 17, 1853. **[197]**

CAMP WRIGHT [California, 1862–1875]. On December 11, 1862, a camp was established in Round Valley, Mendocino County, California, about one mile northwest of present-day Covelo, California. There had been a detachment of troops in the area from December, 1858, to September, 1861, but they did not establish a regular post. The new post was first called Fort Wright, but after August, 1866, it was known as Camp Wright. The post was abandoned on June 17, 1875. **[68]**

117

Y-Z

FORT YAMHILL [Oregon, 1856–1866]. Fort Yamhill was established on August 30, 1856, on the south fork of the Yamhill River to protect the settlers from Indians located on a reservation there. The post was abandoned on June 30, 1866.

FORT YATES [North Dakota, 1874–]. A post was established on December 23, 1874, at the Standing Rock Indian Agency on the Missouri River, to aid in the control of Indians established on reservations on the Missouri. The post was designated Fort Yates on December 30, 1878.

FORT YELLOWSTONE [Wyoming, 1886–]. Troops were sent to protect Yellowstone National Park, arriving on August 17, 1886. They established Camp Sheridan at Mammoth Hot Springs. On May 11, 1891, the name was changed to Fort Yellowstone.

FORT YUMA [California, 1850–1882]. A post, first called Camp Yuma, was established on November 27, 1850, at the confluence of the Colorado and Gila rivers. The post was temporarily abandoned in 1851 and then reoccupied on February 22, 1852. After March, 1882, only a small detachment was left at the post.

FORT ZARAH [Kansas, 1864–1869]. Fort Zarah was established in September, 1864, on the left bank of Walnut Creek, two miles from its confluence with the Arkansas River, to furnish a base of operations against hostile Kiowa and Comanche Indians. The post was abandoned on December 4, 1869.

118

ILLUSTRATIONS

Fort Harmar, Ohio, from S. P. Hildreth, Pioneer History *(Cincinnati, 1848).*

Fort Washington, Ohio, from Benson J. Lossing, The Pictorial Field-Book of
the War of 1812 *(New York, 1868).*

Fort McHenry, Maryland.

Fort Pulaski, Georgia.

Fort Marion, Florida, as it appeared at about the time of the Civil War.

Fort Jefferson, Florida.

Fort Trumbull, Connecticut, from an oil painting by Seth Eastman.

Fort Mifflin, Pennsylvania, from an oil painting by Seth Eastman.

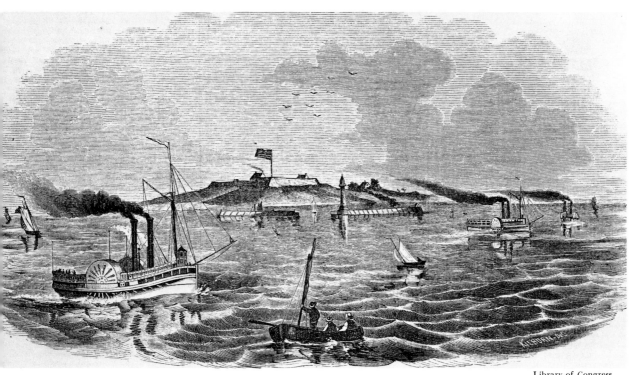

Fort Ontario, New York

Library of Congress

Fort Niagara, New York

Library of Congress

Fort Mackinac, Michigan, from Francis de Castelnau, Vues et
Souvenirs de l' Amerique du Nord *(Paris, 1842).*

Fort Howard, Wisconsin, also from de Castelnau's Vues et Souvenirs.

Fort Snelling, Minnesota, painted by Seth Eastman.

Hexagonal tower at Fort Snelling, 1887.

*Northwest corner of the old quadrangle and parade ground,
Jefferson Barracks, Missouri, about 1890.*

Jefferson Barracks, from J. C. Wild, The Valley of the Mississippi *(St. Louis, 1841).*

Fort Rice, North Dakota, an oil painting by Seth Eastman.

Interior of Fort Rice, North Dakota, in 1864.

Fort Larned, Kansas, as sketched by Theodore R. Davis for
Harper's Weekly, *June 8, 1867.*

*Fort Massachusetts, Colorado, drawn by J. M. Stanley for the reports
of the Pacific Railroad surveys.*

Fort Bowie, Arizona.

Fort Reno, Wyoming, in 1867.

U.S. Signal Corps Photo, The National Archives

Fort Wingate, New Mexico, in 1895.

Fort Apache, Arizona, about 1892.

Fort Leavenworth, Kansas, from Elvid Hunt, History of Fort Leavenworth, 1827–1927 (Fort Leavenworth, 1926).

Fort Keogh, Montana, from a painting by Private Hermann Stieffel of the Fifth Infantry, 1877–1881.

U.S. Signal Corps Photo, The National Archives

Fort Sumner, New Mexico, showing company quarters under construction.

Ruins of Fort Union, New Mexico.

U.S. Department of the Interior,
National Park Service Photo

APPENDIXES

APPENDIX A

Forts of the Seminole Wars

The Seminole Wars of 1836–1843 and 1855–1856 resulted in the establishment of a large number of small forts in Florida and southeastern Georgia. Most of these posts were officially named, and records for some of them exist. Others were designated only by numbers, corresponding to the numbers of territorial squares which were surveyed and marked out by the army as a means of scouting against the Indians. The location of many of the forts is difficult to ascertain with certainty.

The following alphabetical list shows the forts that can be identified. The names are taken from the "Map of the Seat of War in Florida," compiled in 1839 by Captain John Mackay and Lieutenant J. E. Blake, and from the "Map of the Seat of War in Florida," compiled in 1843 by Captain J. McClellan and Lieutenant A. A. Humphreys. To the names of forts included on these official maps have been added the names of forts listed in Thomas H. S. Hamersly, *Complete Regular Army Register of the United States for One Hundred Years (1779–1879)*.

The posts marked with an asterisk (*) are included in the preceding catalog, since they were of more than temporary duration. Plate 21, a contemporary map which copies on a smaller scale the Mackay-Blake map, shows the location of many of these forts.

FLORIDA FORTS

FORT ALABAMA	FORT BARRANCAS *
FORT ANDREWS	FORT BASINGER
FORT ANN	FORT BRADEN
FORT ANNUTEELIGA	FORT BROOKE *
FORT ARBUCKLE	FORT BROOKS
FORT ARMISTEAD	FORT BROWN
FORT ARMSTRONG	FORT BUCKEYE
FORT ATKINSON	FORT BUTLER
FORT BARBOUR	FORT CALL
FORT BARKER	FORT CAPRON

139

FORT CARROLL

FORT CASEY

FORT CENTER

FORT CHIPOLA

FORT CHOKONIKLA

FORT CHRISTMAS

FORT CLARKE

FORT CLINCH *[1]

FORT COOPER

FORT CRABBE

FORT CRANE

FORT CRAWFORD

FORT CROSS [2]

FORT CUMMINGS

FORT DADE

FORT DALLAS *

FORT DAVENPORT

FORT DENAUD

FORT DOANE

FORT DOWNING

FORT DRANE

FORT DULANY

FORT ECONFINEE

FORT FANNING

FORT FOSTER [2]

FORT FOWLE

FORT FRANK BROOKE

FORT FRAZER

FORT FULTON

FORT GADSDEN *

FORT GAMBLE

FORT GARDNER

FORT GATES

FORT GATLIN

FORT GREEN

FORT GRIFFIN

FORT HAMER

FORT HAMILTON

FORT HANSON

FORT HARLLEE

FORT HARRELL

FORT HARRIETT

FORT HARRISON

FORT HARVIE

FORT HEILEMAN

FORT HENRY

FORT HOLMES

FORT HOOK

FORT HULBERT

FORT HUNTER

FORT JACKSON

FORT JEFFERSON *

FORT JENNINGS

FORT JONES

FORT JUPITER

FORT KATE

FORT KEAIS

KEY WEST BARRACKS *

FORT KING *

FORT KINGSBURY

FORT KISSIMMEE

FORT LANE

FORT LAUDERDALE

FORT LAWSON

FORT LLOYD

FORT MACKAY

FORT MACOMB [2]

FORT MAITLAND

FORT MANY

FORT MARION *

FORT MASON

FORT McCLELLAN

FORT McCLURE

FORT McCRABB

FORT McNEILL

FORT McRAE

FORT McREE

FORT MEADE *

FORT MELLON

FORT MICANOPY

FORT MITCHELL

FORT MONIAC

140

FORT MYAKKA
FORT MYERS *
FORT NOEL
FORT OCILLA
FORT PEYTON
FORT PICKENS
FORT PIERCE *
FORT PLEASANT
FORT POINSETT
FORT PRESTON
FORT RUSSELL
FORT ST. MARKS
FORT SANDERSON
FORT SCHACKELFORD
FORT SEARLE
FORT SHANNON
FORT SIMMONS
FORT SIMON DRUM
FORT STANSBURY

FORT STARKE
FORT SULLIVAN
FORT T. B. ADAMS
FORT TAYLOR [2]
FORT THOMPSON
FORT VAN COURTLAND
FORT VAN SWEARENGEN
FORT VINTON
FORT VOSE
FORT WACAHOOTA
FORT WACASASSA
FORT WACISSA
FORT WALKER
FORT WARD
FORT WEKIWA
FORT WESTCOTT
FORT WHEELOCK
FORT WHITE
FORT WOOL

[1] Five forts of this name.   [2] Two forts of this name.

GEORGIA FORTS

FORT A. S. MILLER
FORT BARNUM
FORT DEARBORN
FORT FLOYD
FORT GILMER
FORT HENDERSON
FORT LA MOTTE

FORT MCLANE
FORT MUDGE
FORT MUSE
FORT NORTON
FORT TATNALL
FORT TOMPKINS
FORT WALKER

PLATE 21: EAST FLORIDA, 1840 (OVERLEAF)

Map courtesy of Library of Congress.

MAP
OF
EAST FLORIDA,

Reduced from the Map compiled by

CAPT. JOHN MACKAY & LIEUT. J.E. BLAKE

and published by order of the

SENATE OF THE U. STATES,

FOR THE MONTHLY CHRONICLE.

1840.

Thayer, successor to Moore, Boston

Scale of Statute Miles.

APPENDIX B

Annual Strength of the Regular Army

1789–1895

The aggregate strength of the regular army at stated periods from the beginning of the national government to 1895 is shown in the following table. The figures from 1789 to 1878 are taken from the compilation made by Adjutant General E. D. Townsend, published in *House Executive Document* No. 23, 45 Congress, 3 session, serial 1852. Those from 1879 to 1898 are taken from the annual reports of the Secretary of War for those years.

Year	Aggregate Strength	Year	Aggregate Strength
1789	672[1]	1807[2]	
1790[2]		1808[2]	
1791[2]		1809	6,954
1792[2]		1810[2]	
1793[2]		1811[2]	
1794	3,578[1]	1812	6,686
1795	3,440	1813	19,036
1796[2]		1814	38,186
1797[2]		1815	33,424
1798[2]		1816	10,024
1799[2]		1817	8,220
1800[2]		1818	7,676
1801	4,051	1819	8,688
1802[2]		1820[2]	
1803	2,576	1821[2]	
1804	2,730	1822	5,211
1805[2]		1823	5,949
1806[2]		1824	5,779

Year	Aggregate Strength	Year	Aggregate Strength
1825	5,719	1861	16,422
1826	5,809	1862[3]	
1827	5,722	1863[3]	
1828	5,529	1864[3]	
1829	6,169	1865	22,310
1830	5,951	1866[4]	
1831	5,869	1867	56,815
1832	6,102	1868	50,916
1833	6,412	1869	36,774
1834	6,824	1870	37,075
1835	7,151	1871	28,953
1836	6,283	1872	28,175
1837	7,834	1873	28,652
1838	8,653	1874	28,444
1839	9,704	1875	25,318
1840	10,570	1876	28,280
1841	11,169	1877	23,945
1842	10,628	1878	25,818
1843	8,935	1879	26,389
1844	8,573	1880	26,411
1845	8,349	1881	25,670
1846	10,690	1882	25,186
1847	21,686	1883	25,478
1848	10,035	1884	26,383
1849	10,585	1885	26,859
1850	10,763	1886	26,544
1851	10,538	1887	26,436
1852	11,202	1888	26,738
1853	10,417	1889	27,478
1854	10,745	1890	27,089
1855	15,752	1891	26,175
1856	15,562	1892	26,900
1857	15,764	1893	27,519
1858	17,498	1894	27,934
1859	16,435	1895	27,172
1860	16,367		

[1]Enlisted men only. [2]No returns. [3]Annual returns suspended. [4]No consolidated returns.

APPENDIX C

Army Territorial Commands

The military frontier was of such extent that administrative division became necessary, and in 1813 the army was organized on a territorial basis. The nation was divided into geographical units, variously called divisions, departments, and districts. Each had a headquarters with commanding officer and staff and each served as an intermediate headquarters between the army posts and operational units within the area and the headquarters of the army or the War Department.

The boundaries of the various territorial commands and the terminology used to designate them changed with amazing frequency. Not only were there periodic rearrangements of the whole system, but there were also minor changes in the boundaries of the commands between the major changes. This shuffling and reshuffling of the geographical divisions within which the army operated is indicated in summary form below. The data are taken chiefly from the compilation of Raphael P. Thian, in his *Notes Illustrating the Military Geography of the United States* (Washington, 1881). Thian's printed work covers the years 1813 to 1880; it has been carried down to 1904 in a manuscript revision now in the War Department Records of the National Archives, Record Group 94.

From March 19, 1813, to May 17, 1815

On March 19, 1813, the United States was divided into nine military districts, as follows:

Military District No. 1—Massachusetts and New Hampshire.
Military District No. 2—Rhode Island and Connecticut.

Military District No. 3—New York from the sea to the Highlands and New Jersey.

Military District No. 4—Pennsylvania from its eastern limits to the Alleghenies and Delaware.

Military District No. 5—Maryland and Virginia.

Military District No. 6—North Carolina, South Carolina, and Georgia.

Military District No. 7—Tennessee, Louisiana, and Mississippi Territory.

Military District No. 8—Kentucky, Ohio, and Indiana, Illinois, Missouri, and Michigan territories.

Military District No. 9—Pennsylvania from the Alleghenies to its western limit, New York north of the Highlands, and Vermont.

On April 10, 1813, the southern counties of New Jersey were taken from Military District No. 3 and added to Military District No. 4. On July 2, 1814, an additional jurisdiction was carved out of Military District No. 5, as follows:

Military District No. 10—Maryland, District of Columbia, and Virginia between the Rappahannock and Potomac rivers.

From May 17, 1815, to May 17, 1821

On May 17, 1815, the military district system was abandoned, and the country was divided into a Division of the North, with five subordinate military departments, and a Division of the South, with four subordinate military departments, as follows:

Division of the North—New England, New York, New Jersey, Pennsylvania, Delaware, Maryland, Ohio, and Michigan and Indiana territories.

Military Department No. 1—New York above the Highlands and Vermont.

Military Department No. 2—New Hampshire, Massachusetts, Rhode Island, and Connecticut.

Military Department No. 3—New York below the Highlands and the northern counties of New Jersey.

Military Department No. 4—Pennsylvania, Delaware, Maryland, and the southern counties of New Jersey.

Military Department No. 5—Ohio and Michigan and Indiana territories.

Division of the South—District of Columbia, Virginia, North Carolina, South Carolina, Georgia, Louisiana, Tennessee, Kentucky, and Mississippi, Missouri, and Illinois territories.

Military Department No. 6—Virginia, North Carolina, and District of Columbia.

Military Department No. 7—South Carolina and Georgia.

146

Military Department No. 8—Louisiana and Mississippi Territory.

Military Department No. 9—Tennessee, Kentucky, and Missouri and Illinois territories.

From May 17, 1821, to May 19, 1837

On May 17, 1821, the Division of the North and the Division of the South were abolished and in their place was established a simple two-fold division of the country. A line was drawn between Cape Sable, Florida, and Fond du Lac on Lake Superior. The Western Department embraced the area west of the line and included all of Kentucky and Tennessee. The Eastern Department embraced all the country east of the line, except for the parts of Kentucky and Tennessee.

From May 19, 1837, to July 12, 1842

On May 19, 1837, the country was divided into a Western Division and an Eastern Division by a line beginning at the mouth of the Mississippi, extending up that river to Cassville in Wisconsin Territory, and then north to the Canadian border. Each division had subordinate departments, as follows:

Western Division.

Military Department No. 1—The country north of the 37th parallel, and west of the Mississippi and the line drawn from Cassville to the Canadian border.

Military Department No. 2—The country south of the 37th parallel and west of the Mississippi River.

Eastern Division.

Military Department No. 3—Kentucky, Tennessee, Mississippi, Louisiana east of the Mississippi, Alabama, Georgia, and Florida Territory.

Military Department No. 4—North Carolina, South Carolina, and Virginia.

Military Department No. 5—Maryland, Delaware, Pennsylvania, New Jersey, and New York.

Military Department No. 6—Connecticut, Rhode Island, Massachusetts, New Hampshire, Vermont, and Maine.

Military Department No. 7—Ohio, Michigan, Indiana, Illinois, and Wisconsin Territory east of the line dividing the two divisions.

On September 1, 1841, Military Department No. 7 was transferred from the Eastern to the Western Division, and on March 29, 1842, the part of

Louisiana east of the Mississippi was transferred from the Eastern to the Western Division.

From July 12, 1842, to April 20, 1844

On July 12, 1842, the Western and Eastern Divisions were discontinued, and the United States was divided into nine independent departments. The numbers of the departments in this arrangement pertained to quite different areas from those in the previous enumeration of departments.

Military Department No. 1—West Florida, Alabama, Mississippi, Louisiana, Tennessee, and Kentucky.

Military Department No. 2—The country west of the Mississippi, north of Louisiana and Texas, and south of the 37th parallel.

Military Department No. 3—Missouri north of the 37th parallel, Illinois, Iowa Territory, Wisconsin Territory west of the 90th meridian, and the Indian country north and west of the line indicated.

Military Department No. 4—Indiana, Ohio, Michigan, Wisconsin Territory east of the 90th meridian, and the Indian country north.

Military Department No. 5—Pennsylvania, New York, Vermont, New Jersey, Connecticut, and Rhode Island.

Military Department No. 6—Massachusetts, New Hampshire, and Maine.

Military Department No. 7—Delaware, Maryland, and Virginia.

Military Department No. 8—North Carolina, South Carolina, and Georgia.

Military Department No. 9—East and Middle Florida.

From April 20, 1844, to August 31, 1848

On April 20, 1844, the Eastern and Western Divisions were reconstituted, to be divided again by the Fond du Lac–Cape Sable line. Military Departments Nos. 1, 2, and 3 were included in the Western Division; Military Departments Nos. 5, 6, 7, and 8 were placed in the Eastern Division; Military Departments Nos. 4 and 9 were independent. The arrangement was as follows:

Western Division—The country west of the Fond du Lac–Cape Sable line, embracing Wisconsin Territory west of the line, Iowa Territory, Illinois, Missouri, Kentucky, Tennessee, Arkansas, Louisiana, Mississippi, Alabama, West Florida, and the Indian country west of the Mississippi.

Eastern Division—New England, New York, New Jersey, Pennsylvania, Delaware, Maryland, Virginia, North Carolina, South Carolina, and Georgia.

Military Department No. 4—Ohio, Indiana, Michigan, and the part of Wisconsin Territory not contained in the Western Division.

Military Department No. 9—East and Middle Florida.

On September 14, 1845, Military Department No. 9 was discontinued, being absorbed by Military Departments Nos. 1 and 8. On June 1, 1844, Rhode Island was transferred from Military Department No. 5 to Military Department No. 6. On November 3, 1846, two new departments were created, as follows:

Military Department No. 9—To embrace so much of the Mexican province of New Mexico as has been or may be subjected to the arms or the authority of the United States.

Military Department No. 10—To consist of the Territory of Oregon and so much of the Mexican provinces of the two Californias as has been or may be subjected to the arms or the authority of the United States.

From August 31, 1848, to October 31, 1853

On August 31, 1848, the old arrangement was discontinued and a new arrangement of Eastern and Western Divisions with eleven subordinate departments was instituted. The numbers of the departments were again thoroughly shuffled, as follows:

Eastern Division—The country east of a line drawn from Fond du Lac on Lake Superior to Cape Sable in Florida, including Indiana and Georgia, but excluding Illinois, Kentucky, and Tennessee.

Military Department No. 1—New England.
Military Department No. 2—Michigan, Wisconsin east of the Fond du Lac–Cape Sable line, Ohio, and Indiana.
Military Department No. 3—New York, New Jersey, Pennsylvania, Delaware, and Maryland.
Military Department No. 4—Virginia, North Carolina, South Carolina, Georgia, and Florida east of the Fond du Lac–Cape Sable line.

Western Division—The country west of the Fond du Lac–Cape Sable line, excluding Indiana and Georgia, but including Illinois, Kentucky, and Tennessee.

Military Department No. 5—Alabama, Louisiana, Mississippi, Tennessee, Kentucky, and Florida west of the Fond du Lac–Cape Sable line.
Military Department No. 6—Wisconsin west of the Fond du Lac–Cape Sable line, Iowa, Illinois, and Missouri north of the 37th parallel.

Military Department No. 7—The country west of the Mississippi, south of the 37th parallel, and north of Louisiana and Texas.

Military Department No. 8—That part of Texas south and east of a line drawn from a point on the Rio Grande south of El Paso, at 32° north latitude, to the junction of Choctaw Creek with the Red River, and down the Red River to Arkansas.

Military Department No. 9—New Mexico Territory and the country north and west of the line marking Military Department No. 8.

Military Department No. 10 (Independent)—California.

Military Department No. 11 (Independent)—Oregon Territory.
On October 10, 1848, Departments Nos. 10 and 11 were assigned to a newly created Pacific Division.

This general arrangement underwent a number of modifications before it was replaced in 1853. These changes were in three areas. First, Florida east of the Fond du Lac–Cape Sable line was transferred to the Western Division on August 7, 1849, changed back to the Eastern Division on November 25, 1850, and returned to the Western Division on February 11, 1852. Second, the line dividing Military Department No. 8 and Military Department No. 9 was shifted back and forth as new posts were established in Texas and New Mexico. Changes were made in the boundary between the departments on December 15, 1849, November 14, 1851, and February 15, 1853. Third, some of the subordinate departments were discontinued and merged into the parent division. Thus, on May 17, 1851, Military Departments Nos. 1 and 2 were merged into the Eastern Division, Military Department No. 5 was merged into the Western Division, and Military Departments Nos. 10 and 11 were merged into the Pacific Division. Military Department No. 5, however, was revived on March 8, 1852, and Military Department No. 1 on August 14, 1852. On October 25, 1852, Military Department No. 5 was again discontinued.

From October 31, 1853, to the Civil War

The system of divisions and numbered departments was abandoned on October 31, 1853, and a system of departments with descriptive names was set up in its place. In this period there were no divisions; each department reported directly to the Headquarters of the Army.

Department of the East—The country east of the Mississippi River.

Department of the West—The country west of the Mississippi River and east of the Rocky Mountains, except the Departments of Texas and New Mexico.

Department of Texas—Texas south of the 33rd parallel.

Department of New Mexico—New Mexico Territory east of the 110th meridian.

Department of the Pacific—The country west of the Rocky Mountains, except Utah Territory and the Department of New Mexico.

This simple division into five departments was soon changed, both by the creation of new departments carved out of the original ones, and by repeated changes in the boundaries between the various departments. Changes in the department arrangement were as follows:

Department of Florida created (March 27, 1856)—Florida except that part west of the Chattahoochee and Apalachicola rivers.

Department of Utah created (January 1, 1858)—Utah Territory.

Department of the Platte created (March 27, 1858)—The line of communication to the west through Nebraska Territory.

Department of Florida discontinued (August 1, 1858)—Merged into the Department of the East.

Department of California created (September 13, 1858)—The country west of the Rocky Mountains and south of Oregon and Washington territories, including the Rogue River and Umpqua districts, and excluding Utah east of the 117th meridian and New Mexico east of the 110th.

Department of Oregon created (September 13, 1858)—Oregon and Washington territories, except Rogue River and Umpqua districts.

Department of the Platte discontinued (May 16, 1859)—Merged into the Department of the West.

Department of the Pacific revived (January 15, 1861)—Formed by the consolidation of the Departments of California and Oregon.

Changes in the boundaries of the departments also occurred, of which the following may be noted. Fort Bliss, Texas, was transferred from the Department of Texas to the Department of New Mexico from November 11, 1853, to December 8, 1860. The Department of Texas was extended to include the northern part of Texas (February 28, 1857) and the Indian Territory south of the Arkansas River and Fort Smith (August 19, 1859). The latter additions were returned to the Department of the West on December 8, 1860. On January 14, 1858, the Department of the Pacific gained the Territory of Utah west of the 117th meridian from the Department of Utah.

The Civil War Period

The Civil War upset the normal military command situation. Although the frontier areas still presented serious defense problems and special arrangements had to be made to provide for crises—for example, the creation of a separate Department of the Northwest as a result of the Sioux outbreak of 1862—most of the additions and changes in the territorial departments had to do with the war against the Confederacy. Thian's *Notes* lists ninety changes between April, 1861, and the rearrangement of divisions and departments which took place in August, 1866.

From August 6, 1866, to July 3, 1891

In August, 1866, a new organization of territorial commands was instituted, reflecting in part the post-Civil War needs in the South and East, and in part the frontier situation in the West. The arrangement originally consisted of two divisions with subordinate departments and eight independent departments. This general setup continued through the century, with a good many variations, however, as new divisions and departments were created. Sometimes all the departments were subordinated to divisions; sometimes there were a number of independent departments which reported direct to the Headquarters of the Army. From March 11, 1867, to March 31, 1870, special military districts, similar to departments, were established in the South as part of Reconstruction.

On August 6, 1866, the general pattern was determined. This was modified on August 11 by the creation of the Department of Dakota and modifications in the Departments of the Platte and of the Missouri. The following listing reflects the situation as of the latter date.

Division of the Missouri—Missouri, Kansas, Minnesota, Iowa, Arkansas, Indian Territory, and the Territories of Colorado, New Mexico, Nebraska, Dakota, Utah, and Montana.

> Department of Arkansas—Arkansas and Indian Territory.
> Department of the Missouri—Missouri, Kansas, and New Mexico and Colorado territories.
> Department of the Platte—Iowa and the Territories of Nebraska, Utah, Dakota west of the 104th meridian (which became the Territory of Wyoming on July 25, 1868), and so much of Montana as lay contiguous to the road from Fort Laramie to Virginia City.
> Department of Dakota—Minnesota, Dakota Territory east of the 104th meridian, and Montana Territory, except that part contiguous to the road from Fort Laramie to Virginia City.

Division of the Pacific—California, Oregon, Nevada, and the Territories of Arizona, Washington, and Idaho.

> Department of California—California, Nevada, and Arizona Territory.
> Department of the Columbia—Oregon and the Territories of Washington and Idaho.

Department of the East—New England, New York, New Jersey, and Pennsylvania.

Department of the Gulf—Florida, Louisiana, and Texas.

Department of the Lakes—Ohio, Michigan, Indiana, Illinois, and Wisconsin.

Department of the Potomac—Virginia, except the counties of Alexandria and Fairfax, and West Virginia.

Department of the South—North Carolina and South Carolina.

Department of the Tennessee—Kentucky, Tennessee, Georgia, Alabama, and Mississippi.

Department of Washington—Delaware, Maryland, District of Columbia, and Alexandria and Fairfax counties of Virginia.

For this period Thian's *Notes* indicates sixty changes in the territorial commands. Some of these, however, concerned only the switch of a single post from one department to another for convenience of administration.

In the East there were numerous changes, as new departments were created and old ones changed or discontinued. On March 11 and 12, 1867, the Departments of the Gulf, Potomac, South, Tennessee, and Arkansas were discontinued. The areas belonging to the discontinued departments were reconstituted into five military districts established for Reconstruction purposes and a new department, as follows:

First Military District (ended January 29, 1870)—Virginia.
Second Military District (ended July 28, 1868)—North Carolina and South Carolina.
Third Military District (ended July 28, 1868)—Georgia, Florida, and Alabama.
Fourth Military District (ended February 26, 1870)—Mississippi and Arkansas.
Fifth Military District (ended March 31, 1870)—Louisiana and Texas.
Department of the Cumberland—West Virginia, Tennessee, and Kentucky.

There soon began a general abandonment of the military districts, as they were replaced by the reconstitution of old departments or the erection of new ones. In the East after the discontinuation of the districts, the following commands were in existence, including those which were part of the arrangement of August, 1866.

Division of the Atlantic—February 12, 1868, to July 2, 1891.
Division of the South—March 16, 1869, to January 15, 1872, and November 25, 1872, to June 26, 1876.
Division of the Gulf—December 18, 1880, to May 6, 1881.

Department of the East—January 3, 1863, to October 31, 1873, and November 8, 1877—.

Department of the Gulf—November 1, 1871, to July 17, 1878.

Department of the Lakes—August 6, 1866, to October 31, 1873.

Department of Louisiana—July 28, 1868, to March 31, 1870.

Department of the South—July 28, 1868, to November 1, 1883.

Department of Virginia—January 29, 1870, to April 30, 1870.

Department of West Point—March 2, 1877, to July 13, 1882.

Department of the Cumberland—March 12, 1867, to May 4, 1870.

Department of Washington—February 2, 1863, to March 16, 1869.

District of Georgia—January 4, 1870, to May, 1871.

There were a good many changes in the boundaries of these commands.

Aside from the military occupation of the South, the focus of attention after the Civil War was on the Indian regions of the West. Here, as in the East, there were many changes in the organization and boundaries of the territorial commands. In addition to the Departments of the Missouri, Platte, Dakota, California, and Columbia, which continued in existence throughout the whole period, the following new departments were created.

Department of Alaska—Established on March 18, 1868, and discontinued on July 1, 1870, merging into the Department of the Columbia.

Department of Texas—Established on March 31, 1870 (Louisiana and Texas).

Department of Arizona—Established on April 15, 1870 (Arizona Territory and California south of a line from the northwest corner of Arizona to Point Conception).

Department of Arkansas—Re-established from December 18, 1880, to May 6, 1881 (Arkansas, Louisiana, and Indian Territory), then merged into the Departments of the Missouri and of the South.

Within this arrangement of commands the following transfers of territory took place:

The Indian Territory was transferred to the Department of the Missouri when the Department of Arkansas was discontinued on March 12, 1867. On November 1, 1871, it was changed to the Department of Texas, then on July 10, 1874, the part of Indian Territory north of the Canadian River was returned to the Department of the Missouri, and on March 11, 1875, the remainder also was transferred. From December 18, 1880, to May 6, 1881, the Indian Territory was part of the Department of Arkansas, then returned to the Department of the Missouri.

Further changes in the boundary between the Department of the Missouri and the Department of Texas involved the part of Texas north of the Canadian River, which was transferred to the Department of the Missouri on July 10, 1874, and returned on March 11, 1875. The portion of El Paso

County, Texas, lying north of an east-west line passing immediately south of the town of San Elizario was transferred from the Department of Texas to the Department of the Missouri on December 15, 1877, then passed to the Department of Arizona when it acquired New Mexico Territory on November 30, 1885, and was returned to the Department of Texas on January 7, 1887.

The Department of Arizona on February 14, 1883, lost the portion of California it originally held to the Department of California, but on December 15, 1886, regained the portion of California south of the 35th parallel. The Territory of New Mexico was transferred from the Department of the Missouri to the Department of Arizona on November 30, 1885.

The Department of the Platte on June 22, 1875, gained from the Department of the Columbia the part of Idaho Territory lying east of a line formed by the extension of the western boundary of Utah to the northeastern boundary of Idaho, and on January 21, 1891, gained from the Department of Dakota the part of South Dakota south of the 44th parallel.

Transfers of states from one department to another during this period may be noted. Arkansas was transferred to the Department of the Missouri on March 31, 1870, to the Department of the Gulf on November 1, 1871, to the Department of the South on July 1, 1878, to the Department of Arkansas on December 18, 1880, to the Department of the South on May 6, 1881, to the Department of the East on November 1, 1883, and back to the Department of the Missouri on July 19, 1889. Illinois was transferred from the Department of the Lakes to the Department of the Missouri on March 16, 1869, and Wisconsin from the Department of the East to the Department of Dakota on April 6, 1889.

From July 3, 1891, to March 11, 1898

On July 3, 1891, the military divisions (Atlantic, Missouri, and Pacific) were discontinued and eight military departments retained, the commanders of which reported direct to the Major General Commanding the Army.

Department of the East—New England, New York, New Jersey, Pennsylvania, Ohio, Delaware, Maryland, Virginia, West Virginia, North Carolina, South Carolina, Georgia, Florida, Louisiana, Mississippi, Alabama, Kentucky, Tennessee, and District of Columbia.

Department of the Missouri—Michigan, Wisconsin, Indiana, Illinois, Missouri, Kansas, Arkansas, Indian Territory, and Oklahoma Territory.

Department of the Platte—Iowa, Nebraska, Colorado, South Dakota south of the 44th parallel, Wyoming (except Fort Yellowstone), Idaho east of a line formed by the extension of the western boundary of Utah to the northeastern boundary of Idaho, and Utah Territory.

155

Department of Dakota—Minnesota, North Dakota, South Dakota north of the 44th parallel, and Fort Yellowstone, Wyoming.

Department of Texas—Texas.

Department of California—California north of the 35th parallel and Nevada.

Department of Arizona—Arizona and New Mexico territories and California south of the 35th parallel.

Department of the Columbia—Oregon, Washington, Idaho west of a line formed by the extension of the western boundary of Utah to the northeastern boundary of Idaho, and Alaska Territory.

In this arrangement two changes were made. On June 30, 1893, the Department of Colorado was created (Colorado and the Territories of Arizona, New Mexico, and Utah) and the Department of California gained the part of the state south of the 35th parallel. The Department of Arizona was thus discontinued, being absorbed by the Departments of Colorado and California. On July 20, 1895, the Department of the Platte gained the part of South Dakota lying between the 44th and 45th parallels west of the Missouri River.

BIBLIOGRAPHY

Bibliography

I. COMPREHENSIVE LISTINGS OF MILITARY POSTS

A number of lists of regular army military installations have been compiled which aim at providing a full list of posts, both those in existence at the time the list was compiled and those which had been abandoned. These lists vary in completeness, in amount of information provided for each entry, and in accuracy.

Hamersly, Thomas H. S. *Complete Regular Army Register of the United States for One Hundred Years (1779 to 1879).* Washington, 1880.   [1]
    In Part II, pp. 122–162, there is a "List of Military Forts, Arsenals, Camps, Barracks, &c.," which lists posts alphabetically and indicates their location and usually the dates of establishment and abandonment. The list contains 979 entries, but some of these are cross references. The list includes temporary Florida forts and Civil War installations, as well as more permanent types of military stations. This is a generally accurate and useful list and has been much relied upon by other compilers.

Heitman, Francis B. *Historical Register and Dictionary of the United States Army, from Its Organization, September 29, 1789, to March 2, 1903.* 2 vols. Washington, 1903.   [2]
    Volume II, pp. 475–559, contains a "List of Forts, Batteries, Named Camps, Redoubts, Reservations, General Hospitals, National Cemeteries, etc., Established or Erected in the United States from Its Earliest Settlement to Date." This list, of 4,911 entries, gives only the name and location (often in very general terms) of the installations.

Ledyard, Edgar M. "American Posts," in *Utah Historical Quarterly*, 1:56–64, 86–96, 114–127 (1928); 2:25–30, 55–64, 90–96, 127–128 (1929); 3:27–32, 59–64, 90–96 (1930); 5:65–80, 113–128, 161–176 (1932); 6:29–48, 64–80 (1933).   [3]

This is a listing of 2,386 posts, including early settlers' forts and trading posts as well as regular army forts. The work is miscellaneous in character and is of very limited value.

List of Military Posts, Etc., Established in the United States from Its Earliest Settlement to the Present Time. Washington, 1902.   [4]

This list of 4,573 entries was prepared by the Returns Division of the Adjutant General's Office and carries the following warning: "This list has been prepared only for convenience of reference. The data available for consultation is known to be incomplete, and may be erroneous in some instances." The list is similar to that in Heitman and contains only the name of the post and a very brief notation of its location.

Outline Index of Military Forts and Stations.   [5]

This compilation of data on military posts consists of twenty-six folio volumes in manuscript, one for each letter of the alphabet. It was prepared in the Adjutant General's Office late in the nineteenth century and is the most valuable single listing of posts. It contains information about the location and dates of establishment and abandonment of the posts, and for most items includes also numerous references to official orders and other records. Unfortunately, the material was compiled at different times by different persons and is often incomplete and sometimes inaccurate. The *Outline Index* is now in the National Archives, Records of the Adjutant General's Office (Record Group 94).

Preliminary Checklist of Records of Army Commands: Post Records, 1813–1942.   [6]

This checklist consists of a series of mimeographed sheets, briefly describing the extant post records in the Records of United States Army Commands (Record Group 98) in the National Archives. There is a separate sheet devoted to each post for which records—letter books, order books, guard reports, quartermaster records, and the like—are on file. The series by no means includes all posts, since in the period before the Civil War especially many post records are entirely missing, but the list as it stands is very valuable. A brief history is given for the posts included in the checklist.

II. OFFICIAL LISTINGS OF MILITARY POSTS AT GIVEN DATES

ANNUAL RETURNS

Annual Reports of the Secretary of War.   [7]

These reports contain tables prepared by the Adjutant General which show the breakdown of army strength by station for the year in question.

The tables thus provide an annual list of military posts, with notation of size and location of garrison.

REPORTS OF THE SURGEON GENERAL

"Geographical Positions of the Military Posts, with Their Local Topography and Altitudes Above the Sea," in *Statistical Report on the Sickness and Mortality in the Army of the United States, Compiled from the Records of the Surgeon General's Office, Embracing a Period of Sixteen Years, from January, 1839, to January, 1855.* Senate Executive Document No. 96, 34 Cong., 1 sess., serial 827, pp. 498–508.   [8]

   This list contains 159 items.

A *Report on Barracks and Hospitals, with Descriptions of Military Posts.* Circular No. 4. Washington, 1870.   [9]

   This volume contains information on 154 installations. The reports for the individual posts are several pages in length and include data on location, description of the country, some historical information, and descriptions of barracks, climate, water supply, and so forth.

A *Report on the Hygiene of the United States Army, with Descriptions of Military Posts.* Circular No. 8. Washington, 1875.   [10]

   This volume lists 238 installations, with information comparable to that in Circular No. 4.

OFFICIAL LISTS FOR THE WHOLE UNITED STATES

Outline Description of U. S. Military Posts and Stations in the Year 1871. Washington, 1872.   [11]

   This volume, issued by the Quartermaster General, contains information on 231 posts arranged by Military Department. Information includes date of establishment, location, description of post buildings, water and wood supply, Indians, communications, reservation, description of country, etc. An appendix, pp. 243–271, includes additional material (brought up to date to 1872) on posts in the Department of the Missouri.

Outline Descriptions of the Posts and Stations of Troops in the Geographical Divisions and Departments of the United States. Compiled by Inspector General R. B. Marcy, by order of the General in Chief of the Army. Washington, 1872.   [12]

   This volume gives descriptions, similar to those in the previous item, of 238 posts. For some posts the information is quite extensive; for others it is very brief.

Alphabetical List of Military Posts, Garrisons, Stations, and National Ceme-

161

teries of the United States, with Their Post Offices and Telegraph Stations, February 28, 1879. Washington, 1879. **[13]**

This fifteen-page pamphlet, issued by the Adjutant General, lists 235 posts.

OFFICIAL LISTS FOR PARTICULAR GEOGRAPHICAL DIVISIONS

Outline Descriptions, Posts & Stations of Troops in the Military Division of the Atlantic. Philadelphia, 1870. **[14]**

This volume gives information as of October, 1870. It includes 60 posts of the Department of the East and 12 posts of the Department of the Lakes.

Outline Descriptions of the Posts and Stations of Troops in the Military Division of the Missouri. Chicago, 1871. **[15]**

This volume, dated December 31, 1870, lists 57 installations in the Department of the Missouri, Department of the Platte, and Department of Dakota.

Outline Descriptions of the Posts in the Military Division of the Missouri ... Accompanied by Tabular Lists of Indian Superintendencies, Agencies and Reservations, a Summary of Certain Indian Treaties, and Table of Distances. Chicago, 1872. **[16]**

This volume, dated June 1, 1872, lists 71 installations in the Department of Dakota, Department of the Missouri, Department of the Platte, and Department of Texas.

Outline Descriptions of the Posts in the Military Division of the Missouri ... Accompanied by Tabular Lists of Indian Superintendencies, Agencies and Reservations, and a Summary of Certain Indian Treaties. Chicago, 1876. **[17]**

This volume contains descriptions of 90 posts in the Department of Dakota, Department of the Platte, Department of the Missouri, Department of Texas, and Department of the Gulf. In addition to the regular descriptive material there are drawings of the post layout and of the military reservation for each post as well as a fold-out map showing the military posts west of the Mississippi.

Outline Descriptions of the Posts and Stations of Troops in the Military Division of the Pacific. San Francisco, 1871. **[18]**

This volume, issued on January 1, 1871, lists 48 installations.

Revised Outline Descriptions of the Posts and Stations of Troops in the Military Division of the Pacific. San Francisco, 1872. **[19]**

This volume, issued on February 1, 1872, describes 40 posts.

Outline Descriptions of Military Posts in the Military Division of the Pacific. San Francisco, 1879. **[20]**

This volume, listing 44 posts, has a fold-out map in the back.

III. PRINTED DOCUMENTS

There are innumerable items dealing with the military frontier or with special aspects of individual posts in the printed Congressional documents, in addition to the Annual Reports of the Secretary of War and the special Surgeon General's Circulars mentioned above, items [7–10]. The *American State Papers: Military Affairs* (5 vols., Washington, 1832–1861) and *American State Papers: Indian Affairs* (2 vols., Washington, 1832–1834) have much information on the early years. For items in the serial set of Congressional documents, see the standard indexes of Poore and of Ames and the *Tables of and Annotated Index to the Congressional Series of United States Public Documents (1817–1893)*. There are excellent materials on the military frontier in Clarence E. Carter, editor, *The Territorial Papers of the United States* (26 vols., Washington, 1934–1962).

IV. RECORDS IN THE NATIONAL ARCHIVES

Information on the military posts must ultimately be sought in the multifarious records of the War Department on file in the National Archives. There is no one file which supplies all the data needed in drawing up a brief historical account of each post; many kinds of records must be appealed to in order to piece out the full story. The following collections proved most useful in furnishing data for the present *Guide*.

Records of the Adjutant General's Office (Record Group 94). [21]
> Since the Adjutant General was chiefly responsible for maintaining records in regard to the posts and their personnel, the record of his office are especially necessary. See the volumes of Letters Sent; the large miscellaneous file called "Post Revolutionary War Papers"; Orders and Circulars; Returns of Departments; Returns of Territorial Divisions, Departments, and Districts; Returns of Military Posts; Military Reservation File; Outline Index of Military Forts and Stations (item [5] above); Medical Histories of Posts; and Miscellaneous File.

Records of the Headquarters of the Army (Record Group 108). [22]
> Letters sent and received by the Commanding General and general and special orders from his headquarters give information on operations, movement of troops, inspections, and other matters. There is a special group of inspection reports covering the years 1830–1866. Of special interest are Book 219, Description of Posts and Camps in the Division of the Pacific, Departments of Columbia and California (1868), and Book 220, Descriptive Book of the District of Texas (July 1, 1868).

Records of the Office of the Inspector General (Record Group 159). [23]
> The reports of the various inspectors general of the army, who made

periodic tours of the military posts and sent detailed reports to the Secretary of War or the Commanding General, are a rich source of data. There are three bound volumes of reports for the period 1814–1836, including some also for 1842, indexed by posts. For the period 1878–1889 the inspection reports are filed with the Letters Received by the Office of the Inspector General, but there is a two-volume index to these reports, arranged by military department and then by post. Some valuable inspection reports are filed in the Records of the Adjutant General's Office and the Records of the Headquarters of the Army. For publications of inspection reports see the following:

Croghan, George. *Army Life on the Western Frontier: Selections from the Official Reports Made Between 1826 and 1845 by Colonel George Croghan.* Edited by Francis Paul Prucha. Norman, 1958. [24]

Freeman, William G. "W. G. Freeman's Report on the Eighth Military Department," edited by M. L. Crimmins, in *Southwestern Historical Quarterly,* 51:54–58, 167–174, 252–258, 350–357 (July, 1947– April, 1948); 52:100–108, 227–233, 349–353, 444–447 (July, 1948– April, 1949); 53:71–77, 202–208, 308–319, 443–473 (July, 1949– April, 1950); 54:204–218 (October, 1950). [25]

Hayne, Arthur P. "Report of Inspection of the Ninth Military Department, 1819," edited by Lester B. Shippee, in *Mississippi Valley Historical Review,* 7:261–274 (December, 1920). [26]

Mansfield, J. K. F. "Colonel J. K. F. Mansfield's Report of the Inspection of the Department of Texas in 1856," edited by M. L. Crimmins, in *Southwestern Historical Quarterly,* 42:122–148, 215–257, 351–387 (October, 1938–April, 1939). [27]

————. *Mansfield on the Condition of the Western Forts, 1853–54.* Edited by Robert W. Frazer. Norman, 1963. [28]

Records of the Office of the Secretary of War (Record Group 107). [29]
Of special value here are the early volumes of letters sent by the Secretary of War (usually referred to as Military Books), which give information about posts not available in other sources.

Records of United States Army Commands (Record Group 98). [30]
The records described in the Checklist noted in item [6] above, as well as records of the various military divisions and departments give important data on the individual posts.

Additional information can be found in the Records of the Chief of Engineers (Record Group 77), Records of the Commissary General of Subsistence (Record Group 192), Records of the General Land Office (Record Group 49), Records of the Quartermaster General (Record Group 92), and Records of the Surgeon General's Office (Record Group 112).

The Cartographic Branch of the National Archives, with its rich collection of manuscript maps, is invaluable for materials concerning military posts.

V. SECONDARY ACCOUNTS

Innumerable histories have been written of military posts. Some of these are the work of skilled historians who have diligently sought out the extant sources and who have fashioned accounts which are as complete and accurate as possible. Others are patriotic addresses, written to extoll the heroism of the men at a given fort. Still others are the reminiscences of some person who served at the installation in question or lived in the vicinity of the post. A few are tourist guides to historic army sites which now, in ruins or in restored form, attract the curious visitor. Many of the accounts are of little value to a person seeking sound historical information, but there is no clear line to be drawn between the useless and the valuable. I have tried to include in the following lists all the histories which seemed to me to be more or less competent accounts; I have eliminated trivial and overly sentimental works, reminiscences, and source material for a post history that is not an analytical history itself.

The lists, in accord with the nature of this *Guide*, center on military posts. There is much material about the military frontier and about individual posts in histories of states and territories, in histories of military units, and in biographies of military men and frontiersmen, but I have made no attempt to list such writings here. Omitted also are unpublished theses and dissertations.

ACCOUNTS COVERING MORE THAN ONE POST

Barrett, Arrie. "Western Frontier Forts of Texas, 1845–1861," in *West Texas Historical Association Year Book*, 7:115–139 (June, 1931). **[31]**

Barry, Louise. "The Fort Leavenworth-Fort Gibson Military Road and the Founding of Fort Scott," in *Kansas Historical Quarterly*, 11:115–129 (May, 1942). **[32]**

Beers, Henry Putney. "The Army and the Oregon Trail to 1846," in *Pacific Northwest Quarterly*, 28:339–362 (October, 1937). **[33]**

――――――. *The Western Military Frontier, 1815–1846.* Philadelphia, Pennsylvania, 1935. **[34]**

Bender, Averam B. "Frontier Defense in the Territory of New Mexico, 1846–1853," in *New Mexico Historical Review*, 9:249–272 (July, 1934). **[35]**

――――――. "Frontier Defense in the Territory of New Mexico, 1853–1861," in *New Mexico Historical Review*, 9:345–373 (October, 1934). **[36]**

――――――. *The March of Empire: Frontier Defense in the Southwest, 1848–1860.* Lawrence, Kansas, 1952. **[37]**

――――――. "Military Posts in the Southwest, 1848–1860," in *New Mexico Historical Review*, 16:125–147 (April, 1941). **[38]**

Brandes, Ray. *Frontier Military Posts of Arizona.* Globe, Arizona, 1960. **[39]**

—————. "A Guide to the History of the U. S. Army Installations in Arizona, 1849–1886," in *Arizona and the West*, 1:42–65 (Spring, 1959). **[40]**

Burlingame, Merrill G. *The Montana Frontier*. Helena, 1942. **[41]**

Clark, Dan Elbert. "Frontier Defense in Iowa, 1850–1865," in *Iowa Journal of History and Politics*, 16:315–386 (July, 1918). **[42]**

Clark, Robert Carlton. "Military History of Oregon, 1849–59," in *Oregon Historical Quarterly*, 36:14–59 (March, 1935). **[43]**

"Dakota Military Posts," in *South Dakota Historical Collections*, 7:77–99 (1916). **[44]**

"Early Military Posts, Missions and Camps," in *Transactions of the Kansas State Historical Society*, 1–2:263–270 (1881). **[45]**

Foreman, Grant. *Advancing the Frontier, 1830–1860*. Norman, 1933. **[46]**

Gallaher, Ruth A. "The Military-Indian Frontier, 1830–1835," in *Iowa Journal of History and Politics*, 15:393–428 (July, 1917). **[47]**

Garfield, Marvin H. "The Military Post as a Factor in the Frontier Defense of Kansas, 1865–1869," in *Kansas Historical Quarterly*, 1:50–62 (November, 1931). **[48]**

Graham, A. A. "The Military Posts, Forts and Battlefields Within the State of Ohio," in *Ohio Archaeological and Historical Publications*, 3:300–314 (1891). **[49]**

Hammond, John Martin. *Quaint and Historic Forts of North America*. Philadelphia, 1915. **[50]**

Hardin, J. Fair. "Fort Jesup, Fort Selden, Camp Sabine, Camp Salubrity: Four Forgotten Frontier Army Posts of Western Louisiana," in *Louisiana Historical Quarterly*, 16:5–26, 278–292, 441–453, 670–680 (January-October, 1933); 17:139–168 (January, 1934). **[51]**

Hart, Herbert M. *Old Forts of the Northwest*. Seattle, 1963. **[52]**

Holden, W. C. "Frontier Defense, 1846–1860," in *West Texas Historical Association Year Book*, 6:35–64 (June, 1930). **[53]**

—————. "Frontier Defense, 1865–1889," in *Panhandle-Plains Historical Review*, 2:43–64 (1929). **[54]**

—————. "Frontier Defense in Texas During the Civil War," in *West Texas Historical Association Year Book*, 4:16–31 (June, 1928). **[55]**

Lockwood, Frank C. "Early Military Posts in Arizona," in *Arizona Historical Review*, 2:91–97 (January, 1930). **[56]**

McElroy, Harold L. "Mercurial Military: A Study of the Central Montana Frontier Army Policy," in *Montana Magazine of History*, 4:9–23 (Fall, 1954). **[57]**

Mattison, Ray H. "The Army Post on the Northern Plains, 1865–1886," in *Nebraska History*, 35:17–43 (March, 1954). **[58]**

————. "The Military Frontier on the Upper Missouri," in *Nebraska History*, 37:159–182 (September, 1956). [59]

Morrison, William Brown. *Military Posts and Camps in Oklahoma.* Oklahoma City, 1936. [60]

National Park Service. *Soldier and Brave: Indian and Military Affairs in the Trans-Mississippi West, Including a Guide to Historic Sites and Landmarks.* New York, 1963. [61]

Prosch, Thomas W. "The United States Army in Washington Territory," in *Washington Historical Quarterly*, 2:28–32 (October, 1907). [62]

Prucha, Francis Paul. *Broadax and Bayonet: The Role of the United States Army in the Development of the Northwest, 1815–1860.* Madison, 1953. [63]

————. "Distribution of Regular Army Troops Before the Civil War," in *Military Affairs*, 16:169–173 (Winter, 1952). [64]

Richardson, Rupert N. *The Comanche Barrier to South Plains Settlement.* Glendale, California, 1934. [65]

Rister, Carl Coke. *The Southwestern Frontier—1865–1881.* Cleveland, 1928. [66]

Rogers, Fred B. "Early Military Posts of Del Norte County," in *California Historical Society Quarterly*, 26:1–11 (March, 1947). [67]

————. "Early Military Posts of Mendocino County, California," in *California Historical Society Quarterly*, 27:215–228 (September, 1948). [68]

Temple, Frank M. "Federal Military Defense of the Trans-Pecos Region, 1850–1880," in *West Texas Historical Association Year Book*, 30:40–60 (October, 1954). [69]

Van der Zee, Jacob. "Forts in the Iowa Country," in *Iowa Journal of History and Politics*, 12:163–204 (April, 1914). [70]

Welty, Raymond L. "The Army Fort of the Frontier (1860–1870)," in *North Dakota Historical Quarterly*, 2:155–167 (April, 1928). [71]

————. "The Frontier Army on the Missouri River, 1860–1870," in *North Dakota Historical Quarterly*, 2:85–99 (January, 1928). [72]

————. "The Policing of the Frontier by the Army, 1860–1870," in *Kansas Historical Quarterly*, 7:246–257 (August, 1938). [73]

Wesley, Edgar B. "The Beginnings of Coast Fortifications," in *Coast Artillery Journal*, 67:281–290 (March, 1927). [74]

————. *Guarding the Frontier: A Study of Frontier Defense from 1815 to 1825.* Minneapolis, 1935. [75]

Whiting, J. S. *Forts of the State of Washington: A Record of Military and Semi-military Establishments Designated as Forts from May 29, 1792, to November 15, 1951.* Seattle, 1951. [76]

———————, and Richard J. Whiting. *Forts of the State of California*. Seattle, 1960. [77]

HISTORIES OF INDIVIDUAL POSTS

Agnew, Daniel. *Fort McIntosh: Its Times and Men*. Pittsburgh, 1893. [78]

Aleshire, Ruth Cory. "Warsaw and Fort Edwards on the Mississippi," in *Transactions of the Illinois State Historical Society for the Year 1930*, pp. 200–209. [79]

Anderson, Harry H. "A History of the Cheyenne River Indian Agency and Its Military Post, Fort Bennett, 1868–1891," in *South Dakota Historical Society, Report and Historical Collections*, 28:390–551 (1956). [80]

Anderson, James. "Fort Osage: An Incident of Territorial Missouri," in *Bulletin of the Missouri Historical Society*, 4:174–176 (April, 1948). [81]

Anderson, Thomas M. "Vancouver Barracks—Past and Present," in *Journal of the Military Service Institution of the United States*, 25:69–78, 267–279 (July-August, September-October, 1904). [82]

Andrews, Roger. *Old Fort Mackinac on the Hill of History*. Menominee, Michigan, 1938. [83]

Arthur, Robert. "Historical Sketch of the Coast Artillery School," in *Journal of the United States Artillery*, 44:15–48, 164–203 (July-August, September-October, 1915). [84]

———————. *History of Fort Monroe*. Fort Monroe, Virginia, 1930. [85]

Ayres, Mary C. "History of Fort Lewis, Colorado," in *Colorado Magazine*, 8:81–92 (May, 1931). [86]

Bald, F. Clever. "Fort Miami," in *Historical Society of Northwestern Ohio Quarterly Bulletin*, 15:127–138 (July, 1943). [87]

Barnes, Frank. *Fort Sumter National Monument, South Carolina*. National Park Service Historical Handbook Series No. 12. Washington, 1952. [88]

Barry, Richard Schriver. "Fort Macon: Its History," in *North Carolina Historical Review*, 27:163–177 (April, 1950). [89]

Beach, James H. "Old Fort Hays," in *Collections of the Kansas State Historical Society*, 11:571–581 (1910). [90]

Bertsch, W. H. "The Defenses of Oswego," in *Proceedings of the New York State Historical Association*, 13:108–127 (1914). [91]

Blades, Thomas E., and John W. Wike. "Fort Missoula," in *Military Affairs*, 13:29–36 (Spring, 1949). [92]

Bradford, S. Sydney. "Fort McHenry, 1814: The Outworks in 1814," in *Maryland Historical Magazine*, 54:188–209 (June, 1959). [93]

Braly, Earl Burk. "Fort Belknap of the Texas Frontier," in *West Texas*

Historical Association Year Book, 30:83–114 (October, 1954). [94]

"A Brief History of Fort Sill and the Field Artillery School," in *Field Artillery Journal*, 23:528–541 (November-December, 1933). [95]

Briggs, John Ely. "The Second Fort Des Moines," in *Palimpsest*, 24:161–172 (May, 1943). [96]

Brindley, William. "Magnificent Mud," in *Field Artillery Journal*, 39:124–125 (May-June, 1949). [97]

Brown, Dee. *Fort Phil Kearny: An American Saga.* New York, 1962. [98]

Caldwell, Norman W. "Cantonment Wilkinsonville," in *Mid-America*, 31:3–28 (January, 1949). [99]

————. "Fort Massac: The American Frontier Post, 1778–1805," in *Journal of the Illinois State Historical Society*, 43:265–281 (Winter, 1950). [100]

————. "Fort Massac: Since 1805," in *Journal of the Illinois State Historical Society*, 44:47–60 (Spring, 1951). [101]

Campbell, Hortense Balderston. "Camp Beecher," in *Kansas Historical Quarterly*, 3:172–185 (May, 1934). [102]

Chambers, Alexander. "Fort Bridger," in *Annals of Wyoming*, 5:91–95 (October, 1927–January, 1928). [103]

Chapman, John. "Fort Concho," in *Southwest Review*, 25:258–286 (April, 1940). [104]

————. "Fort Griffin," in *Southwest Review*, 27:426–445 (Summer, 1942). [105]

————. "Old Fort Richardson," in *Southwest Review*, 38:62–69 (Winter, 1953). [106]

Chase, Lew Allen. "Fort Wilkins, Copper Harbor, Mich.," in *Michigan History Magazine*, 4:608–611 (April-July, 1920). [107]

Clinton, Amy Cheney. "Historic Fort Washington," in *Maryland Historical Magazine*, 32:228–247 (September, 1937). [108]

Covington, James W., editor. "The Establishment of Fort Brooke: The Beginning of Tampa," in *Florida Historical Quarterly*, 31:273–278 (April, 1953). [109]

————. "Life at Fort Brooke, 1824–1836," in *Florida Historical Quarterly*, 36:319–330 (April, 1958). [110]

Cowell, Ray Theodore. "History of Fort Townsend," in *Washington Historical Quarterly*, 16:284–289 (October, 1925). [111]

Crimmins, M. L. "Camp Cooper and Fort Griffin, Texas," in *West Texas Historical Association Year Book*, 17:32–43 (October, 1941) [112]

————. "Fort Elliott, Texas," in *West Texas Historical Association Year Book*, 23:3–12 (October, 1947) [113]

————. "Fort Fillmore," in *New Mexico Historical Review*, 6:327–333

169

(October, 1931).   [114]

————. "Fort McKavett, Texas," in *Southwestern Historical Quarterly*, 38:28–39 (July, 1934).   [115]

————. "Fort Massachusetts, First United States Military Post in Colorado," in *Colorado Magazine*, 14:128–135 (July, 1937).   [116]

————. "Fort Stockton Sixty Years Ago," in *Frontier Times*, 5:390–391 (July, 1928).   [117]

————. "General Mackenzie and Fort Concho," in *West Texas Historical Association Year Book*, 10:16–31 (October, 1934).   [118]

————. "History of Camp Colorado, Texas," in *Frontier Times*, 13:402–408 (May, 1936).   [119]

————. "The Military History of Camp Colorado," in *West Texas Historical Association Year Book*, 28:71–80 (October, 1952).   [120]

————. "Old Fort Duncan: A Frontier Post," in *Frontier Times*, 15:379–385 (June, 1938).   [121]

————. "Old Fort Richardson," in *Frontier Times*, 17:421–424 (July, 1940).   [122]

Crocchiola, Stanley Francis Louis. See Stanley, F.

Cubberly, Frederick. "Fort King," in *Florida Historical Society Quarterly*, 5:139–152 (January, 1927).   [123]

Cullimore, Clarence C. *Old Adobes of Forgotten Fort Tejon*. Bakersfield, California, 1949.   [124]

Culverwell, Albert. "Stronghold in the Yakima Country: Fort Simcoe and the Indian War, 1856–59, in *Pacific Northwest Quarterly*, 46:46–51 (April, 1955).   [125]

————. *Stronghold in the Yakima Country: The Story of Fort Simcoe, 1856–1859*. Olympia, Washington, 1956.   [126]

Davis, Mrs. Elvert M. "Fort Fayette," in *Western Pennsylvania Historical Magazine*, 10:65–84 (April, 1927).   [127]

DeLand, Charles E. "Editorial Notes on Old Fort Pierre and Its Neighbors," in *South Dakota Historical Collections*, 1:317–379 (1902).   [128]

DeNoyer, Charles. "The History of Fort Totten," in *Collections of the State Historical Society of North Dakota*, 3:178–236 (1910).   [129]

Duval, Ruby R. "Fort Severn: The Battery at Windmill Point," in *United States Naval Institute Proceedings*, 59:843–848 (June, 1933).   [130]

Edwards, Paul M. "Fort Wadsworth and the Friendly Santee Sioux, 1864–1892," in South Dakota Department of History, *Report and Historical Collections*, 31:74–156 (1962).   [131]

Ellison, Robert S. *Fort Bridger, Wyoming: A Brief History*. Casper, Wyoming, 1931.   [132]

Emery, B. Frank. "Fort Saginaw," in *Michigan History Magazine*, 30:476–503

(July-September, 1946). [133]

————. *Fort Saginaw, 1822–1823: The Story of a Forgotten Frontier Post.* Detroit, 1932. [134]

————. *Fort Wilkins, 1844–46.* Detroit, 1932. [135]

Fisher, James. "Fort Wilkins," in *Michigan History Magazine,* 29:155–165 (April-June, 1945). [136]

Flagler, Daniel Webster. *A History of the Rock Island Arsenal from Its Establishment in 1863 to December, 1876; and of the Island of Rock Island, the Site of the Arsenal, from 1804 to 1863.* Washington, 1877. [137]

Fletcher, Henry T. "Old Fort Lancaster," in *West Texas Historical and Scientific Society Publications,* No. 4, pp. 33–44 (1932). [138]

Foreman, Grant. "The Centennial of Fort Gibson," in *Chronicles of Oklahoma,* 2:119–128 (June, 1924). [139]

————. *Fort Gibson: A Brief History.* Norman, 1943. [140]

"Fort Abercrombie, 1857–1877," in *Collections of the State Historical Society of North Dakota,* volume 2, part 2:7–34 (1908). [141]

"Fort Atkinson, Iowa," in *Annals of Iowa,* 3d series, 4:448–453 (July, 1900). [142]

Fort Bliss 100th Anniversary Commission. *Fort Bliss One Hundredth Anniversary, 1848–1948.* El Paso, 1948. [143]

"Fort Des Moines (No. 1), Iowa," in *Annals of Iowa,* 3d series, 3:351–363 (April-July, 1898). [144]

"Fort Des Moines, No. 2," in *Annals of Iowa,* 3d series, 4:161–178 (October, 1899). [145]

"Fort Dodge, Iowa," in *Annals of Iowa,* 3d series, 4:534–538 (October, 1900). [146]

Fort Harrison on the Banks of the Wabash, 1812–1912. Terre Haute, Indiana, 1912. [147]

"Fort Niagara," in *Quartermaster Review,* 14:24–29 (January-February, 1935). [148]

"Fort St. Clair: Celebration of St. Clair Day," in *Ohio Archaeological and Historical Publications,* 32:506–529 (1923). [149]

"Fort Sanford, Iowa," in *Annals of Iowa,* 3d series, 4:289–293 (January, 1900). [150]

Foster, James Monroe, Jr. "Fort Bascom, New Mexico," in *New Mexico Historical Review,* 35:30–62 (January, 1960). [151]

Frazier, Ida Hedrick. *Fort Recovery: An Historical Sketch Depicting Its Role in the History of the Old Northwest.* Columbus, Ohio, 1948. [152]

Gallaher, Ruth A. *Fort Des Moines in Iowa History.* Iowa City, 1919. [153]

Giffen, Helen S. "Camp Independence—An Owens Valley Outpost," in *His-

torical Society of Southern California Quarterly, 24:129–142 (December, 1942). [154]

————. "Fort Miller and Millerton: Memories of the Southern Mines," in *Historical Society of Southern California Quarterly*, 21:5–16 (March, 1939). [155]

Goplen, Arnold O. "Fort Abraham Lincoln, a Typical Frontier Military Post," in *North Dakota History*, 13:176–221 (October, 1946). [156]

Graham, Louis E. "Fort McIntosh," in *Western Pennsylvania Historical Magazine*, 15:93–119 (May, 1932). [157]

Grange, Roger T., Jr. "Fort Robinson, Outpost on the Plains," in *Nebraska History*, 39:191–240 (September, 1958). [158]

Grant, Joseph H. "Old Fort Snelling," in *Quartermaster Review*, 13:21–24, 71–72 (March-April, 1934). [159]

Gregg, Kate L. "Building of the First American Fort West of the Mississippi," in *Missouri Historical Review*, 30:345–364 (July, 1936). [160]

————. "The History of Fort Osage," in *Missouri Historical Review*, 34:439–488 (July, 1940). [161]

Grismer, Karl H. *The Story of Fort Myers: The History of the Land of the Caloosahatchee and Southwest Florida*. St. Petersburg, 1949. [162]

Griswold, Bert J., editor. *Fort Wayne, Gateway of the West, 1802–1813.* Indiana Historical Collections, volume 15. Indianapolis, 1927. [163]

————. *The Pictorial History of Fort Wayne, Indiana*. Chicago, 1917. [164]

Griswold, Gillett. "Old Fort Sill: The First Seven Years," in *Chronicles of Oklahoma*, 36:2–14 (Spring, 1958). [165]

Guie, H. Dean. *Bugles in the Valley: Garnett's Fort Simcoe*. Yakima, Washington, 1956. [166]

Hafen, LeRoy R., and Francis Marion Young. *Fort Laramie and the Pageant of the West, 1834–1890.* Glendale, California, 1938. [167]

Hagen, Olaf T. "Platte Bridge Station and Fort Caspar," in *Annals of Wyoming*, 27:3–17 (April, 1955). [168]

Haley, James Evetts. *Fort Concho and the Texas Frontier*. San Angelo, Texas, 1952. [169]

Handy, Mary Olivia. *History of Fort Sam Houston*. San Antonio, 1951. [170]

Hanna, Alfred Jackson. *Fort Maitland: Its Origin and History*. Maitland, Florida, 1936. [171]

Hansen, Marcus L. *Old Fort Snelling*. Iowa City, 1917. [172]

————. *Old Fort Snelling, 1819–1858*. Iowa City, 1918. [173]

Hieb, David L. *Fort Laramie National Monument, Wyoming*. National Park Service Historical Handbook Series No. 20. Washington, 1954. [174]

Hoekman, Steven. "The History of Fort Sully," in *South Dakota Historical Collections and Report*, 26:222–277 (1952). [175]

Holcombe, Return I. "Fort Snelling," in *American Historical Magazine*, 1:110–133 (March, 1906). **[176]**

Holt, John R. *Historic Fort Snelling*. Fort Snelling, Minnesota, 1938. **[177]**

Hoop, Oscar Winslow. "History of Fort Hoskins, 1856–65," in *Oregon Historical Quarterly*, 30:346–361 (December, 1929). **[178]**

Hummel, Edward A. "The Story of Fort Sisseton," in *South Dakota Historical Review*, 2:126–144 (April, 1937). **[179]**

Hunt, Elvid. *History of Fort Leavenworth, 1827–1927*. Fort Leavenworth, Kansas, 1926. **[180]**

Irwin, James R. "Fort Wayne—A Century of Service," in *Michigan Alumnus*, 40:68–79 (Autumn, 1948). **[181]**

Jackson, Donald. "Old Fort Madison, 1808–1813," in *Palimpsest*, 39:1–64 (January, 1958). **[182]**

Jenks, William L. "Fort Gratiot and Its Builder Gen. Charles Gratiot," in *Michigan History Magazine*, 4:141–155 (January, 1920). **[183]**

Jennings, Richard H. "Fort Wayne," in *Detroit Historical Society Bulletin*, 6:5–8 (May, 1950). **[184]**

Johnson, Richard W. "Fort Snelling and Its History," in *Western Magazine*, 15:44–46, 170–173 (July, October, 1920). **[185]**

——————. "Fort Snelling from Its Foundation to the Present Time," in *Minnesota Historical Collections*, 8:427–448 (1898). **[186]**

Johnson, Sally A. "Cantonment Missouri, 1819–1820," in *Nebraska History*, 37:121–133 (June, 1956). **[187]**

——————. "Fort Atkinson at Council Bluffs," in *Nebraska History*, 38:229–236 (September, 1957). **[188]**

——————. "The Sixth's Elysian Fields: Fort Atkinson on the Council Bluffs," in *Nebraska History*, 40:1–38 (March, 1959). **[189]**

Jones, Robert Ralston. *Fort Washington at Cincinnati, Ohio*. Cincinnati, 1902. **[190]**

Kellogg, Louise Phelps. "Old Fort Howard," in *Wisconsin Magazine of History*, 18:125–140 (December, 1934). **[191]**

Kendall, Jane R. "History of Fort Francis E. Warren," in *Annals of Wyoming*, 18:3–66 (January, 1946). **[192]**

Kenny, Judith Keyes. "The Founding of Camp Watson," in *Oregon Historical Quarterly*, 58:5–16 (March, 1957). **[193]**

Kindervater, E. A. "Fort Sam Houston: An Historical Sketch," in *Quartermaster Review*, 15:27–31, 67–68 (November-December, 1935). **[194]**

King, Arthur G. "The Exact Site of Fort Washington and Daniel Drake's Error," in *Bulletin of the Historical and Philosophical Society of Ohio*, 11:128–146 (April, 1953). **[195]**

Kinney, Sheldon H. "Dry Tortugas," in *United States Naval Institute Pro-

GUIDE TO MILITARY POSTS

ceedings, 76:425–429 (April, 1950). [196]

Knight, Oliver. *Fort Worth, Outpost on the Trinity.* Norman, 1953. [197]

Knopf, Richard C., Raymond S. Baby, and Dwight L. Smith. "The Rediscovery of Fort Washington," in *Bulletin of the Historical and Philosophical Society of Ohio*, 11:3–12 (January, 1953). [198]

Lattimore, Ralston B. *Fort Pulaski National Monument, Georgia.* National Park Service Historical Handbook Series No. 18. Washington, 1954. [199]

Lessen, Harold I., and George C. Mackenzie. *Fort McHenry National Monument and Historic Shrine, Maryland.* National Park Service Historical Handbook Series No. 5. Washington, 1950. [200]

McClellan, S. Gove. "Old Fort Niagara," in *American Heritage*, 4:32–41 (Summer, 1953). [201]

Mahan, Bruce E. "Old Fort Atkinson," in *Palimpsest*, 2:333–350 (November, 1921). [202]

————. "Old Fort Crawford," in *Palimpsest*, 42:449–512 (October, 1961). [203]

————. *Old Fort Crawford and the Frontier.* Iowa City, 1926. [204]

Mantor, Lyle E. "Fort Kearny and the Westward Movement," in *Nebraska History*, 29:175–207 (September, 1948). [205]

Mattes, Merrill J. "Fort Laramie Centennial: 1849–1949," in *Westerners Brand Book* [Chicago], 6:9–11, 13–16 (April, 1949). [206]

————. "Fort Laramie, Guardian of the Oregon Trail: A Commemorative Essay," in *Annals of Wyoming*, 17:3–20 (January, 1945). [207]

————. "Fort Mitchell, Scotts Bluff, Nebraska Territory," in *Nebraska History*, 33:1–34 (March, 1952). [208]

————. "A History of Old Fort Mitchell," in *Nebraska History*, 24:71–82 (April-June, 1943). [209]

————. "Revival at Old Fort Randall," in *Military Engineer*, 44:88–93 (March-April, 1952). [210]

Mattison, Ray H. "Fort Rice—North Dakota's First Missouri River Military Post," in *North Dakota History*, 20:87–108 (April, 1953). [211]

————. "Old Fort Stevenson—A Typical Missouri River Military Post," in *North Dakota History*, 18:53–91 (April-July, 1951). [212]

Miller, W. C. "History of Fort Hamilton," in *Ohio Archaeological and Historical Publications*, 13:97–111 (1904). [213]

Millis, Wade. "Fort Wayne, Detroit," in *Michigan History Magazine*, 20:21–29 (Winter, 1936). [214]

Milner, P. M. "Fort Macomb," in *Publications of the Louisiana Historical Society*, 7:143–152 (1913–1914). [215]

Mokler, Alfred James. *Fort Caspar (Platte Bridge Station).* Casper, Wyoming, 1939. [216]

Montgomery, Mrs. Frank C. "Fort Wallace and Its Relation to the Frontier," in *Collections of the Kansas State Historical Society*, 17:189–283 (1926–1928). [217]

Morrison, William Brown. "Fort Arbuckle," in *Chronicles of Oklahoma*, 6:26–34 (March, 1928). [218]

————. "Fort Towson," in *Chronicles of Oklahoma*, 8:226–232 (June, 1930). [219]

————. "Fort Washita," in *Chronicles of Oklahoma*, 5:251–258 (June, 1927). [220]

Mueller, Esther. "Old Fort Martin Scott, at Fredericksburg," in *Frontier Times*, 14:463–468 (August, 1937). [221]

Mullin, Cora Phoebe. "The Founding of Fort Hartsuff," in *Nebraska History Magazine*, 12:129–140 (April-June, 1929). [222]

Murbarger, Nell. "When the Troopers Came to Nevada," in *Desert Magazine*, 16:12–16 (December, 1953). [223]

Nankivell, John H. "Fort Crawford, Colorado, 1880–1890," in *Colorado Magazine*, 11:54–64 (January, 1934). [224]

————. "Fort Garland, Colorado," in *Colorado Magazine*, 16:13–28 (January, 1939). [225]

Norton, W. T. "Old Fort Belle Fontaine," in *Journal of the Illinois State Historical Society*, 4:334–339 (October, 1911). [226]

Nye, Wilbur Sturtevant. *Carbine and Lance: The Story of Old Fort Sill.* Norman, 1937. [227]

Official Book of the Fort Armstrong Centennial Celebration, June 18th–24th, 1916. Rock Island, Illinois, 1916. [228]

Oneal, Ben G. "The Beginnings of Fort Belknap," in *Southwestern Historical Quarterly*, 61:508–521 (April, 1958). [229]

Peck, Maria. "Fort Armstrong," in *Annals of Iowa*, 3d series, 1:602–613 (January, 1895). [230]

Pfanner, Robert. "The Genesis of Fort Logan," in *Colorado Magazine*, 19:43–50 (March, 1942). [231]

————. "Highlights in the History of Fort Logan," in *Colorado Magazine*, 19:81–91 (May, 1942). [232]

Pierson, Lloyd. "A Short History of Camp Verde, Arizona, to 1890," in *El Palacio*, 64:323–339 (November-December, 1957). [233]

Prance, Lois, and James R. Irwin. "History of Fort Wayne," in *Michigan History Magazine*, 30:5–40 (January-March, 1946). [234]

Pride, Woodbury Freeman. *The History of Fort Riley.* Fort Riley, Kansas, 1926. [235]

Prucha, Francis Paul. "Fort Ripley: The Post and the Military Reservation," in *Minnesota History*, 28:205–224 (September, 1947). [236]

Pugh, Edwin V. "Fort McIntosh," in *Pitt*, 47:14–17 (Autumn, 1952). **[237]**

Quaife, Milo M. *Chicago and the Old Northwest, 1673–1835: A Study of the Evolution of the Northwestern Frontier Together with a History of Fort Dearborn.* Chicago, 1913. **[238]**

————, editor. "Fort Knox Orderly Book, 1793–97," in *Indiana Magazine of History*, 32:137–168 (June, 1936). **[239]**

Randall, E. O. "Fort St. Clair," in *Ohio Archaeological and Historical Publications*, 11:161–163 (1902). **[240]**

Reinhardt, George C. "Fort Leavenworth Is Born," in *Military Review*, volume 33, no. 7:3–8 (October, 1953). **[241]**

————. "Fort Leavenworth Grows Up," in *Military Review*, volume 33, no. 12:16–33 (March, 1954). **[242]**

Riley, Edward M. "Historic Fort Moultrie in Charleston Harbor," in *South Carolina Historical and Genealogical Magazine*, 51:63–74 (April, 1950). **[243]**

Rister, Carl Coke. "The Border Post of Phantom Hill," in *West Texas Historical Association Year Book*, 14:3–13 (October, 1938). **[244]**

————. "Fort Griffin," in *West Texas Historical Association Year Book*, 1:15–24 (June, 1925). **[245]**

————. *Fort Griffin on the Texas Frontier.* Norman, 1956. **[246]**

Rothermich, Albert E., editor. "Early Days at Fort Missoula," in *Frontier and Midland*, 16:225–235 (Spring, 1936). **[247]**

Samonisky, Harris. "Fort Delaware," in *Coast Artillery Journal*, 76:137–138 (March-April, 1933). **[248]**

Sanger, Donald Bridgman. *The Story of Old Fort Bliss.* El Paso, 1933. **[249]**

Scanlan, Peter L. *Prairie du Chien: French, British, American.* Menasha, Wisconsin, 1937. **[250]**

Scobee, Barry. *Old Fort Davis.* San Antonio, 1947. **[251]**

Scott, Julia G. "Old Fort Massac, Illinois," in *Magazine of History*, 10:287–292 (November, 1909). **[252]**

————. "Old Fort Massac," in *Transactions of the Illinois State Historical Society for the Year 1903*, pp. 38–64 (1904). **[253]**

Sheldon, Addison E. "Old Fort Kearny," in *Publications of the Nebraska State Historical Society*, 21:269–279 (1930). **[254]**

Sides, Joseph C. *Fort Brown Historical: History of Fort Brown, Texas, Border Post on the Rio Grande.* San Antonio, 1942. **[255]**

Slaughter, Linda W. "Fort Abercrombie," in *Collections of the State Historical Society of North Dakota*, 1:412–423 (1906). **[256]**

————. "Fort Randall," in *Collections of the State Historical Society of North Dakota*, 1:423–429 (1906). **[257]**

Sleight, Eleanor Friend. "Fort Defiance," in *El Palacio*, 60:3–11 (January, 1953). [258]

Snow, Edward Rowe. *Historic Fort Warren*. Boston, 1941. [259]

Spear, Elsa. *Fort Phil Kearny, Dakota Territory, 1866–1868*. Sheridan, Wyoming, 1939. [260]

Spring, Agnes Wright. "The Founding of Fort Collins, United States Military Post," in *Colorado Magazine*, 10:47–55 (March, 1933). [261]

Stanley, F. [Stanley Francis Louis Crocchiola]. *Fort Bascom, Comanche-Kiowa Barrier*. Pampa, Texas, 1961. [262]

————. *The Fort Conrad, New Mexico, Story*. Dumas, Texas, 1961. [263]

————. *Fort Craig*. Pampa, Texas, 1963. [264]

————. *The Fort Fillmore, New Mexico, Story*. Pantex, Texas, 1961. [265]

————. *Fort Union (New Mexico)*. Privately printed, 1953. [266]

Sweet, J. H. "Old Fort Kearny," in *Nebraska History*, 27:233–243 (October-December, 1946). [267]

Swett, Morris. *Fort Sill: A History*. Fort Sill, Oklahoma, 1921. [268]

Tenny, Walter H. "History of Fort Ethan Allen," in *Vermont Quarterly*, 19:26–30 (January, 1951). [269]

Thomlinson, M. H. *The Garrison of Fort Bliss, 1849–1916*. El Paso, Texas, 1945. [270]

"Three Forts Des Moines: Celebration of the Hundredth Anniversary of Establishment of the Military Post at Des Moines," in *Annals of Iowa*, 25:3–60 (July, 1943). [271]

Toler, Grace Cabot. "Old Fort Wilkinson," in *National Historical Magazine*, 74:46–47 (July-August, 1940). [272]

Turner, Andrew J. "The History of Fort Winnebago," in *Collections of the State Historical Society of Wisconsin*, 14:65–103 (1898). [273]

United States Work Projects Administration, Florida. *History of the Fort Jefferson National Monument. Part One: The Fort at Garden Key, 1846–1860*. Key West, Florida, 1936. (Typescript copy in the Library of Congress). [274]

Unrau, William E. "The Story of Fort Larned," in *Kansas Historical Quarterly*, 23:257–280 (Autumn, 1957). [275]

Utley, Robert M. "Fort Union and the Santa Fe Trail," in *New Mexico Historical Review*, 36:36–48 (January, 1961). [276]

————. *Fort Union National Monument, New Mexico*. National Park Service Historical Handbook Series No. 35. Washington, 1962. [277]

"Vancouver Barracks," in *Quartermaster Review*, 13:18–21, 69–70 (May-June, 1934). [278]

Van der Zee, Jacob. *Old Fort Madison*. Iowa City, 1918. [279]

Waitman, Leonard. "The History of Camp Cady," in *Historical Society of Southern California Quarterly*, 36:49–91 (March, 1954). [280]

Walsh, Richard. "Fort McHenry, 1814: The Star Fort," in *Maryland Historical Magazine*, 54:296–309 (September, 1959). [281]

Watkins, Albert. "History of Fort Kearny," in *Collections of the Nebraska State Historical Society*, 16:227–267 (1911). [282]

Webb, Henry W. "The Story of Jefferson Barracks," in *New Mexico Historical Review*, 21:185–208 (July, 1946). [283]

Wentworth, John. *Early Chicago: Fort Dearborn*. Chicago, 1881. [284]

Wesley, Edgar Bruce. "Life at a Frontier Post: Fort Atkinson, 1823–1826," in *Journal of the American Military Institute*, 3:203–209 (Winter, 1939). [285]

_____. "Life at Fort Atkinson," in *Nebraska History*, 30:348–358 (December, 1949). [286]

Williams, Ames W. "Stronghold of the Straits: A Short History of Fort Zachary Taylor," in *Tequesta: The Journal of the Historical Association of Southern Florida*, No. 14, pp. 3–24 (1954). [287]

Willman, Lillian M. "The History of Fort Kearny," in *Publications of the Nebraska State Historical Society*, 21:211–249 (1930). [288]

Wilson, Frazer Ells. *Fort Jefferson: The Frontier Post of the Upper Miami Valley*. No place given, 1950. [289]

Wilson, Frederick T. "Old Fort Pierre and Its Neighbors," in *South Dakota Historical Collections*, 1:263–311 (1902). [290]

Wilson, W. Emerson. *Fort Delaware*. Newark, Delaware, 1957. [291]

Winans, W. P. "Fort Colville 1859 to 1869," in *Washington Historical Quarterly*, 3:78–82 (October, 1908). [292]

Wood, Henry. "Fort Union: End of the Santa Fe Trail," in *Westerners Brand Book* [Denver Posse], 3:205–256 (1947). [293]

Woodward, Arthur. "Fort Tejon—A Nursery of the Army," in Helen S. Giffen and Arthur Woodward, *The Story of El Tejon*. Los Angeles, 1942. Pp. 57–137. [294]

Wright, Muriel H. "A History of Fort Cobb," in *Chronicles of Oklahoma*, 34:53–71 (Spring, 1956). [295]

Young, Rogers W. "The Construction of Fort Pulaski," in *Georgia Historical Quarterly*, 20:41–51 (March, 1936). [296]

_____. "Fort Marion During the Seminole War, 1835–1842," in *Florida Historical Society Quarterly*, 12:193–223 (April, 1935). [297]

A NOTE ON DESIGN

The text of this volume was set in Linotype Electra, the boldface headings in Caledonia, and the initials and display type in Caslon Old Style. It was printed on Warren's Olde Style, substance 70, and cased in Interlaken Homespun binding cloth. The end papers are in Tweedweave, substance 80. The eagle design was adapted by Herman J. Viola from a brass army uniform insignia of the 1830's.